Imperial Leather

Cambridge Imperial and Post-Colonial Studies Series

General Editors: Megan Vaughan, Kings' College, Cambridge and Richard Drayton, Corpus Christi College, Cambridge

This informative series covers the broad span of modern imperial history while also exploring the recent developments in former colonial states where residues of empire can still be found. The books provide in-depth examinations of empires as competing and complementary power structures encouraging the reader to reconsider their understanding of international and world history during recent centuries.

Titles include:

Sunil S. Amrith
DECOLONIZING INTERNATIONAL HEALTH
India and Southeast Asia, 1930–65

Tony Ballantyne
ORIENTALISM AND RACE
Aryanism in the British Empire

Robert J. Blyth
THE EMPIRE OF THE RAJ
Eastern Africa and the Middle East, 1858–1947

Roy Bridges (*editor*)
IMPERIALISM, DECOLONIZATION AND AFRICA
Studies Presented to John Hargreaves

L. J. Butler
COPPER EMPIRE
Mining and the Colonial State in Northern Rhodesia, c.1930–64

Hilary M. Carey (*editor*)
EMPIRES OF RELIGION

T. J. Cribb (*editor*)
IMAGINED COMMONWEALTH
Cambridge Essays on Commonwealth and International Literature in English

Michael S. Dodson
ORIENTALISM, EMPIRE AND NATIONAL CULTURE
India, 1770–1880

B. D. Hopkins
THE MAKING OF MODERN AFGHANISTAN

Ronald Hyam
BRITAIN'S IMPERIAL CENTURY, 1815–1914: A STUDY OF EMPIRE AND EXPANSION
Third Edition

Robin Jeffrey
POLITICS, WOMEN AND WELL-BEING
How Kerala became a 'Model'

Gerold Krozewski
MONEY AND THE END OF EMPIRE
British International Economic Policy and the Colonies, 1947–58

Sloan Mahone and Megan Vaughan (*editors*)
PSYCHIATRY AND EMPIRE

Javed Majeed
AUTOBIOGRAPHY, TRAVEL AND POST-NATIONAL IDENTITY

Francine McKenzie
REDEFINING THE BONDS OF COMMONWEALTH 1939–1948
The Politics of Preference

Gabriel Paquette
ENLIGHTENMENT, GOVERNANCE AND REFORM IN SPAIN AND ITS EMPIRE 1759–1808

Jennifer Regan-Lefebvre
COSMOPOLITAN NATIONALISM IN THE VICTORIAN EMPIRE
Ireland, India and the Politics of Alfred Webb

John Singleton and Paul Robertson
ECONOMIC RELATIONS BETWEEN BRITAIN AND AUSTRALASIA 1945–1970

Kim A. Wagner (*editor*)
THUGGEE
Banditry and the British in Early Nineteenth-Century India

Jon E. Wilson
THE DOMINATION OF STRANGERS
Modern Governance in Eastern India, 1780–1835

Cambridge Imperial and Post-Colonial Studies Series
Series Standing Order ISBN 978–0–333–91908–8 (Hardback)
978–0–333–91909–5 (Paperback)
(*outside North America only*)

You can receive future titles in this series as they are published by placing a standing order. Please contact your bookseller or, in case of difficulty, write to us at the address below with your name and address, the title of the series and the ISBN quoted above.

Customer Services Department, Macmillan Distribution Ltd, Houndmills, Basingstoke, Hampshire RG21 6XS, England

Cosmopolitan Nationalism in the Victorian Empire

Ireland, India and the Politics of Alfred Webb

Jennifer Regan-Lefebvre

palgrave
macmillan

© Jennifer Regan-Lefebvre 2009

All rights reserved. No reproduction, copy or transmission of this publication may be made without written permission.

No portion of this publication may be reproduced, copied or transmitted save with written permission or in accordance with the provisions of the Copyright, Designs and Patents Act 1988, or under the terms of any licence permitting limited copying issued by the Copyright Licensing Agency, Saffron House, 6-10 Kirby Street, London EC1N 8TS.

Any person who does any unauthorized act in relation to this publication may be liable to criminal prosecution and civil claims for damages.

The author has asserted her right to be identified
as the author of this work in accordance with the Copyright,
Designs and Patents Act 1988.

First published 2009 by
PALGRAVE MACMILLAN

Palgrave Macmillan in the UK is an imprint of Macmillan Publishers Limited, registered in England, company number 785998, of Houndmills, Basingstoke, Hampshire RG21 6XS.

Palgrave Macmillan in the US is a division of St Martin's Press LLC,
175 Fifth Avenue, New York, NY 10010.

Palgrave Macmillan is the global academic imprint of the above companies and has companies and representatives throughout the world.

Palgrave® and Macmillan® are registered trademarks in the United States, the United Kingdom, Europe and other countries.

ISBN-13: 978–0–230–22085–0 hardback

This book is printed on paper suitable for recycling and made from fully managed and sustained forest sources. Logging, pulping and manufacturing processes are expected to conform to the environmental regulations of the country of origin.

A catalogue record for this book is available from the British Library.

A catalog record for this book is available from the Library of Congress.

10 9 8 7 6 5 4 3 2 1
18 17 16 15 14 13 12 11 10 09

Printed and bound in Great Britain by
CPI Antony Rowe, Chippenham and Eastbourne

À Thomas

Contents

Preface	ix
Abbreviations	xii
A Note on Terminology	xiii

1 'How rich my life has been, not in itself but in its associations': An Introduction to Alfred Webb ... 1

2 'Interested in people of all countries, especially of America': A Quaker Family in the Atlantic World ... 13
   A Quaker family in Victorian Ireland ... 13
   Transatlantic social justice and anti-slavery ... 17
   A print network ... 24
   Webb and Quakerism ... 28

3 'The labours and responsibilities nearly killed me': Webb and Social Activism in Victorian Dublin ... 34
   Social activism in Ireland ... 35
   Suffragism and the Contagious Diseases Acts ... 42
   Representing and exhibiting in Dublin ... 51
   Literary reputation ... 56

4 'Some curious characters floated on the surface': Webb's Entry into Nationalist Politics ... 60
   The road to the Home Government Association ... 61
   The Home Government Association ... 66
   Evolution of the Home Rule League ... 74
   Viable alternatives ... 80

5 'I am willing to take any dangerous part': Webb in the World of Parnell and Gladstone ... 85
   Land, the law and the National League ... 85
   'Phantoms of the Irish Protestant conscience' ... 92
   'Led to our doom with Machiavellian ingenuity' ... 100

6 'A union of hearts firmly based on love of Ireland': Cosmopolitan Friendship in the Imperial Metropolis	106
The liberal face of Irish nationalism	107
Cosmopolitan London	114
Friendship and nationalism	118
7 'I stand beside you as a comrade': Irish and Indian Political Collaboration	128
Webb the internationalist in the Irish Party	128
Four international approaches in the Irish Party	132
Internationalism in practice: Irish and Indian political strategies	136
An Irish president for an Indian Congress	146
8 'Politics is a difficult and anxious game': An Assessment of Webb	154
Webb in political life, 1895–1908	154
Irish–Indian relations after 1894	156
Losing faith in the Imperial Parliament	160
Webb and the Irish Party post-1895	162
An assessment of Webb	169
Notes	174
Bibliography	208
Index	221

Preface

This biography began life as a doctoral thesis at Queen's University Belfast, where I had the pleasure of being supervised by Sean Connolly, the late Martin Lynn, and Robert Blyth. I would also like to thank Keith Jeffery and Tom Bartlett, who examined the thesis, and Mary O'Dowd and the late Peter Jupp, who conducted the thesis differentiation: all four offered encouragement and helpful advice. My greatest intellectual debts are to Sean Connolly, who was an outstanding supervisor, and to Peter Gray, Director of Graduate Studies. Both Sean and Peter were unfailing in their encouragement and kindness, rigorous in their approach to my work and full of wit and humour. They led by example and I am humbled when I think that, in the time it took me to produce this book, each of them produced a tome twice its length.

I must thank the Deputy Keeper of the Records of the Public Records Office of Northern Ireland for permission to quote from the Rev. J. B. Armour papers, the Joseph Biggar papers, the Home Rule Association Letterbook, the Jeremiah Jordan papers and the John Pinkerton papers. I was granted permission of the Board of the National Library of Ireland to quote from the 20 collections I consulted there, which are fully listed in my bibliography. I apologise to any copyright holders who I have been unable to trace, who I have accidentally overlooked, or to whom I have been unaware of my duties. I would like to thank the staff of the other libraries and archives where I conducted my research: the Boston Public Library, the British Library Office of India and Oriental Collections, the Dublin City Archives, the Linen Hall Library, the National Archives of India, the National Archives of Ireland, the Newspaper Library of Belfast Central Library, the Trinity College Dublin Library and Manuscripts and the University College Dublin Library and Archives. I would like to thank the staff of the Friends Historical Library in Dublin for making special arrangements for me to work longer hours and for their insight into the Society of Friends. I thank Deepa Bhatnagar, Research Officer in the Nehru Memorial Museum and Library, for her warm welcome, encouragement and efficiency. At Queen's University Belfast, I have enjoyed the encouragement of Deirdre Wildy, a true historian's librarian, who was always on the lookout for resources for me and who was a great friend in the Library and its Special Collections. I would particularly like to thank the staff of the National Library of

Ireland for being so consistently pleasant, helpful and enthusiastic. Tom Desmond deserves special thanks: had he not engaged me in conversation in the lift of the Manuscripts building, I never would have known about Webb's 1886 autograph letter to Charles Oldham, one of the single most important documents I used in writing this book. The National Library of Ireland kindly also provided the cover image from the *Irish Weekly Independent*. One of the things I enjoyed most in preparing this book was the research I undertook in two beautiful private clubs in London. I would like to thank Simon Roberts, Secretary of the National Liberal Club, and Simon Blundell, Librarian of the Reform Club, for their permission to undertake research and their hospitality. In the National Liberal Club, where I worked in the reading room at a desk flanked by marble busts of Bright and Cobden, I was quite charmed by the Club members who expressed enthusiasm about my research and stopped by for regular updates on my progress.

The research for this book was made possible through a Queen's University International Student Award, travel grants through the Queen's University William and Betty MacQuitty Award, Alumni Fund and Helena Wallace Award, and grants from the Institute of Irish Studies and the School of History. David Hayton, as head of the School of History, granted me visiting research status for the 2007–2008 academic year. I am very grateful to Emma Rothschild and Gareth Stedman Jones for supporting my post-doctoral research as a Mellon Visiting Scholar and for providing such a congenial environment at the Centre for History and Economics at King's College, Cambridge. Also in Cambridge, Chris Bayly brought the Reform Club archives to my attention, was generous with his time and was encouraging of my work. His 2007 Wiles Lectures at Queen's were crucial in helping me to crystallise my thoughts on Webb, liberalism and India, and I would like to thank the Boyd family for endowing and continuing to support this marvellous lecture series.

In India I am extremely grateful to Purnima Mehta and the staff at the American Institute of Indian Studies. Ambassador Kieran Dowling, Modhrima DasGupta, Chris Pepe, Ed Henry, Chelsea Booth and Stephanie Booth all helped me to remain sane (just) and to enjoy Delhi. Satish Kumar and Lord Rana of Malone assisted me in applying for visas. I am very grateful to Emma Reisz, not only for her friendship but also for her much-needed practical advice in planning my trip. Peter Marshall also provided encouragement and introductions for my trip.

Elleke Boehmer and Susheila Nasta, through their AHRC-funded Making Britain project, have provided great stimulation, feedback and encouragement for my work. Carla King generously shared her work on Michael Davitt – a fitting tribute to Webb and Davitt's own friendship. Marie-Louise Legg was kind enough to meet me and field my questions about Webb. Richard Harrison corresponded with me about Quaker research and resources. Neal Garnham read sections on masculinity and friendship. My colleagues in the Queen's Postcolonial Forum – Anthony Soares, Maeve McCusker, Eamonn Hughes, Stefan Andreasson, Jonathan Skinner and Satish Kumar – were great fun, and a real lifeline when I was trying to convert the thesis into the book. At Queen's I have enjoyed advice, encouragement or moral support from Paul Bew, Dominic Bryan, Catherine Clinton, Marie Coleman, Elaine Doyle, Richard English, Liam Kennedy, Danny Kowalsky, Peter Ludlow, Patrick Maume, Raoul McLoughlin, Sean McDaid, Caoimhe Nic Dhaibheid, Sean O'Connell, Colin Reid, Nini Rodgers and Jonathan Wright. At conferences I have enjoyed enlightening conversations with Frank Bouchier-Hayes, Michael Keyes, Jen Moore, James O'Connel, Alan O'Day, Kate O'Malley and Michael Silvestri. Many more friends provided moral support, and I would like to particularly thank Joanna Brennan and Jan Muench whose wonderful hospitality allowed me to carry out research in London. I apologise to anyone whose name I have overlooked, and of course any errors or omissions in the text are mine and mine alone.

Richard Drayton first suggested that I publish the book in this series; I would like to thank him, his co-editor Megan Vaughan, and Michael Strang and Ruth Ireland at Palgrave for their support and guidance. I am also grateful to the anonymous reviewer for such insightful and beautifully written comments, which have, I believe, strengthened the book. Two other mentors deserve mention: Judith Kisor and Alice Leader, both teachers and scholars, determined my decision to become a historian. Their passion for history still motivates me and influences the way I think and write.

Finally, I have been fortunate to have a wonderfully supportive family, who have intervened at crucial moments to prevent me from starving or, worse, taking myself too seriously. I am grateful for the love of my parents, Dick and Judi Regan, my sisters, Deirdre and Colleen Regan, and my extended Regan and Murray families. Last of all, Thomas Regan-Lefebvre has tolerated my obsession with another man over the past five years, and this book is dedicated to him.

Jennifer Regan-Lefebvre
Paris, February 2009

Abbreviations

BLOIOC	British Library Oriental and India Office Collections
BPL	Boston Public Library
DFHL	Dublin Friends Historical Library
DNB	*Oxford Dictionary of National Biography* (Oxford, 2004)
NAI	National Archives of India
NLC	National Liberal Club Archives
NLI	National Library of Ireland
NMML	Nehru Memorial Museum and Library
PRONI	Public Record Office of Northern Ireland
TCD	Trinity College Dublin Manuscripts
UCD	University College Dublin Archives

A Note on Terminology

The Irish Parliamentary Party, the official political party of Irish nationalism in the Westminster Parliament, is also referred to as the Irish Party and the Nationalist Party. When the word 'party' is not capitalised, it does not refer to a specific political party. 'Westminster', 'Parliament' and the 'Imperial Parliament' all refer to the same institution. The terms 'home rule', 'home ruler' and 'home rule movement', all of which refer to the constitutional movement for an Irish domestic parliament and the pieces of legislation dedicated to this end, have not been capitalised except when used in the title of an organisation or document.

When the word 'Liberal' is capitalised it refers to a person or idea belonging to the British Liberal Party. Occasionally the uncapitalised word 'liberal' is used to refer to a person or idea that is associated with progressive thought, but does not necessarily belong to the Liberal Party. The same is true of the words 'Conservative' and 'conservative', 'Nationalist' and 'nationalist'. When the word 'Empire' is capitalised it refers to the institution commonly known as the British Empire. The word 'British' is often omitted from this title to emphasise how non-British people used and controlled the Empire. The word 'imperial' has not been capitalised except in official titles of organisations.

1
'How rich my life has been, not in itself but in its associations'[1]: An Introduction to Alfred Webb

Alfred John Webb was born in Ireland as a citizen of the world. This is the first full biographical study of Webb (1834–1908): a Dublin printer, Quaker, social activist, Irish nationalist MP and president of the Indian National Congress. Using Webb as a window, this study tracks the movement of ideas through the Atlantic World, Britain and Ireland, and across the Empire. It begins by analysing Webb's upbringing in Dublin by Quaker printers who were deeply involved in the Garrisonian anti-slavery movement and had contacts across the Atlantic World. It then traces how Webb's belief in social justice was translated into his support for Irish nationalism and a range of social and women's issues. As an Irish nationalist MP in Westminster, Webb made contacts within the Indian nationalist community and the British Liberal establishment. His involvement in a complex network of progressive social organisations led to his invitation to preside at the Congress: in particular, Webb developed a close personal friendship and political relationship with the Indian politician, Dadabhai Naoroji, whose social and political interests neatly overlapped with Webb's.

Many of the major themes of nineteenth-century Irish history appear in Webb's story: family emigration, Famine relief and the growth of Irish nationalism. But Webb's life appears, in other respects, an unusual one for a Victorian Irishman. He was a member of a religious minority, a businessman in a largely agrarian economy, and a home ruler who rejected ethnic nationalism and provincialism. Throughout his life he made intellectual journeys to the heart of liberalism, nationalism and anti-imperialism. Yet in examining Webb's life closely, it emerges that he was not an anomaly, but is a window into a vibrant community within late-Victorian Ireland that embraced social activism, international responsibility, multiculturalism and anti-imperialism. Although Webb made three major transoceanic voyages in his life – to Australia, to India and on a global trip via the United States – he did not need to travel to sustain or develop his internationalist beliefs, which were cultivated within Dublin, where he lived most of his life, and then flourished in London, where he spent 5 years as an MP.

This biographical study is organised thematically as well as chronologically, so a brief overview of Webb's life may serve as an introduction. Webb was born into a Dublin Quaker family of printers. His father, Richard Davis Webb, acquired his own print shop in downtown Dublin in 1828. Webb began working in the business at a young age and acquired sole responsibility after his father's death, finally selling the business in 1894. The Webbs were the type of Quaker who espoused many reformist ideas, in particular temperance, suffragism, the abolition of slavery and the extension of political franchise throughout the British Empire. They frequently printed pamphlets and books for these causes. Alfred Webb became an Irish home ruler and undertook printing for various nationalist organisations, including the Ladies' Land League and the Irish Protestant Home Rule Association. The printing business brought together various kinds of progressive thinkers and fostered a culture of social activism, and the Webbs' wide-ranging interests defeat the view that nineteenth-century Dublin had little significant intellectual activity beyond nationalism. Webb's familiarity with literature and history enabled him to write the *Compendium of Irish Biography*.[2]

Webb became interested in Irish nationalist politics in 1865, when, despite his non-violent tendencies, he was inspired by the Fenians. In 1870, he became a founding member of Isaac Butt's Home Government Association and its acting secretary. Webb's business acumen and his moral standards made him a competent and respected treasurer, and while running his printing shop he took on that role in subsequent nationalist organisations, spanning the period 1873–1900: the Home Rule League, the National League, the Irish Parliamentary Party, the Irish National Federation and the United Irish League. In 1890 he was elected MP for West Waterford. Traumatised by the Parnell Split and always acting on strict moral principles, Webb joined McCarthy as an anti-Parnellite and resigned from Parliament in 1895 in protest at T. M. Healy's behaviour.

One issue in which Webb took a life-long interest was the welfare of Britain's colonies. His father had campaigned against the Opium Wars of the 1840s and Webb spoke about the opium traffic in India and China in Parliament. Webb's interest was timely, as moderate Indian nationalism was attracting adherents among educated Indians in London. I use the term Indian, rather than South Asian, to reflect nineteenth-century usage; I also use the term nationalist advisedly, as these Indians were not nationalists in the sense of being separatists: their demands were for more representation in the government of India and did not extend even as far as home rule. However, for simplicity, and in recognition of the fact that they were thinking on an all-India basis, the supporters of the Indian National Congress will be referred to in this study as nationalists. One of them was Dadabhai Naoroji, who was a founder of the Indian National Congress and a personal friend of Webb. Naoroji was known to many other Irish nationalists, including Michael Davitt and Frank Hugh O'Donnell, who were involved in schemes to have Naoroji elected to Parliament for an Irish seat. In recognition of his support for Indian issues, Webb was invited to be president of the Indian National Congress in 1894. Webb was extremely proud of his invitation to Madras and it was a fitting achievement for a man who saw himself as both an Irishman and a global citizen.

Webb's life is a manifestation of the role of associational culture in shaping political life and the centrality of personal networks in building social capital. Webb hated the Empire and imperialism in all its forms. However, he also realised that the Empire was, in a sense, a complex communications network through which ideas spread; this is how Irish and Indian nationalists, from opposite ends of the globe, could unite in London and find that their goals and ideas were very similar. The emphasis on networks has been made by, among others, Tony Ballantyne, who in his admirable study of Aryanism in the British Empire sought to reject 'both the metropolitan-focused project of imperial history and the tradition of colonial history that accepts the bounded and self-sufficient nation-state as its analytical frame'.[3] He advocates study of networks across such boundaries, real and imagined, to more effectively understand the workings of Empire.

This poses something of a challenge when analysing the actions of individuals whose own efforts were both nationalistic and focused on London. How do we reconcile a view of Empire as a system of overlapping networks, and an understanding of the growth of nationalism? How, also, do we examine the experience of these individuals in the geographic centre of the Empire, without falling into the trap of writing metropolitan-centred history that discounts the experiences of those in the peripheries? My study has a metropolitan focus and it profiles individuals who campaigned for recognition of their own imagined

4 *Cosmopolitan Nationalism in the Victorian Empire*

nation-states.[3] In terms of analytical framework, I must differentiate between the language of Empire and nation as contemporary theoretical buzzwords and those ideas as they were held by the individuals I study. In other words, though we might reject the ideas of metropole and periphery as historiographical markers, they are useful concepts and terms to explain nineteenth-century perspectives. Scholars may not believe that the metropole was the point from which all ideas, people and capital flowed in the Empire, but Webb largely believed this to be true. Webb and Naoroji understood Parliament to be the centre of imperial power, and while both tried to challenge that power by strengthening nationalist bodies in their 'peripheral' locations, both viewed Parliament as the legitimate forum through which to express their demands, and Gladstonian liberalism as the framework through which those demands would be understood and, hopefully, met.

This study does not attempt to be subaltern; it is concerned with the experiences of political and social elites. It seeks to understand why a group of individuals thought it personally satisfying and politically strategic to participate in cosmopolitan networks in late-Victorian London, and why and how those networks revolved around the British Liberal Party and progressive social activist groups. It seeks to reveal the political connections between Irish and Indian nationalists in Britain, and in particular to examine how the ideology and administration of the Irish Nationalist Party both allowed for and hindered collaboration between Irish and Indian men.

I use the term cosmopolitan to describe those individuals who think there is something inherently good in interacting with those who are culturally different from themselves, and who believe that such interaction holds promise and status. By promise, I mean that they believe multicultural interaction suggests the potential to come into contact with new ideas, networks and skills. By status, I mean not only that multicultural interaction can appeal as sophisticated and worldly, but more specifically that it lends an air of universality to their arguments. The cosmopolitans in this book met through progressive societies and high politics. By claiming an internationalised consensus for their ideas, they gained political status. Nowhere is this more apparent than in nationalism itself. Those nationalists who embraced internationalism felt that their arguments for self-government were strengthened by the fact that other individuals around the world, removed from their specific situation, agreed that political rights were deserved by all. I refer to Webb and Naoroji as cosmopolitan nationalists to explain the fact that their nationalism stressed universal rights, rather than exclusive ethnicity.

Leela Gandhi's *Affective Communities*, a book that appeared when this manuscript was nearing completion, also rehabilitates lesser-known anti-imperialists in late-Victorian London and examines the ethical causes and social organisations that brought them together and allowed them to form cross-cultural relationships.[4] Her larger concern is how these individuals can be understood within post-colonial theory and how cross-cultural friendship and utopianism can be appreciated as political acts in the colonial sphere. This is less of a theoretical problem for me because my biographical subject was a self-proclaimed nationalist and nationalist theory is, in essence, a framework for understanding kinship that bridges cultural difference. Most frequently the cultural differences that nationalism claims to overrule are those of class, educational level, gender and urbanism/ruralism. Nationalism is the result of individuals believing or imagining that their shared, common support for the nation or the national ideal is more important than their socioeconomic differences.[5]

Webb's story is somewhat exceptional in that I argue that his nationalism allowed him to cross ethnic and racial boundaries, and to form friendship with those who identified with other nations, but this is not inherently contradictory. Nationalism requires a degree of imagination: though they may claim otherwise, nationalists must imagine the boundaries of their nations. Second, Webb's nationalism was civic, not ethnic, in nature. His ideas about nationalism were created through his own colonial and imperial predicament, that of being a member of a religious minority within Ireland, one that had its own historical narrative of discrimination and oppression but which had also enjoyed certain social and political privileges over the religious majority. Webb's writings diagnose guilt and preach responsibility on Irish Quakers specifically and Irish Protestants more generally, and on the part of Irish people broadly within the imperial political system. In this regard a biography of Webb will hopefully contribute to the large body of literature on the history of Irish nationalism, as well as two strong and growing areas of historical research: connections between Ireland and India and the stories of South Asians in Britain.

Interest in Ireland and India stems from a wider and older field of research on Ireland's status within the United Kingdom, that of whether or not Ireland was a British colony.[6] In the nineteenth century Ireland was a constitutive part of the United Kingdom, but it retained some semi-colonial features, such as a lord lieutenant, and a strong popular narrative of colonisation; in this regard the nineteenth-century Irish had both (even simultaneously) a colonial and an imperial experience.

Questions about the racial and ethnic dimensions of this experience – where the Irish were seen to be, or saw themselves, in a Victorian racial taxonomy – have been hotly debated and likely will remain important.[7]

Some long-established areas of research into modern Irish history segue neatly into recent discussion of Ireland's place in the Empire. Ireland's pan-imperial connections have often been expressed in terms of enduring relationships with Irish emigrants in the colonies (especially Canada, Australia and New Zealand).[8] Historians have also noted the disproportionately high percentage of Irish participation in the British military and East India Company army, and the Irish role in Imperial policing.[9] Irish historians have become concerned about the cultural norms Irish people exported throughout the Empire and the ways in which Irish people also imported Imperial norms and experienced the Empire 'at home'.[10]

There has been a great deal of recent scholarship specifically on Irish–Indian connections, much of it focusing on literary–cultural connections and figures such as Annie Besant, Margaret and James Cousins, Rabindranath Tagore and W. B. Yeats.[11] Recently Tadhg Foley and Maureen O'Connor have produced an edited collection titled *Ireland and India: Colonies, Culture and Empire*, covering a range of facets to the Irish–Indian relationship, including religion, literary exchange, political inspiration and administrative overlap. Webb, however, is mentioned in only one essay, and in the context of his position as an Irish Quaker nationalist, 'a minority several times over'.[12] Recent work on political connections in the twentieth century has explained ventures such as the Indian–Irish Independence League and the League Against Imperialism.[13]

Older works that laid the foundations for current research include those of Scott B. Cook and Howard V. Brasted. Cook has examined Ireland on the receiving end of imperial legislation, and persuasively argued that Ireland's relationship with India was always special in the eyes of British imperialists: British policy makers tended to compare Ireland with India, and not Australia or Canada, and were happy to extend self-government to New South Wales but not to Ireland or India.[14] Brasted has written on Irish–Indian political developments, and particularly on the roles of Davitt and O'Donnell, but not on Webb.[15]

Webb's Congress presidency, perhaps the most significant single event in the history of Irish–Indian political collaboration, has received very little scholarly attention. Webb's position in late-Victorian London does feature in Jonathan Schneer's *London 1900*, a fascinating study of the political landscape of the capital in its imperial moment.[16] Schneer's study situates Webb in a complex and exciting network that is composed of individuals from throughout the Empire. I have tried to flesh out some of these networks in more details here, and to demonstrate, as Antoinette Burton writes, 'some of the ways imperial power relations were challenged and remade by colonial subjects not just in the far-flung territories of the empire but more centrally, in the social spaces of "domestic" Victorian imperial culture itself.'[17] Given the recent scholarly attention to South Asians in Victorian Britain and Edwardian Britain, it is suitable that the experience of that community be explored in relation to Britain's largest 'ethnic minority' community at the time, the Irish.[18]

Webb's life tied together diverse areas of history that are not often studied in tandem, and perhaps he has been largely forgotten because his life revolved around several movements and ideas that failed, were short-lived, or were politically overshadowed after he retired. Although many ideas shared by Irish and Indians may not have resulted in political change, and although the sense of civic duty that characterised Webb's circle in Dublin may have been eclipsed by nationalism, these ideas were interesting in their own time and deserve study. Webb is barely mentioned in the literature on Ireland and India, Irish nationalism, Dublin civic life, printing and Quakerism, but his life, as well as being fascinating in its own right, yields information and new perspectives to all these areas of inquiry. In light of Webb's experiences, some of the appellations cast on nineteenth-century Ireland, both then and more recently, now seem unfair: isolated, deteriorating (especially Dublin), Catholic and dogmatic, parochial, inward-looking and obsessed with nationalism. Likewise, certain adjectives can here be put together in unexpected combinations: nationalist and Quaker, nationalist and imperialist, anti-imperialist and business-oriented, proudly Irish and devoutly Protestant.

The dearth of scholarly work on Webb has not been due to lack of archival material; sources for Webb's life are plentiful. The best starting point is his autobiography, handwritten around 1904–1906 and held at the Dublin Friends Historical Library (DFHL). Excerpts from this autobiography have been edited and published by Marie-Louise Legg, and her introduction has proved an important foundation for this author.[19] Webb's autobiography is not a spiritual one in the Quaker tradition, nor does it deal extensively with political events, curious for a man best known for his political career. The autobiography is a rambling narrative of Webb's life, roughly chronological but frequently digressing. It is full of charming anecdotes and rich material for a social historian, but is a trying source for the biographer. Webb explains in the text that he had begun an autobiography 20 years earlier but had it destroyed. 'I can now take a fairer view of the relative importance of the various events of my life',[20] he wrote, and certainly in the intervening 20 years he had achieved what he would be best remembered for: representing Waterford in Parliament and presiding at the Indian National Congress. However, his account of his early life is inevitably shaped by his later experience, and his descriptions of his thoughts, feelings and beliefs as a young person cannot always be taken at face value. They are an older man's memory of his youth; they are not necessarily inaccurate, but they must be weighed against other available evidence.

As a business owner and political administrator, Webb created a paper trail that was probably larger than that of many of his parliamentary colleagues to begin with, and subsequently better preserved after his death.

He had strongly encouraged the establishment of the National Library of Ireland and donated three of his scrapbooks to its collection. The scrapbooks contain approximately 350 newspaper clippings (mentions of Webb, speeches he had written and letters he wrote to the editor), with some annotations. In addition, there are draft letters, invitations to events and a few cartoons drawn by Webb. His dedication in collecting newspaper articles may suggest pride or even hubris, but it is also possible that Webb subscribed to a clipping service once he had become a public figure.[21] Webb's donation also suggests false modesty in his constant protests that he was not an important individual, and instead belief that his life's work would be of use to future historians. Webb also left several volumes of the records of his printing business to the National Library, forming one of the most comprehensive records of a nineteenth-century Irish printing business, and his sister gave a collected volume of Webb's pamphlets to the National Library after his death.

In addition, Webb had a voluminous correspondence with nearly all of the major figures in the home rule movement. Most of these collections are held in archives in the Republic of Ireland. The most important sources are his correspondence with Davitt, J. F. X. O'Brien and William O'Neill Daunt, but he also corresponded with John Dillon, Isaac Butt, Charles Stewart Parnell and T. M. Healy. His correspondence with Naoroji is held in the National Archives of India.

Webb wrote regularly and self-published when necessary. Most famous for his *Compendium*, he also wrote approximately 150 pieces for newspapers (letters and articles) and published a range of articles on social and political issues including 'The propriety of conceding the elective franchise to women' and *The Opinions of Some Protestants regarding Their Catholic Fellow-Countrymen*.[22] Towards the end of his life he produced a short pamphlet stating many of his philosophies, titled *Thoughts in Retirement*.[23]

This is, in fact, the principal source problem in writing a biography of Webb: there is abundance, not paucity, of archival material on Webb, but most of it was created by the man himself. This does lead to instances where Webb's account of a story is the only surviving one. While always trying to remain critical, I had to place a certain amount of trust in Webb (as have other historians of the Home Rule era, who have relied on his emotive accounts of the Parnell Split). As this is the first full-length study of Webb, I have, in turn, tried to earn the trust of my reader by offering a detailed account constructed from the large amount of source material available. In telling a detailed story, I am also mindful of Linda Colley's statement in her masterful biography of Elizabeth Marsh: 'adopting a purely abstract approach to changes and influences that transcend continents means that we understand them only imperfectly. There can and should be no Olympian version of world history, and there is always a human and individual dimension.'[24] Without an exploration of Webb's trials as the treasurer of a cash-strapped political organisation, or his sensitivity to personal attacks from colleagues, his Indian political intervention is just an abstract historical anecdote, rather than the result of a series of political and social roles and decisions.

These overlapping roles are presented in the next six chapters, roughly following the chronology of Webb's life. This progression can also be understood as six ideological building blocks: in successive chapters, Webb builds on his beliefs in Quaker conscience and justice, racial and gender equality and human rights, and these beliefs manifest themselves in social activism, nationalism and anti-imperialism. Over the course of Webb's career his personal networks also shift and overlap and as a general trend his spheres of influence move eastward around the globe: from Australia, to Boston, to Dublin, to London, to India. Soon after his return from India as Congress President in early 1895, he took a major trip with his wife to retrace his youthful travels, such that he circumnavigated the globe in fewer than 18 months; literally, his influences and beliefs came full circle, such that at the peak of his career he could be described as a truly global thinker.

Chapter 2 explores Webb's upbringing by progressive Quaker printers. The atmosphere in which Webb grew up was simultaneously self-contained and universal: although the family life was physically centred around the small world of the family printing shop and the Society of Friends community, Webb's parents brought the world's problems and treasures to their children's doorstep. Through their involvement in myriad progressive causes they educated their children to believe in social justice for all people. These views placed them firmly in the radical political side of the major debate within Irish Quakerism. His parents' brand of Quaker societal responsibility is explored through their social and political contacts and contextualised within the history of Quakerism. Their close relationship with prominent American abolitionists, especially William Lloyd Garrison and Frederick Douglass, is explained. The Webbs' printing business made the family a major ally for many progressive causes; the prime example is their printing of the first European edition of Douglass's autobiography, using the proceeds to organise and fund his 1845 Irish lecture tour.

Chapter 3 demonstrates how Webb entered public life in mid-Victorian Dublin, transferring his parents' beliefs in social justice into a wide range of progressive activities. In particular, I analyse Webb's involvement in the movements for temperance, women's suffrage and the repeal of the Contagious Diseases Acts, and the relationship between these organisations and their sister societies in Britain. What begins to emerge most strikingly is the fact that Dublin was home to many progressive, cosmopolitan individuals and to a healthy civic life. For the most part, this activity had nothing to do with national politics, nor was it isolated within Ireland's borders. Webb's printing business made him a central and intermediary figure in many of Dublin's progressive societies. Although there has been ample scholarly work on Irish social activism, most of it has been written in an Irish women's history framework, and neither the experience of men nor the international context has been emphasised.[25]

Chapter 4 explains how Webb translated his sense of social justice into support for the fledgling home rule movement. Recruited by Isaac Butt in 1870 as a token Protestant home ruler, Webb occupied a series of administrative positions in the movement. He experienced frustration and disappointment when the movement did not progress according to his wishes and embrace policies in support of female suffrage and international responsibility. This chapter draws on the records of the Home Rule League which allow me to refocus the history of the Irish Party of this period, concentrating on its internal workings, its efforts to court Irish Protestants and its strained relationship with Irish nationalists in Britain.

Chapter 5 reveals Webb's forgotten role in one of the most-studied areas of Irish history, from the rise of the Parnellite Irish Party in 1880 to the failure of the second home rule bill in 1893. Webb offers new insights into Parnell's management style and the way in which decisions were made in the Party. As a treasurer and insider in the Party, Webb expressed frustration at the Party's loose financial management, yet he also revelled in the alliance with the British Liberal Party as he felt that his nationalism was finally re-converging with his social activism. Webb also began to find his voice as an advocate for increased justice and responsibility in international affairs through his writings in Irish, British and American newspapers and through his friendship with his colleague Davitt. Chapters 4 and 5 may appear to be anti-cosmopolitan in their detailed focus on the organisation of Irish home rule, but it is in this experience that we can understand how Webb's cosmopolitan vision for political justice was both logistically frustrated and allowed the ideological space in which it could develop.

Chapter 6 bridges the national and the international dimensions of Webb's political life by exploring the personal friendships between members of the Irish Party, members of the Liberal Party and some Indian nationalists living in London. Webb's friendships reveal much about the character of the nationalist movement, the communities, identities and relationships that were behind decisions, and of course about Webb himself. Building on the political framework to Webb's career detailed in the two previous chapters, a structure of friendships within the Party can be outlined and the allowances these friendships made for a cosmopolitanism subculture can be understood. Close examination of correspondence between members of the Party is used to explore the nature of late-Victorian masculinity, and most significantly how masculinity was shaped by racial theories and nationalism.

In Chapter 7 Webb's cosmopolitan nationalism results in the most important event in his political career. As an MP in London Webb found common cause with individuals from across the British Empire. This chapter explores in detail how Webb's internationalism culminated in his selection for the presidency of the tenth annual Indian National Congress in 1894. This chapter will trace the events leading up to Webb's presidency, first identifying Webb within the strands of thought in Irish nationalist internationalism, using the Parnell–Rhodes correspondence and offerings some corrections to other interpretations of the writings of the controversial yet much-cited O'Donnell. Second, the chapter describes how and why Irish nationalists like Webb formed relationships with other cosmopolitans, particularly Indians, in late nineteenth-century London.

Chapter 8 concludes the study with the aftermath of Webb's Congress presidency in terms both of Indian–Irish affairs and of the progress of the home rule movement. In spite of his continued contact with his Indian friends, Webb entered the twentieth-century feeling frustrated about the Irish and Indian nationalist movements. He was confused by some of the cultural changes taking place in Ireland and was concerned about political apathy. He remained entirely committed to the constitutional goals of the home rule movement and of the potential for Irish people to effect change in international affairs.

2
'Interested in people of all countries, especially of America': A Quaker Family in the Atlantic World

Alfred Webb was born into the Religious Society of Friends and it was this organisation that shaped his early personal and political networks. Webb's parents espoused a particularly radical form of Quakerism that laid the foundations for Webb's future involvement in political and civic life, and they also shaped Webb's intellectual spheres of reference. They negotiated the demands and responsibilities of Quakerism in a time in which Quakers were divided over the ethics of public engagement. In the name of social responsibility and justice, Webb's parents became vigorous campaigners for political causes, particularly the abolition of American slavery. They used their printing business to further their progressive causes and they amassed a transatlantic network of activists, writers and philanthropists. Webb inherited both this network and the fraught relationship with the Society of Friends, and these shaped his political actions later in life.

A Quaker family in Victorian Ireland

To understand Webb's socialisation within the Religious Society of Friends, it is important to note the political and social position of the Society, and Webb's family, in nineteenth-century Ireland. In nineteenth-century Ireland members of the Religious Society of Friends were deeply divided over the propriety of their participation in broader political and social life. At the same time, the religious community was extremely close-knit, even exclusive. Webb's family was at the centre of these changes: they challenged traditional teachings, flouted rules and eventually resigned in protest from the Society.

Alfred Webb's parents, Richard Davis Webb ('R. D.', 1805–1872) and Hannah Waring Webb (1810–1862), were both born into long-standing Irish Quaker families. Webb was the eldest child and had three younger siblings, Richard, Deborah and Anne. Hannah Webb was born in Waterford and had been educated at a girls' school in Clonmel, County Tipperary. R. D. was born in Dublin, attended the Ballitore Quaker school in County Kildare and was apprenticed to a printer in Dublin. Neither R. D. nor Hannah attended university, which was still considered unusual and unnecessary for non-conformists who usually planned on entering a trade. However, they read extensively, engaged in intellectual debates and encouraged learning in their children. They spoke French well, took German lessons together as adults and corresponded with each in Latin.[1] William Lloyd Garrison described R. D. as,

> Though not a graduated scholar, he was, nevertheless, very broadly educated by his own industry and aptitude for the acquirement of general knowledge; and his reading was of the more varied and extensive character. His epistolary correspondence was far-reaching, and with some of the brightest and best men and women of the age.[2]

Webb himself was taught by private tutors at home and then sent to Dr Hodgson's high school in Manchester. It is not clear why Webb did not go to Ballitore, but correspondence between R. D. and the Scottish phrenologist George Combe on scientific schooling shows that he took his sons' education seriously and sought the best tutors for them; Combe and Hodgson were both closely associated with Manchester Quakers and educationalists, including Jacob Bright.[3] Webb's brother Richard also attended Dr Hodgson's for 3 years and was then apprenticed at Shackleton's Mill (run by the Quaker Shackleton family in Kildare), and his sister Anne attended teacher training college in Nottingham.[4] Webb, like his parents, was strongly encouraged to marry within the Irish Quaker community, and in 1861 he married Elizabeth Shackleton.

The preference for Quaker associations evident in Webb's life – in terms of education, apprenticeships and marital partner – reflects an insularity that the community perhaps developed through its history of persecution and withdrawal from mainstream societal mores. The Religious Society of Friends is a Christian, Protestant, non-conformist sect founded by George Fox in England in 1652. The Society that George Fox established was a reaction to the turbulence of the English Civil War and the tumultuous religious climate of the Reformation. His Society based itself on a commitment to quiet reflection, simplicity and the avoidance of conflict.

The Quakers faced suspicion and even persecution in England for their non-conformist views and quickly established communities in Ireland and the American colonies. The first Quaker settlement in Ireland was established by William Edmondson in 1654 in Lurgan.[5] At the beginning of the nineteenth century approximately 4500 Quakers lived in Ireland, and a small but vibrant Quaker community of 650 was well-established in Dublin.[6] Other centres of Quaker settlement were in County Kildare and in southern parts of the country, including Cork, Waterford and Clonmel. Webb recalled in his youth that Quaker social events were scheduled during the 9-day annual meeting, when Quakers from across Ireland would come to Dublin and stay with their relatives and friends. He remembered 70 people meeting for tea, conversation and parlour games, 'in a house at which no Friend would now [1904] invite more than a dozen'.[7] The social circle was tightly knit and meetings were social as well as religious events for the highly self-contained community.

The Society was formative for its members in part, perhaps, because it was so unusual in its devotional practices. Quaker worship is based on silence and the belief that members will access God and experience divine light through prayerful reflection.[8] Meeting houses are usually simply constructed buildings and worship is often conducted with the congregation sitting in a circle. The term 'meeting' is used to describe both an occurrence and a community, such that the Dublin Monthly Meeting refers both to the event and to the congregation. As Quakerism rejects hierarchy before God, there is no clergy. Simplicity is encouraged in every aspect of daily life, in the nineteenth century most noticeably in dress. The pursuit of peace, not only in terms of denouncing warfare but also in maintaining peaceful dealings with other individuals, is an important tradition. In the nineteenth century Irish and British Quakers were divided as to whether this peace testimony required them to take direct political action for peaceful causes, or to withdraw and distance themselves from potential controversy.

The Society did not set doctrine, although decisions reached at meetings were recorded and printed as *Rules of Discipline of the Yearly Meeting of Friends in Ireland*. R. D. Webb printed the 1841 version of this text, which set down behavioural guidelines for every aspect of Quaker life, from treatment of servants to choosing suitable reading material. The Webbs often disregarded the *Rules*. They purchased a piano for their two daughters to play,[9] even though the *Rules* prohibited music and dancing, 'which have no better object than sensual gratification'.[10] They also hired apprentices from a range of religious denominations[11] although the *Rules* argued that Friends should 'give preference to our own members' and ensure that apprentices take part in Quaker worship.[12] The *Rules* warned that novels were corrupting,[13] but the Webb children were allowed to read novels; a favourite was *Jane Eyre*.[14] Since R. D. himself had printed the *Rules*, he could not claim ignorance of its content. He was not alone in disregarding some of the Society's traditions in his private life. Within some of the most fundamental and widely accepted traditions of the Society of Friends there was tension in the nineteenth century, and the Webbs represent the faction within the Society that embraced political and social radicalism in favour of isolationism.

The Quaker community in Ireland also courted controversy in terms of its attitudes towards the law. As non-conformists, they often refused to take the religious oaths that were demanded in the Penal Era. Waterford City allowed Quakers to trade without taking oaths and this led to the growth of a Quaker community there.[15] Many Quakers also refused to pay tithes to the established Church of Ireland; Webb recalled that his father's refusal to pay tithes resulted once in the police confiscating furniture from the family home.[16] The Society viewed 'the imposition of religious exercises by the civil government...[as] an infringement of the rights of conscience'.[17] Therefore, Quakers were encouraged not to observe public fast days or religious holidays, but to keep their shops open and go about business as usual.[18] However, the Society of Friends did not promote widespread civil disobedience: taxpaying was encouraged so that Friends would not 'defraud the king in any branch of his revenues'.[19]

As in Great Britain, the Quaker business community in Ireland flourished. Quakers tended to employ themselves as craftsmen or merchants, rather than as farmers; in seventeenth- and eighteenth-century Dublin they could be found working as grocers, tanners, glovers, bakers and shopkeepers.[20] In the nineteenth century in the greater Dublin area most of life's necessities and some luxuries could be supplied by Quaker businesses, including the Edmondson laundry, Bewley's importers and restaurants, Barrington's soap, Allen's clothing shops, Jacob's grocers, Webb's printing shop and Shackleton's mill.[21]

The *Rules* strongly advised Friends against entering politics, due to the 'lamentable extent to which political animosity prevails amongst the inhabitants of this land'. Its 1835 decision concluded that political life was not Christian life, and, 'on seeking to be redeemed from the world and its spirit', Friends should set 'an instructive example of the meek, loving, and inoffensive deportment which characterizes the true Christian'.[22] For reformist Friends this attitude was evidently inadequate. Quakers like the Webbs disavowed neutrality: rather than avoiding politics they hoped to defeat sectarianism and temper animosity in Irish politics.

Transatlantic social justice and anti-slavery

As believers in the Quaker responsibility to lobby for social justice, R. D. and Hannah Webb had a natural sociopolitical network of like-minded Friends. Their home and their printing business were natural meeting places, real and virtual, for the exchange and productions of ideas across a large network of activists. R. D. and Hannah's activism spanned a broad range of social causes, which can be seen to reflect major Quaker theological concerns, and most particularly the cause of the abolition of American anti-slavery.

'We were interested in people of all countries, especially of America,' Alfred Webb argued in his autobiography.[23] Dubbed 'anti-everythingarians', R. D. and Hannah kept their home open to liberal-minded and often radical philanthropists and thinkers, both male and female.[24] Reminiscing about his childhood in his autobiography, Webb presented his young self as well aware of the changes happening in the world, and his memoirs give the impression that as a child he believed he was living in an exhilarating age.[25] His involvement in foreign affairs as an adult may have led him to overemphasise his interest in the same as a child, but it is indisputable that his parents took a profound interest in the extra-Irish world.

Visitors to the Webb household during Webb's youth included the American Quaker Lucretia Mott, the economist and essayist Harriet Martineau, and Asenath Nicholson, an American Quaker philanthropist and 'pronounced vegetarian' who wrote testimonies about the Irish Famine.[26] The Webbs were very involved in the Garrisonian movement to abolish slavery and American abolitionists Frederick Douglass and William Lloyd Garrison were invited to visit. They shared this interest in abolitionism with visitors Daniel O'Connell and Dr R. R. Madden, the historian of the United Irishman and an ex-colonial medic.[27] Other visitors from the United States included a group of Native American Indians, who visited the Webbs in the 1840s. He recalls these visitors having breakfast at the Webb home dressed in animal skins and feathers, attracting a considerable crowd on the street outside the window of the breakfast room.[28]

R. D. and Hannah read widely and their children were exposed to new literature. Favourites included *Uncle Tom's Cabin*, which Hannah read to the children as a serial in an American newspaper.[29] The family also subscribed to Garrison's abolitionist newspaper *The Liberator* and Joseph Barker's English Chartist paper *The People*.[30] Webb vividly recalled reading new literature on Irish antiquities, especially the debates on the origin of round towers, and the report of the Ordnance Survey when he was a teenager.[31] His uncle read John Mitchel's *United Ireland* to him and his cousins and Webb remembered feeling strongly inspired by the rebellion of 1848.[32] Such autobiographical memories, written more than 50 years after the events, are tinted with a humour that lends credibility. Webb seems to have been amused when he recalled how, at the age of 14, he and the printing apprentices made plans to construct barricades to take part in the 1848 revolution, and 'promised at all events to stand firmly by each other when we found ourselves in the dock'.[33]

Events in far-off lands such as the American South or British India were very real to Webb, and his and his parents' interest in these places and their inhabitants bore no recognisable trace of exoticism. News of the progress of the Mexican War, the Opium Wars in China and the Crimean War (all of which the Webbs opposed) was eagerly consumed by the family. In his late teens Webb was sent to Australia to improve his health. He took to the physical life, at one point walking some 500 miles across the continent, and worked as a ship hand on his return journey to Ireland. The trip was the first of several long-distance journeys across the Indian Ocean and perhaps gave him confidence that the world was a small and navigable place. The Webbs' interaction with foreigners through their progressive interests also normalised far-off lands decades before the Irish middle classes indulged in regular transoceanic (and non-emigratory) travel.

Webb's retrospective judgement was that, as a man in his twenties, he interpreted the world as one in which a struggle was taking place between large powers and newly empowered nations: 'The horrors of the Indian Mutiny – horrors mainly discreditable to England – war between France and Austria on the plains of the Piedmont – and then most exciting of all, Garibaldi's progress in the liberation of Italy, profoundly moved us.'[34] Again, Webb may be overemphasising his own interest at the time, but his parents were certainly moved, so much so that they invited some Italian exiles to dine at their home. Years later, Webb still had romantic memories of Italian radicals and tried to publish Mazzini's letters (Mazzini also had anti-slavery interests),[35] but found his Irish parliamentary career too demanding of his time.[36]

Not all of the Webbs' interests were in distant lands. Ireland was fertile ground for Quaker philanthropy. A Central Relief Committee was established in Dublin to coordinate Quaker Famine relief efforts in the 1840s and the Webbs printed most of its documents. Some Quakers in Britain and Ireland made an effort to tour the areas affected by the Famine to assist with relief and report back their findings to their communities. In 1847 Webb toured famine-affected regions with his father and the Quaker philanthropist William Forster (father of the future Lord Lieutenant of Ireland), and future MP and confectionary magnate Joseph Rowntree also attributed his interest in the relief of poverty to his visit to Ireland in that same year.[37] One English Quaker who visited affected areas found the Central Relief Committee to be very well organised, and was impressed that 'some Friends devote almost all their time, giving up day and night to its concerns and management.'[38]

The Webbs' attitudes towards domestic politics are slightly more ambiguous. 'I cannot recall a time,' Webb claimed in his autobiography, 'when I was not deeply interested in the history, antiquities, and politics of Ireland', although he never mentions his parents pushing him in a nationalistic direction. Certainly, young Webb remembered hearing stories of the French revolution and the rebellions of 1798 and 1803 from witnesses.[39] It is known that R. D. was a friend of O'Connell, principally because the two shared an interest in abolitionism. However, this does not mean that R. D. was necessarily nationalistic: both he and O'Connell were politically at ease within a larger British liberal tradition. Before Irish politics became polarised between nationalists and unionists, Catholic emancipation and electoral reform were issues that many liberals, regardless of their religious or family background, could support. In that sense, there is nothing unusual about a Quaker businessman and a Catholic politician being friends in 1840s Dublin. However, R. D. probably felt less comfortable with O'Connell's focused targeting of the Catholic masses and Catholic priests in his campaigns. In a letter to an American abolitionist R. D. wrote, 'I know what an abominable thing is Popery...I see how it breeds and fosters ignorance, lies, cruelty, fanaticism – I know it is the curse of Ireland.'[40] His correspondence with some American abolitionists is also tinged with anti-Catholicism, and fears that Irish Catholic superstition was rubbing off on American visitors to Ireland.[41]

Just as R. D. could detest Catholicism as a social phenomenon and be friends with O'Connell, he had many English friends but could be anti-English in political terms. R. D. boycotted Queen Victoria's first visit to Ireland because he believed that the English 'despised' the people of

Ireland.⁴² He also collected, with James Haughton, 25,000 signatures on a petition for mercy for the lives of convicted Young Irelanders in 1848,⁴³ although their campaign may have been motivated by the Quaker disapproval of the death penalty, and not by nationalistic feelings.

One more bizarre story concerning the Webbs' interest in the Irish past deserves scrutiny. In his autobiography and in several public speeches, Webb remarked that inside the family home had been the 'dried, mummy-like head' of John Sheares, who was executed by hanging and subsequently beheaded for his involvement in the 1798 rebellion.⁴⁴ Beheading was punishment for high treason and bodies of traitors were not always rejoined with their respective heads. The head, which bore an anguished expression and a rope-burned neck, was displayed in a glass case, having been removed from Sheares's coffin in what Webb described simply as a 'prank'. Webb apparently was not frightened by the head, but took it as a reminder of the sacrifice men like Sheares had made for Ireland. The historian Dr Madden spotted the head on a social visit to the Webb home and with R. D.'s permission returned it to the grave.⁴⁵ Webb gives few details about the appearance and condition of the head or the way in which it was reinterred.

The fact that a future Irish Party MP grew up with the severed head of an Irish nationalist hero could not be a trivial detail. Unfortunately, it is difficult to contextualise this grotesque feature of the Webbs' home life. Although Irish Protestants are often associated with the Gothic, the Webbs were not members of the Anglican Ascendancy and did not have the class anxieties or sense of social instability that is seen as contributing towards a self-association with the macabre.⁴⁶ Besides, an actual severed head is a step beyond Gothic literary tropes of monsters in Big Houses. In her study of the middle-class Victorian parlour, Thad Logan explains that Victorian interest in the natural world led many Victorians to display shells, fossils and geological curios in 'cabinets of curiosity' in their parlours.⁴⁷ She also explains that taxidermy had evolved into a 'perfectly acceptable hobby for young ladies' in the mid-Victorian era and these ladies were encouraged to create items for display in the parlour, such as screens made from the wings and head of dead birds. Stuffed animals were very popular decorative items in the Victorian home, and 'stuffed birds, in particular, were not only common but the sign of a certain refinement.'⁴⁸ However, Logan makes no mention of stuffed human heads on display in curio cabinets, and Webb's description of the Sheares head does not suggest that it was trussed up to serve as decoration. In terms of nationalist history, the cult surrounding national heroes meant that 'relics' of these individuals were often claimed by private individuals. In some cases it was a desire to maintain the dignity of the hero's body that led to the remains going missing; one example is that of Robert Emmet, whose remains were buried and later moved, and whose head and body were buried separately.[49] However, the Webbs' case, of actually keeping such a relic on display in their home, seems to be an extreme and unique one.

The Webbs' home – which often must have felt like a hostel for the world's travelling progressives, or a museum of radicals, both living and mummified – was also shaped by the omnipresence of their religious community. It is possible to illustrate some of the changes and disharmony by examining how the Webbs still incorporated three broad Quaker traditions into their international radicalism: the avoidance of conflict, the belief in sobriety and the pursuit of justice. Translated into actual campaigns, these traditions can be explored as pacifism, the temperance movement, and several of the movements for social justice.

Avoiding conflict is an important Quaker tradition, both in everyday personal relationships and with regard to armed conflict. The Quakers refused to take part in wars and have long been associated with pacifism, particularly in Ireland where they were caught in the midst of the 1798 rising but refused to take arms on either side of the struggle. In the nineteenth century interpretations of the Quaker peace testimony were challenged; Friends in Britain and Ireland were unsure about, for example, whether or not they could support the anti-slavery North in the American Civil War because it was fighting a just cause.[50] Friends also seemed confused about what the correct attitude was to take in relation to British imperial expansion and imperial wars.[51] Webb appears to have been reluctant to privilege pacifism over civil rights. Although he did not condone or encourage warfare, he often argued that the right to bear arms was crucial and that the Irish deserved this right as the British did. Writing to the editor of the *New York Nation* in 1875, he argued forcefully against the Coercion Act, which he insisted 'has deprived five and a half millions of people of the most dearly-prized political rights – the right to carry arms'.[52]

Sobriety, in the widest sense of the word, is another aspect of Quaker heritage. The tradition of sober and simple dress, decorum and behaviour fed into the temperance movement. The *Rules* argued that excessive drinking was sinful, although it did not demand total abstention from alcoholic beverages.[53] R. D. Webb founded the Irish Temperance Union (ITU, later known as the Hibernian Temperance Society) in 1829 with Richard Allen and James Haughton, in the hope that temperance would become a mass movement. Both Allen and Haughton were brought up Quaker; Haughton formally withdrew his membership in the 1830s but continued attending meetings all his life. The three men, who shared so many overlapping progressive interests, came to be known locally as 'the Faction'. Their temperance ambitions were fulfilled by Father Theobald Mathew, who did achieve a mass movement and became friendly with the founders of the ITU.

Webb was teetotal and supported the temperance movement throughout his entire life. He did not make temperance a cornerstone of his public policy because he saw it as a matter of personal choice over which he had little hope of influence: drink is consumed 'by those fully informed and who are free agents'.[54] Still, he claimed at the height of the home rule crisis that 'Drinking is the greatest bar to our political advancement,' and 'total abstinence is one of the greatest discoveries of the age.'[55] Throughout his career he also opposed measures which he believed would strengthen the 'drink interest' in Ireland, such at the 1904 Government Licensing Bill.[56]

Social justice, as a broad term, was held by many Quakers as the most important crusade in society. It can be understood as stemming from a belief in total egalitarianism among people, and the right of all to enjoy the same rights and protection under the law. It has been combined with a witness to alleviate suffering: Quaker relief and charity work falls also into this category. Quakers who held these values in high esteem have felt compelled to campaign on a wide range of issues, but social justice became problematic when it moved beyond local poor relief into the realm of global politics. The anti-slavery campaign is the best example.

The anti-slavery movement in Britain and Ireland thrived on the involvement of many Quakers and the Society had been concerned with anti-slavery since the early eighteenth century.[57] However, the issue was not universally accepted by Quakers: Webb recalled one of his Quaker cousins expressing the view that 'slavery was very bad; but that Anti-Slavery was worse'.[58] Friends who opposed slavery saw it as an immoral practice and affront to their egalitarian values, in which all people were equal before God and should be treated equally by their fellow men and women. Other Friends did not support the anti-slavery movement, not necessarily because they supported slavery (though some did) but because they shunned politics, which they saw as inherently antagonistic.

For the Webbs, Haughtons and Allens, slavery was an abhorrent practice and an example of the weak being exploited by the strong.[59] Their dedication to the cause was rooted in Quaker egalitarianism, and not any sense of special Irish identification with enslaved people. These

Dublin abolitionists' interest began in the 1830s and received a great boost when several of them attended the World Anti-Slavery Convention in 1840 in London. There they made contact with American abolitionists, including Garrison. Their efforts back in Dublin were based on raising awareness and funds for the campaign, especially through printing books and pamphlets on the subject, writing letters to various newspapers and inviting speakers to give public lectures. Anecdotal evidence exists that some Quakers outside urban areas took the movement to heart, such as Enniscorthy shop-owner and Quaker Francis Davis (1807–1890) who refused to sell sugar because it was produced by slave labour;[60] no anecdotal evidence has been unearthed to measure the Enniscorthy consumers' reaction. However, there is evidence of what the American abolitionists thought of their Irish counterparts: R. D.'s death was noted in several American newspapers, and Garrison argued that R. D. 'deserves to be long and well remembered on both sides of the Atlantic... To him the anti-slavery movement in the United States was largely indebted for his efficient cooperation from 1840.'[61]

The ITU, which met weekly at the Royal Exchange, did not simply consider temperance but became a forum for discussing all these topics related to justice. Haughton's son remembered that those meetings in the 1840s and 1850s were chiefly devoted to 'temperance, peace, anti-slavery and British India'.[62] Their reaction to India and China combined justice, sobriety and pacifism: the Faction objected to both the opium trade and the wars into which the two countries were dragged as a result. Beginning in the 1830s they held public meetings, in cooperation with the English MP James Silk Buckingham, to campaign to abolish the East India Company's monopoly and promote free trade with India and China.[63] The Faction also formed the Dublin British India Committee in the 1840s and the Hibernian Peace Society.[64] The differences between all these societies are not clearly defined in the available sources, probably because of the large overlap in membership and leadership.

Although three prominent Dublin Quakers were actively campaigning for these progressive causes, which they saw as vital expressions of Quaker justice, these issues became fault lines between members of the Society. Ironically, the family printing business, which gained much business from the Society of Friends, also fuelled the Webbs' rift with the Society. In 1846 the American abolitionist and freed slave Frederick Douglass visited Ireland on a lecture tour. Douglass's memoir of slavery, *Narrative of the Life of Frederick Douglass, an American Slave*, was first published in Boston in 1845 by the Anti-Slavery Office. The preface, written by Garrison, quoted O'Connell in support of abolitionism, and described O'Connell as 'the distinguished advocate of universal emancipation, and the mightiest champion of prostrate but not conquered Ireland'.[65] R. D. was eager to bring the cause of abolitionism to the wider Irish public and he and Douglass arranged to reprint the narrative for the first time in Europe. R. D. printed and sold 4000 copies in 1845, and used the proceeds to defray the cost of an Irish lecture tour for Douglass.[66] R. D. arranged most of the details of Douglass's tour, including lectures in Quaker meeting houses and accommodation with extended members of the Webb family in Wexford, Waterford, Cork and Limerick.

On a personal level, the tour was edifying but not entirely successful for R. D. Webb. R. D. decided that he disliked Douglass, and found him haughty; he also believed that Douglass was trying to make personal financial gains from the tour,[67] which was perhaps somewhat unfair because Douglass was dependent on public speaking for his income. R. D. also seems to have wanted Douglass to be more humble and more grateful, which may reveal something about R. D.'s attitudes and should not be taken at face value as a verdict on Douglass's character.

R. D. was understandably frustrated with Douglass, though, for criticising American Quakers and Methodists during a speech in the Dublin Quaker Meeting House, because as a result Douglass and Webb were subsequently banned from using the House for anti-slavery events.[68] The incident reinforced the Webbs' frustration with Irish Quakers at their failure to adopt the anti-slavery movement in the way they wished. In response, R. D. resigned from the Society, marking his displeasure with the Society's refusal to campaign for various social issues which he felt were consistent with their Christian witness. His biographer argues that R. D. felt 'intellectual claustrophobia from the implicit claims which he felt his own closely inbred Quaker community made on him'.[69] R. D.'s resignation seems to have made little practical difference but was a statement of principle. In 1857, aged 23, Alfred Webb also resigned in protest: as explained below, it was a grand gesture but did not lead to a permanent estrangement.

A print network

Douglass's autobiography is a chief example of how the Webbs used their family printing business to garner support for causes in which they believed. Webb's printing would prove to be another stepping stone in his public life. The relationship between printing and politics, from the French Revolution to the growth of nationalism, has been the subject of much scholarly work.[70] Webb was no exception: his printing proved to be a springboard into his own political career, and he had local, national and international printing clients and audiences. Printing was a growing but volatile trade in nineteenth-century Ireland, but the Webbs shielded themselves from economic downturns by printing a diverse range of material.

R. D. completed a standard printing apprenticeship and opened his own printing business in 1828. By the spring of 1829 he had nine employees listed regularly in his wage books.[71] He took on a business partner, another Quaker named Richard Chapman, and a larger print shop in 1832.[72] The partnership lasted nearly 20 years, and ended amicably when Chapman decided to open his own print business in the back of his house.[73] Chapman's decision happily coincided with Alfred Webb's return from Australia and R. D. renamed his business R. D. Webb and Sons. As the eldest, Webb was the heir apparent to the business, and had begun working alongside his father as a child. His younger brother Richard also worked in the press for pocket money but was apprenticed out since 'there would not have been room for both of us'.[74] After R. D.'s death in 1872 Alfred Webb ran the business on his own until he sold it in 1890. Printing was a major and burgeoning industry in nineteenth-century Ireland. In 1870, R. D. Webb and Sons was one of 73 Dublin printing works and by 1890 printing employed approximately 13 per cent of Dublin's manufacturing workforce.[75]

Webb donated three volumes of business records to the National Library of Ireland the year before his death.[76] Although these do not give a complete record of every aspect of the business, they are still one of the most comprehensive sources on a nineteenth-century Irish printing business. Combined with a range of anecdotal sources and extant printed material, it is possible to explore how the Webbs stayed in business so long while taking on a range of philanthropic and social printing projects. The bill book lists printing jobs which can be grouped into types, in approximate descending order of importance: business-related printing, including printing for the railways; printing for philanthropic, social and political organisations; printing for religious organisations; printing for private individuals; and finally printing of non-fiction literature. Webb remembered that his father's business partner, Chapman, was a strict Quaker and as such would 'not take share of the profits of the printing of any novel, nor even of the book catalogue',[77] and there are few jobs that appear to be fiction.

Business-related printing made up the bulk of the Webb's work 1846–1850. Many of the businesses were Quaker-owned, including Bewley and

Evans, who imported and sold tea, coffee and other victuals long before the first Bewley's Café opened in 1894. Most of their printing orders were for labels for bottled beverages. The Webbs printed for cousins, also named Webb, who owned a clothing store. Orders included receipts, reports, circulars, advertisement posters and printed and ruled account books for the running of the business. A third, frequent Quaker customer was George Shackleton of Shackleton Mills in Ballitore, where Richard Webb was apprenticed; he ordered shop bills[78] and labels.[79] The Allens, a Quaker family who owned a clothing shop, ordered broadsides to advertise their frock coats.[80] The railways were important customers for the Webbs, especially the Dublin Kingstown Railway and the Midland Railway lines. During one typical week in 1846, the Webbs printed 400 receipts and 250 circulars for the Midland Railway, and 100 statements of accounts and 500 documents listing proprietors' names for the Dublin Kingstown Railway.[81]

The business printing demonstrates how members of the Quaker community patronised each others' businesses, and how the Webbs could rely on steady business printing to finance their charitable printing. In terms of the number of entries in the bill book, the second largest type of printing done by the Webbs was for philanthropic, social and political organisations. Following on the success of Douglass's narrative, William Brown's *Narrative of William W. Brown, an American Slave* was printed by Webb in 1849. Like Douglass, Brown stayed at the Webb home on his visit to Dublin and was introduced to the Webbs's circle of friends. A number of other short tracts relating to the anti-slavery cause appear in the bill book.

Ironically, the Webbs were at their busiest during Ireland's greatest economic disaster in the nineteenth century, the Famine. Famine-related printing is first noticeable in the bill book in the autumn of 1846, when over 3000 circulars on 'Distress in Ireland' were printed.[82] Over the next few years tens of thousands of circulars were printed for the Central Relief Committee of the Society of Friends – 12,000 alone in July 1848. One particular order of 250 circulars is marked 'clothing affairs' and another is a 'Notice to Pawnbrokers', suggesting that the Committee was concerned with many details regarding the welfare of Famine victims. The obvious issue of supplying food also appears in the form of Indian meal receipts.[83] 'Letters from Kerry' was printed in 1846, and is believed to be a letter concerning Famine conditions in that area. Ironically, due to their high involvement in Famine relief through printing, the Webbs stood a chance of profiting from the Famine; however, all the bill book can prove is that workers were paid for printing, and it is impossible to know whether the Webbs did the work gratis or at a reduced cost.

Anecdotal evidence is available of printing carried out by the Webbs after 1850. One work of major significance that the Webbs printed was Thomas Haslam's 1868 pamphlet 'The marriage problem'. Thomas and his wife Anna Haslam knew the Webbs; like many members of the first wave of Irish feminism they were Quakers.[84] The pamphlet argued for the necessity of limiting family size, and as such is believed to be the earliest printed work on family planning in Ireland, and possibly Britain. The pamphlet distinguished Thomas Haslam as, according to his biographer, 'unique as a nineteenth-century Irishman writing in favour of birth control'.[85] Haslam followed this with a second pamphlet, 'Duties of parents', which advocated sexual abstinence as the most responsible form of birth control.[86] This pamphlet was published in London by Burns in 1872 and the printer is unknown. Not only were the pamphlets courageous achievements by Haslam, they were controversial and bold pamphlets for Webb to print. Webb also printed Haslam's short pamphlet, 'A few words on prostitution and the Contagious Diseases Acts', in 1870. Again, the relationship between the Webbs and their client was enhanced by the fact that they also belonged to the organisation: as described in the next chapter, Webb and Haslam both had leadership roles in the Dublin Branch of the National Association for the Repeal of the Contagious Diseases Acts.[87]

Webb's involvement in Irish nationalism brought much material to be printed, but these projects were not without their complications. Writing in 1881 on behalf of the Ladies' Land League, Anna Parnell implored him: 'I hope you won't boycott us – we have Athy and Riley working for us as well as your house, because we have too much printing for one house to manage.' It seems doubtful that Webb was upset, given Anna's expectations: 'We are not getting too many forms printed, for it is necessary for the forms to be in the hands of the branches before they are required. . . . I ordered 100,000 of each of the three kinds.'[88] Most of the Webb's print jobs for which the number of copies is known were under 3000 copies.

The Webbs have been described as prosperous printers,[89] though in printing for philanthropic causes they often ran the risk of not being paid, or they poured much of their own money back into the causes they supported.[90] In the absence of records of invoices and receipts for the business, it is not possible to know how much printing the Webbs actually did at a discount or for free. However, records of their client organisations often reveal bills unpaid or overdue. The Dublin Women's

Suffrage Association, established in 1876 and of which Webb and his cousins Emily and Helen Webb were members, was running a deficit but its members worried that 'Mr. Webb's printing bill had not been paid.'[91] Webb was also unable to get Haslam to pay for some printing,[92] although their relationship remained amicable.[93]

Likewise, the Irish Parliamentary Party was always cash-strapped and, as one of its treasurers, Webb knew this well. Still, he printed large amounts of material for the cause to which he was devoted, and paid the price. 'The [Irish] Press Agency died £230 in R. D. Webb and Son's debt', Webb noted to another treasurer in 1891, but he refused to take any payment that could instead be directed to the Evicted Tenants Fund. Rather, he agreed to try to make up some of his losses by selling off Press Agency literature 'at less than cost price'.[94]

In spite of the Webbs' business' obvious reliance on Quaker interests, they were not model Quaker employers. Many of Webb's Quaker contemporaries translated their religious ethos into their business models and cast themselves as paternalistic employers who saw it as their mission to care for both the temporal and spiritual well-being of their employees. At a basic level this often included a semi-democratic business structure, where workers had some degree of input into the way the business worked; the Quaker practice of avoiding conflict would also be carried into the work place, particularly with regards to strikes. Larger corporations carried these values a step further, and provided housing, education and healthcare for their employees; for example, Thomas Edmondson of Dublin built houses for his laundry workers, and paid for the medical care if his workers became injured or ill; the Cadbury family built the Bourneville village to house their factory employees; and William Forster established a school for his mill workers.[95]

There is little information about the pastoral care of the Webbs' employees, although Webb did emphasise how they avoided an elitist, hierarchical working set-up.[96] However, the wages that he paid his employees do not seem particularly high, compared to those offered in other trades, and he did not offer any unusual social benefits to his workers.[97] In fact, a flexible labour force, based on the use of many casual workers, seems to have been one of tools the Webbs used to minimise outgoings when business was slow.

Webb and Quakerism

Webb's personality as an employer leads us to the question of the depth of his Quaker beliefs. His early life was indelibly shaped by the experience of being a Quaker, although his relationship with the Society of Friends was, like his parents', fraught. His resignation from the Society of Friends indicated how seriously he took the issues being debated within Quakerism, but he remained in essence a Quaker for the rest of his life and was always considered one by his political colleagues.

Despite the very public and social nature of membership in the Society of Friends, Webb kept his spiritual life private. He offers little information on his spirituality in his autobiography: this could indicate either that it was not important to him, or that it was a private issue that he did not want to share with his audience. However, in order to have some idea what impact his Quaker upbringing may have had on his life and thought, his spirituality deserves what examination is possible from limited sources.

Webb's resignation letter to the Society was polite:

> Never have been more than one [a Quaker] in name, it does not appear to me right or straightforward to continue so, when I do not hold the opinions or act in life as would become a consistent friend – for otherwise than a *consistent* member of any religious persuasion I would not wish to remain. But while thus wishing to withdraw from you in a religious capacity, I expect always to number my most esteemed friends, and those I respect most in life, amongst the members of your body.[98]

After a cooling-off period the Society sent several members to visit Webb at home and ascertain whether he could be persuaded to rethink his decision. Their report back to the Dublin meeting echoed some of the sentiments in his resignation letter, but revealed another factor in Webb's departure:

> Finding he could not unite with some of the opinions of Friends, and desiring to act consistently with any profession he makes, he came to the conclusion he did after much thoughtfulness. Although he states that he does not agree with some of the tenets of the Church of England yet he has for some time past been an attender of the worship of that body, and having found satisfaction in so doing, he expressed his intentions of continuing in the practice.[99]

There is an apparent contradiction in Webb's statement of principle: he resigned because he could not agree with opinions of the Society, but could attend Anglican services without accepting all its tenets. The reference to the Church of England, and not Ireland, is curious, and perhaps indicates the Anglo-centric attitudes of some Dublin Quakers. Webb did not deny his interest in the Anglican communion, and his print business again played a role. While working on a print job for the Marlborough Street National Infant School he travelled to Kingstown to show the proofs to the clients, Mr and Mrs Thomas Young. The couple asked him to dine with them, and they struck up a friendship; soon, he began attending church with them.

How long Webb continued to attend Anglican services is unknown, but he seems to have struggled to find peace with a spiritual tradition throughout his life. According to his autobiography he realised, probably in the 1860s or 1870s, that his parents had not been 'orthodox' Friends, and therefore 'were condemned'. It seems impossible that Hannah and R. D. could have sheltered Webb from orthodox Quakerism and led him to believe that the politics of the Faction were entirely orthodox. Or, Webb may have been completely aware of his parents' differences with the Society, but the reality did not truly sink in until they died and he was forced to consider their fate. Unable to accept that his parents, whom he viewed as ideal Christians, could be slated for damnation, he recalled that 'the edifice of my orthodoxy crumbled beneath and around me.'[100] Webb could hardly have thought of himself as orthodox, but he certainly was deeply troubled by the idea of eternal damnation. In 1876 he rejected the idea, in a pamphlet that was probably written for a non-Quaker audience, and argued that there was no such thing as everlasting punishment after death, even for serious moral transgressions.[101] In spite of Webb's inconsistencies, these instances give the impression that Webb was seriously considering moral and theological questions in his thirties. He may have initially resigned from the Society of Friends out of guilt, perhaps feeling that he was a Quaker 'only in name' because he failed in following the Society's traditions; later in life, he might have gained confidence in his decision to disagree with the 'orthodoxy' that was claimed by the leaders of the Society. Webb had an unfaltering conviction in the moral rectitude of his parents' social crusades; if it led to the conclusion that his parents were damned, then orthodoxy made no sense to Webb.

Ultimately, there are too few sources and too many contradictions to understand Webb's spiritual life, but he seems not to have been alone in his quest for spiritual fulfillment outside of the Society of Friends in this time period. In the 1870s he seems to have abandoned his Anglican worship and began to join Anna and Thomas Haslam (themselves brought up Quakers) and other friends 'on Sunday evenings for social Theistic religious services', taking place in their homes on a rotating basis.[102] Interestingly, he does not reveal his wife's attitudes towards religion, although it seems that she accompanied him to such services.

Although the exact state of his spiritual life in the intervening years is unknown, at the time of writing his autobiography (1904–1906) Webb had come to terms with the Society of Friends and was apparently attending meetings again. He mentions being on his way to the yearly meeting in 1882 when he learned of the Phoenix Park murders.[103] He also wrote, with deep nostalgia, 'While now I could not profess the current beliefs of Friends, or seek formal admission into the Society, I must say that I enjoy the quiet, non-committal hours spent in Friends meeting [sic], so suggestive of thoughts connected with the past,' and admitted a view which was absent from his resignation letter written nearly 50 years earlier: 'I appreciate the many advantages of having been brought up a Friend.'[104] Whether Webb was really appreciating the Society in itself, or simply longing for his lost youth and his family (only his sister Deborah was alive in 1904), is impossible to know.

Webb accepted that throughout his life he was 'regarded as being a Friend, tho I never claimed the appellation'.[105] He did not refute the appellation either. On one occasion, when he was criticised by Quakers for discussing Quaker resistance to law at a public meeting, he made a public apology that explained his mindset:

> It was doubtful taste of one who has left the body to draw its name into such a discussion; but my interests are so much bound up with the Society, and I live so much under the influence of its teachings and history, that it is difficult for me upon all occasions not to have its name on my lips in the discussion of moral questions.[106]

Webb also wrote a number of articles late in his life for Quaker periodicals, including the *British Friend*, on political and social issues. He wrote articles for a variety of other British, Irish and American newspapers so evidently he did not lack other outlets, but wanted to reach a Quaker audience with his views. He also gave 34 papers at the Friends Institute over his lifetime.[107]

The most difficult position for Webb to take, as an Irish Quaker, was one in support of home rule. The size of the rift in the Dublin Monthly Meeting can be measured through a brief examination of the 1893 home rule debate which illustrates the extent to which political attitudes polarised the community and members associated themselves with different factions. Most Friends opposed home rule; they feared that they would be alienated from Friends in Great Britain and they worried about the economic impact upon their businesses. Twenty-two pro-home rule Friends made a statement to the Irish Society of Friends encouraging Friends to support the movement. Furthermore, they accused all Friends who did not support the second home rule bill of belonging to 'that political party which opposed the Abolition of the Slave Trade, Catholic Emancipation, Parliamentary Reform, the Repeal of the Corn Laws, Free Trade, in fact all the great reforms of the century'.[108] The pro-home rule accuser (who could have possibly been Webb) evidently felt that the Society was deeply divided between those who supported reforms and those who had opposed them. There were obvious exceptions that the accuser does not take into account: the Haslams, although not active as Friends by this stage, were reform-minded but anti-home rule. Crucially, the accuser felt that the home rule debate was not an isolated issue, but one that formed part of a wider progressive movement.

In response an anonymous Friend published an open letter, arguing that those Friends who opposed home rule were certainly not Tories, and retorting (rather vaguely) that in fact 'Irish Friends have been actively concerned in promoting all the reforms mentioned.'[109] However, anger and frustration had clearly been building over a 70-year period between two factions. Such issues were not merely political either: they represented fundamentally different interpretations of Quaker witness. Conservatives felt that Friends risked losing necessary focus on peace and divine light by engaging in wider, antagonistic society, and were angered that progressives had created conflict within the Society of Friends. Progressives felt that these conservatives were hiding behind a neutrality testimony that turned a blind eye to injustice throughout the world, and viewed many of the Society's stances as more repressive than benign. The tendency of these liberal Friends to resign from the Society cannot be seen simply as a rejection of that Society, but as one type of experience that was common to a small minority of Friends. What all these Friends – conservative and progressive – had in common is that the Society still played a formative role in their lives and thought. Even many Friends who resigned, including Webb, kept returning to the Society and participating in its practices. The Society gave Webb the support of a close-knit and prosperous community network, a strong sense of social duty and egalitarianism and a belief in self-reliance.

Victorian British liberalism was notable for its Quaker participation, particularly in the leadership of several generations of the Bright family.

It would be erroneous, though, to simply categorise Webb as a prototypical mid-Victorian Quaker politician. As will become evident in the next chapters, Webb's sense of social justice was strongly informed by his Quaker upbringing, but it was articulated and put into action through his primary self-identification as Irish.

3
'The labours and responsibilities nearly killed me'[1]: Webb and Social Activism in Victorian Dublin

Webb's Quaker network and printing business were the springboard from which he became involved in social activism in the greater Dublin area. This activism was then, in turn, the springboard for him to become involved in national elected politics. Social activism can be understood as a broad umbrella term to encompass activity done on a voluntary basis in the public sphere with the intention of building social capital, with particular emphasis on improving the lives of the less fortunate.[2] It covers many social, progressive or reformist organisations and it is a vital form of political expression, particularly for those who are excluded from the elective process, most obviously women. In Webb's case, these activities included the Dublin Statistical Society, the Dublin Women's Suffrage Association, the National Association for the Repeal of the Contagious Diseases Acts (NARCDA) and the Dublin Exhibition committee. As we shall see in Chapters 5 and 6, although more source material is available on Webb's Dublin social activism, he continued in the same activities when he became an MP in London. What is detailed in this chapter, then, could be considered Webb's mid-Victorian liberal and progressive apprenticeship, which ultimately paved the road towards his involvement in much larger imperial concerns.

Webb shared many of these interests with members of his family, and in exploring his civic life it is possible to also comment upon his family life. In addition, Webb became involved in tangential governmental bodies and local politics. Webb's literary life is also relevant, as it was fuelled by the same theories of self- (and social) improvement as his other activist projects. There is a generous amount of scholarly literature on social activism in Ireland that deals with the societies Webb joined and the types of people he knew, and this is a good starting point before revealing the organisations Webb joined, his family relationships, his entry into Dublin politics and his literary contributions.

Social activism in Ireland

Mary Daly's history of the Statistical Society argues that 'in many respects the Society can be seen as an Irish variant of the many moral and social reform movements that were so typical of mid-Victorian England.'[3] On its own, the Society would seem to mimic such a movement: yet in combination with many other social movements in which Webb was involved there is proof that reforming movements in Dublin were rich, varied and deep-rooted. The names of the individuals involved tend to crop up repeatedly, such that it is possible to think of these individuals as part of a recognisable network, despite certain religious faultlines.

Most of Webb's social activism can be characterized as reformist in nature, as opposed to 'benevolent' social work. In her comprehensive study of women philanthropists in nineteenth-century Ireland, Maria Luddy explains that 'benevolent institutions were expressions of a desire on the part of the majority of philanthropic women to do good within a specific organisation which limited both the scope and recipients of its charity.'[4] Examples include schools, orphanages and refuges for the aid of the poor, especially children and 'fallen women'. Reform movements were those that sought 'to improve the plight of the poor and outcast generally through public and political action'.[5] Luddy emphasises that benevolent societies often focused on counselling or 'rescuing' individuals, and not on addressing the underlying social causes of their troubles.[6] In contrast, reformers examined and questioned the existing social order and sought legal overhaul for social problems. Reform societies could sometimes be considered more academic or intellectual.

Reformist groups were usually interdenominational and they often offered opportunities for men and women to work together. The gender divide is evident in the secondary literature on social activism within Ireland and Great Britain.[7] Because much benevolent work was considered women's work – particularly when it involved working with women and children – it is an excellent means of studying women's lives in the nineteenth century. However, because this type of social history has often been written as women's history, the experiences of men involved in social activism have not been emphasised. Webb's experiences of social activism in Ireland are fascinating for what they reveal of individuals coordinating actions and political campaigns across religious and gender lines.

Webb's social activism was rarely benevolent in character. More often Webb devoted his time, resources and talent to activism through the vehicle of the printed word, whether he printed material for a cause or wrote his own opinion pieces. He wrote on politics, on social issues, and in support of organisations of which he was a member. Webb estimated that he wrote between 150 and 175 letters to newspapers, to the *Nation* and *Freeman's Journal* in Ireland, to the *Manchester Guardian* in Great Britain and to papers in the United States and the antipodean colonies. His estimate is confirmed because he clipped these articles and added them to his 'scrapbook'.[8] Most of these letters were written between 1865 and 1905, so on average he might have been contributing four letters per year. In 1883 he was commissioned to write a series of articles on Irish politics for the *New York Nation* under the pseudonymous initials 'D. B.', the last letter in his first and last names.[9] Webb also offered four papers to the Statistical Society, 34 papers for the Friends Institute, and wrote 21 pamphlets and magazine articles.[10]

Webb's experience of social work was as supervisor rather than attendant. One illustration is the Cork St. Fever Hospital, of which Webb was one of the governors for some years (probably in the 1870s, although he does not gives the exact dates).[11] As part of his duties he attended monthly breakfast meetings and occasionally toured the wards.[12] Certainly, he was not directly involved with nursing patients, a feminine preserve. It is easy to sneer at Webb, so proud of his charitable efforts, when (usually female) hospital nurses took on the dirty work. However, Webb's distance from the patients, who were probably overwhelmingly poor, should not be simply construed as social (or gender) superiority or paternalism. He remarked in his autobiography that some friends were shocked that he was willing to visit patients at all, but that he never became ill with fever himself. Reformists like Webb did not necessarily think themselves above the poor or the ill; they recognised the reality of disease and found other ways of working without endangering their own health.

However, some reformist societies largely removed the human aspect from their investigations; those that based their inquiries and analyses on scientific principles could not have been more different from benevolent women who thought of morality in terms of individual self-control. That is not to say that reformists were not moralists; some simply manipulated their 'scientific' findings to justify moral agendas. Webb himself held both progressive and conservative views, sometimes in contradiction. Although Webb was a suffragist who was most interested in affecting legal change for women, he also believed in personal responsibility and self-control, and could be highly critical of women who did not accept responsibility for their families or who could not behave in a 'moral' way.

One of the foremost reformist societies in Victorian Dublin, and also one of Webb's earliest ventures into public life, was the Dublin Statistical Society, founded in 1847 and renamed the Statistical and Social Inquiry Society of Ireland in 1862 (both are referred to here simply as the Statistical Society). The Statistical Society was not merely devoted to statistics as the manipulation of quantitative data according to statistical rules, but took a wide interest in the social sciences and in conducting research into Irish society.[13] Founding members included men from legal, economic and other professional backgrounds; women were not admitted until 1862. From its inception the Statistical Society had a close connection with the Whately Chair of Political Science at Trinity College Dublin and counted many former Whately professors among its members.

Founded at the height of the Irish famine, the Statistical Society endeavoured to diagnose and heal Ireland's economic and social problems. It prohibited discussion of party politics and instead hoped that scientific principles would offer true and neutral resolution for Ireland's issues. Popular issues for discussion included land reform, legal change and laissez-faire economic principles, and members sought answers to problems of public health, work and education. Beginning in 1856, the papers were published annually by the Society. As well as frequent meetings in Dublin, the Society organised the Barrington lectures, which brought speakers on political economy on a tour of small Irish cities. In addition, the Statistical Society struck links with sympathetic societies in Ireland – normally literary societies and Mechanics' Institutes – and statistical societies in the United States and the rest of Europe.[14] Statistical societies had multiplied across 1830s Britain, including in Belfast, but most of them were short-lived. The Dublin Statistical Society was unusual in that it was both founded after the trend had nearly died out and had impressive longevity. In a history of statistical societies M. J. Cullen makes no reference to the Dublin success story, but one of his explanations for the decline of other societies clearly would not have applied to Ireland: 'the long period of mid-Victorian prosperity and comparative tranquility did not favour theories which stressed the urgency of certain kinds of social reforms.'[15]

Webb was one of the significant number of Quakers who joined, including members of the Pim, Shackleton, Haughton and Barrington families. The Barringtons were soap manufacturers and they endowed the lecture series in their name. The most active member of the Statistical Society (based on the number of papers he gave) was William Neilson Hancock, who married the niece of James Haughton, a Quaker grain merchant and member of the so-called Faction.[16] Haughton was the second-most-active member of that era, offering 24 papers between 1847 and his death in 1873. His papers covered imperial affairs, abolitionism, capital punishment, and of course temperance, for which he became almost notorious for his zeal: Daly describes his papers as 'the most overt instances of statistics being employed to disguise propaganda as fact',[17] although in his centennial history of the Society the economist R. D. Collison Black was much more forgiving. Webb's father R. D. was also a member; though he never gave a paper, he served as librarian for the Statistical Society starting in 1850. As with his interests in abolitionism and temperance, Webb may have become a member of the Society by following in the footsteps of his father. Webb eventually became librarian himself, although the exact dates are unknown. Unsurprisingly, the Webbs also undertook printing for the Statistical Society.[18]

The Statistical Society could boast well-known members, including Archbishop Whateley, John Kells Ingram, the economist John Elliott Cairnes, Samuel Ferguson, Isaac Butt, the printer and almanac producer Alexander Thom and the Ordnance Surveyor and Under-Secretary Thomas Larcom. In membership, the Society reflected the composition of the Dublin bourgeoisie and was largely male, Protestant and educated, and of the unionist persuasion associated with that group. However, since debate about political parties was prohibited any unionist/nationalist divide within the Society was largely irrelevant; all of the members participated because they believed that Ireland's problems could be resolved through the better application of the law and political economy. As a result the Statistical Society could also incorporate individuals who supported both Liberal and Conservative parties in Britain.

Many of the papers presented to the Statistical Society have not aged well, but some were far ahead of their time, such as James Lawson's 1849 denunciation of Malthusian principles, 'The over-population fallacy considered'.[19] Black argues that in the 1860s the Statistical Society encouraged 'free and favourable discussion of social changes which it is now customary to regard as unheard of until much more recent days'.[20] To illustrate his point, he notes papers given on the rights of women, including one presented by Webb.

Black describes Webb as 'an active member',[21] although he presented only four papers in 40 years. However, he evidently assisted as librarian and attended meetings frequently. The four papers that Webb presented reflect his range of interest in social causes, though he admitted that the research drew 'not so much from statistical detail as from my own observations made on the spot'.[22] The papers, spaced roughly 10 years apart, offer insight into the development of Webb's social beliefs.

Webb's first contribution was an 1856 paper titled 'Progress of the colony of Victoria'. Based on his experiences of living in Australia from 1853 to 1855 (where he had been sent to improve his health), he explained that the relative failure of the colony was due to the high price of land. When gold was discovered in the colony, workers made huge wages (Webb states that labourers made 15 shillings a day, while we know that he paid his unskilled workers only 7 or 8 shillings a week). However, land prices skyrocketed, and the result was that workers were 'spending their earnings in gross excess and licentiousness'.[23] Webb's shock at the 'dissolute and intemperate habits of the labouring classes'[24] was matched by his disgust with the newly rich gold prospectors, whom he described as having so much wealth that 'some ate banknotes between slices of bread and butter, as sandwiches.'[25] Webb was only 22 when he wrote and delivered this paper, but he spoke with the great confidence of a moralist, castigating the culture of drink and wild spending and blaming it for social ills. However, he also believed that this behaviour was an inevitable product of the land problem, and that the solution lay in government intervention to set realistic prices on land. Since such reform had begun, Webb was confident that Victoria had returned to sobriety and would become prosperous.[26]

Webb's paper also made one remark on the race problems in Victoria. As with the social problems, he described the situation as deplorable but inevitable. The first European settlers in Australia suffered

> from the incursions and determined hostility of the blacks [aborigines]. Doubtless this hostility was owing, in the first instance, to the white man's aggressions on their territory, and to the violence and injustice with which the settlers often acted towards them. It is hard to say how far civilized nations are justified in the means they take to establish their authority in barbarous regions; but wherever the white man plants his foot, a baptism of blood is almost sure to follow before he establishes his claim to possession.[27]

Webb does not suggest any restitution or compensation for the aboriginal population, but his comment was still sensitive for a man of his time.

He accepts the assumption that aboriginal life was 'barbarous' and that his own was civilized, but also expresses discomfort with imperialism.

Webb's second paper to the Statistical Society, 'Propriety of conceding the elective franchise to women' (1867), was what attracted the attention of Black.[28] It was the only paper offered to the Statistical Society on the topic of suffrage for women. Webb's paper corresponded with his involvement in suffragist societies in Dublin, as described in detail below. His paper began with a long quote from the Irish-born Quaker feminist Frances Power Cobbe,[29] describing how she exceeded all of the requirements for voting, with the exception of gender. Webb's argumentation relies on logic: he addresses the common arguments against extending the vote to women and gives rebuttals to each point. Some points are straightforward: he argues that just because all women do not want suffrage, 'we should not refuse equal rights to some because others do not appreciate them,' and points out that many men waste their votes. Other answers are clever and designed as logical traps: for example, he argued,

> It is asked, have not women power enough already? Do they not sway matters quite as much now as is necessary, by home influence and cajoling men? I ask, would it not be much better to give them direct power, since underhand influence is not considered peculiarly beneficial to anyone.[30]

The preachy, moralistic tone from his previous submission to the Statistical Society had gone and, to the modern reader, it speaks much more convincingly. His paper also reveals his philosophy with regard to politics and public life, and his deep sense of political responsibility, for he argued 'It appears to me intense selfishness for men or women to shut their minds to public affairs... All obtain the advantages conferred by the state: all are responsible for the evils caused by bad laws or the maladministration of good ones.'[31] It is easy to understand Webb's own drive, and also how he was setting himself up for a frustrating life in politics. As long as he believed that individuals had a responsibility to take an interest in politics, he was going to be disappointed when the level of public interest in politics did match his own.

Webb's third paper demonstrated that his interests lay in local as well as in international issues. 'Impediments to savings from cost and trouble to the poor of proving wills' (1880–1881) explained the difficulty that the poor could face in trying to secure funds that they had inherited from deceased family members. At the time of writing this paper *agnes Webb's papers were more unrealistic than statistical*

Webb was deeply involved in Irish politics yet, in unusual 'hands on' mode, found the time to tell the story of a widow who he personally assisted in claiming £100 of Post Office life assurance after the death of her husband. Claiming her benefit took nearly 1 month and cost £4 10s in administration fees. Webb was convinced that she could not have continued without his assistance, and he used this anecdote to draw the Society's attention to a larger dilemma: the fate of those people 'utterly unused to business and to whom the simplest transaction – writing a letter or procuring a post office order – is embarrassing and formidable'.[32] Webb, never really an original social thinker, is more diagnostic than prescriptive in his speech; the suggestions he makes for changes to the system are drawn from papers previously delivered to the Statistical Society. His tone is sincere and he seems genuinely indignant at the difficulties this woman faced, but his confidence in his own duty, and ability, to help the less fortunate is the foundation of the paper.

Fourth and finally, a paper on the 'Sherborn, Massachusetts Reformatory Prison for Women' was presented in 1896. Webb visited this prison on a trip to the United States following his resignation from parliament. His paper was also published in the *New Age* magazine. The paper is a classic moralistic account celebrating the efforts of this prison in rehabilitating wayward women by offering them opportunities to train as domestic servants. Webb expressed the belief that the best prisons are those that educate prisoners, and argued that the all-female staff treated the prisoners in a humane way, and so the prisoners responded in similar fashion.[33] In this paper it is possible to see Webb the moralist, just as in his business he employed some young women in the 'hope of reformation'.[34] But by 1896, when the Statistical Society (though largely in decline) was seeing more papers based on pure statistical analysis, Webb's moralistic contribution seems slightly anachronistic.

In addition to the Statistical Society there were several other organisations with which Webb was affiliated and for which there are far fewer sources. One was the Friends Institute, run by the Dublin Society of Friends. The Statistical Society rented rooms in the Friends Institute from 1862 until 1910 to hold its meetings and house its growing library of sociological and economic literature. The Friends Institute, like the Mechanics Institutes that also enjoyed affiliation with the Statistical Society, was founded as an improvement society. It held weekly meetings where papers were presented and discussed; the usual suspects, Webb and Thomas Haslam, participated frequently.[35] Haslam was also involved in debates and discussions at Charles Oldham's Contemporary Club and it is possible that Webb was also; R. F. Foster lists him as a member in the 1880s along with George Russell (Æ), Michael Davitt, Douglas Hyde, George Sigerson and John O'Leary and occasionally William Butler Yeats – a wide spectrum of politicians and intellectuals.[36]

Suffragism and the Contagious Diseases Acts

The greatest cause that brought Haslam, Webb and many of their Quaker contemporaries together was the women's movement. Webb's speech on enfranchisement has been cited as a notably early Irish statement on women's rights, delivered less than a year after the first official suffrage society was formed in Manchester in January 1867. A National Society for Women's Suffrage (NSWS) was established in London in the autumn of 1867.[37] Webb's speech alludes to petitions submitted to Parliament and indicates that much activity preceded the official establishment of suffragist societies.

The suffragist John Stuart Mill was pleased to know that Mr Webb from Dublin had joined the suffrage campaign in 1867, though disappointed that he had declined a place on the executive committee. Writing to John Elliot Cairnes in September 1867, Mill hoped to convince 'your friend Mr Webb' to join the committee, since 'such men as he is are very much wanted on the Committee.'[38] Carmel Quinlan has referred to this Webb as Alfred Webb,[39] but the editors of Mill's correspondence identify him as Richard Davis Webb. Although there is other correspondence from Mill addressed to R. D.[40] and none that specifically identifies Alfred Webb, Quinlan is probably correct: by 1867 R. D.'s activity in public life was waning as his son's was waxing. Mill had reasons to want Alfred Webb on the committee: R. D. had an established reputation as an abolitionist, but Webb was young and energetic and obviously thinking about women's issues, since he delivered his paper 'Propriety of conceding' only 3 months after Mill's letter was written. Both Webbs would have been friendly with Cairnes through the Statistical Society.

A watershed moment in the history of Irish feminism was an April 1870 public meeting organised in Dublin by Annie Robertson. The English feminists, Millicent Fawcett and her husband Henry Fawcett MP, addressed the crowd and Sir Robert Kane presided. Kane, director of the Museum of Irish Industries in Dublin, was a member of the Statistical Society, as were the other distinguished Dubliners who shared the platform: John Kells Ingram, Sir John Gray and Sir William Wilde. Trinity classicist John P. Mahaffy, educationalist Isabella Tod,[41] Orange-advocate William Johnston MP, radical stationer Charles Eason and Webb's fellow temperance advocate T. W. Russell MP were also involved in the movement from its early days.[42] These individuals ranged across the British and Irish political spectrum, including Orange loyalists, liberal unionists, Irish home rulers and radical members of the British Liberal Party. That meeting was reported as having been well attended, although there is no record of whether or not Webb was in the audience.[43]

Anna Haslam took the next step in establishing the Dublin Women's Suffrage Association (DWSA) in 1876. The tactics of the DWSA, its later incarnations and the NSWS, were typically the organisation of public meetings with speakers, the distribution of literature to reading rooms and libraries and the circulation of parliamentary petitions (an impressive 26 in 1886).[44] Unfortunately few records exist from the DWSA.[45] It is not known if Webb joined the DWSA, but he definitely attended meetings of the NSWS when its lecture tours came to Dublin. At one 1876 meeting that Webb attended, the speakers were Lydia Becker of Manchester, Lillian Ashworth of Bath, Eliza Sturge of Birmingham and Isabella Tod of Belfast.[46] Like Webb, Sturge was a Quaker, born into a family of philanthropists and anti-slavery activists.[47] The issue of women's suffrage, as well as women's education and employment, were certainly part of the public debate in 1870s Dublin: a flurry of letters to the editor of the *Freeman's Journal* followed the above 1876 meeting. The newspaper was unwilling to take a side, declaring itself 'too well acquainted with the female method of warfare to engage in a contest'.[48] However, it is not clear to what extent Webb became a part of the debate; although he was highly regarded by suffragists for his paper, he seems to have made no effort to distribute 'Propriety of conceding' as a political pamphlet.

A major issue that complemented the suffragist struggle in the public sphere, although it may have sapped resources from the suffragist societies, was that against the Contagious Diseases Acts (CDAs). The Acts tackled several major concerns in the Victorian Empire: the overall state of public morality, the 'great social evil' of prostitution, the growth of venereal disease and threats to public health and the fitness of the military following the Crimean War. The differences between reformist and benevolent groups are starkest when the issue of prostitution is considered. Women who ran Magdalene laundries tended to view prostitution as the failure of individual women, whereas the campaigners for the repeal of the CDAs pointed out sexual double standards and even the economic causes of prostitution.

Three acts, in 1864, 1866 and 1869, formed the CDAs. These three acts sought to control venereal disease by allowing for the compulsory medical examination of all women presumed prostitutes in areas surrounding military barracks. In Ireland these three areas were in Cork, Cobh and the Curragh. The three Acts that related to Ireland became gradually wider in scope. The 1864 Act was aimed at catching 'known' prostitutes – often when their names were supplied by soldiers being treated for venereal disease. The two further Acts extended these powers so that any woman in the 10-mile vicinity of a military base and thought to be a prostitute by a member of the police could be apprehended and examined. Men were not covered under the CDAs, even though it was recognised that they harboured diseases as well; rather, in what Webb believed was an obvious double standard, 'fallen women' were seen as the sole propagators of vice.

The spread of venereal disease in the military was a matter of governmental concern because it impacted on the fitness of soldiers; in addition, the CDAs had a role in the development of public health, as one doctor who examined statistics on venereal disease pointed out, 'the army and navy are the only fields for exact observation [of the spread of disease] we at present possess.'[49] It was also taken for granted that the 'professional bachelors' in the army would seek out prostitutes since they were discouraged from marrying. In the name of raising morale among soldiers, an 1857 Royal Commission actually recommended that soldiers not be subjected to regular exams for venereal disease, but instead that the causes of disease be addressed.[50] As Quinlan argues, the CDAs were aimed at providing healthy prostitutes for military men, not addressing the causes of prostitution. This argumentation infuriated Webb. He wrote to MPs that 'I cannot regard these Acts in any other light than as a State acknowledgement of fornication as a necessity and as an entirely venial sin.'[51]

When the impact of the 1866 and 1869 Acts became known, and a private campaign to extend the Acts to civilians was launched in England, reformers began to form campaigns to repeal the Acts. The NARCDA was formed in 1869 in Bristol. A sister organisation, the Ladies' National Association for the Repeal of the Contagious Diseases Acts (LNA), was formed in the following year under the charismatic leadership of Josephine Butler.[52] The LNA was formed for several reasons, first because women were initially not allowed to join the NARCDA. Second, a major obstacle to women's participation in the campaign for repeal was the belief that bourgeois women should not even know of such improper issues as prostitution and venereal disease.

In Ireland branches of these repeal organisations, the NARCDA and the LNA, were formed in Dublin, Cork and Belfast. Many members of the repeal organisations were Quakers, including the Webbs, the Haslams and the Harveys. Some, like James Haughton and Francis W. Newman,[53] were also radical vegetarians and abolitionists. Luddy explains that the LNA was a 'very localised and small affair', with many Irish women reluctant to get involved, in part because of the disapproval of some Catholic clergy.[54] The women of the LNA were high-profile, though, including Belfast reformer Isabella Tod and Dubliner Anna Haslam, and Webb's cousins Maria and Helen Webb. The NARCDA and the LNA relied on similar techniques to the suffrage movement: public meetings with speakers, pamphlets for distribution to libraries and reading rooms, parliamentary petitions and media reporting. Webb helped, in addition to attending the NARCDA meetings, by printing for the cause, including Thomas Haslam's 1870 pamphlet 'A few words on prostitution and the Contagious Diseases Acts'. He also lobbied his friends in Parliament. His campaign was supported by some Home Rule MPs and humoured by others; Charles Stewart Parnell gently reassured Webb in a note that 'by a reply which the Government gave today to a question in reference to the Contagious Diseases Acts, Dublin, you will see that they do not intend to extend them'.[55]

Webb's reaction to the Acts reveals something of his social thought. He was disgusted by the business of prostitution, but he could differentiate between the individuals and the institution. There is an anonymous pamphlet titled 'Private advice to boys and young men', which was deposited in the National Library of Ireland by Webb's sister in a collection of Webb's pamphlets. We can safely assume that the pamphlet, dated 1870, was written by Webb. The pamphlet is addressed to adolescent boys and it urges them to avoid 'sensual temptations', either through 'secret or private indulgence' or 'by intercourse with some of those unhappy women who walk the streets at night'.[56] By frequenting prostitutes, Webb argues that men 'help still further to degrade wretched women who were once as pure as your own sisters or your mother'.[57]

Webb's objection to the Acts was based on the sexual double standard and on the fact that tax money was being spent enforcing the Acts. He believed that the Acts had two real results: 'the liberty and honour of our countrywomen endangered' and 'our young men tempted to sin'.[58] He argued against this double standard in an 1876 pamphlet:

> I do not consider them [prostitutes] any more blameworthy or impure than the men who lead them on to continue such a course of life; and when sincerely penitent and resolved to amend, I believe they should be received back into society, as we now receive penitent

young men. In contradistinction to its estimate of these unfortunates, society is strangely lenient towards their male partners in guilt.[59]

Furthermore, Webb found the concept of regulating prostitution absurd and the argument that prostitution could not be stopped defeatist, somewhat akin to 'the "regulation" of murder or robbery'.[60] Thus, he believed that prostitution was a crime, though a crime that claimed the prostitutes themselves as victims. Webb's ideas about prostitution were far from typical of his time: he did not see prostitutes as a class apart but believed that, through bad circumstance, any woman had the potential to become a prostitute and that equally any prostitute had the right and ability to reform and reintegrate into society.

The CDAs were ultimately repealed in 1886 to the great satisfaction of Webb and his colleagues. By that time interest in the campaign, at least in terms of the number of subscribers to repeal organisations, had dropped. In 1886, of course, people like Webb were deeply concerned about the first Home Rule bill, and the repeal campaign may have been put on a back burner.

Beyond Britain, the Acts were extended to the colonies in various legislative packages, including the Cape Colony in South Africa, India, Hong Kong, Fiji and Gibraltar. In the Cape Colony the CDAs were only repealed in 1919.[61] In India the CDAs were repealed in 1888, but a previous Cantonment Act remained in place to regulate prostitutes in military cantonments; British repealers were horrified to realise that women were still subjected to examination in India well into the 1890s. However, as Antoinette Burton writes, Butler and her colleagues in the LNA did not focus on India until repeal was won at home.[62] Curiously, there is no evidence that Webb was very active in campaigning about the plight of women in the colonies. His speech to the Indian National Congress in 1894 shows that he was aware of attempts to regulate 'vice' and regretted that the government had tried to cover up evidence of prostitution, but he did not go into much detail and instead argued that it was further evidence of the need for better local government.[63] This may, however, have been Webb's way of sneaking the issue into his Congress speech without violating the Congress's unofficial ban on discussing matters of society and morality.

The history of social activism in nineteenth-century Dublin is tied up with the history of women and feminism, but understanding the true nature of Webb's feminism is difficult. He argued that he supported suffragism because women 'were oppressed [and] could not help themselves';[64] he does not specify whether women were helpless by nature or by situation. Successful feminist writers tailored their arguments to convince their audiences, so it is difficult to know whether Webb believed this or simply thought it persuasive. Clues to Webb's true beliefs might lie in his personal relationships with women, especially his mother, wife and sisters. The influence of his mother Hannah is the most obvious: she was a feminist and she corresponded with English Quaker feminists such as Anne Knight.[65] Hannah and R. D. also entertained many learned women at their house, like Harriet Martineau, who supported educational reforms for women. Furthermore, there is the point, though so easily overstated, of the relative independence of Quaker women. Typically, Quaker women had their own separate women's meetings, although these meetings tended to deal only with 'women's issues', such as appropriate dress, marriage and rearing of children. However, the fact that they existed at all seems to have impressed non-Quaker women.

The influence of Elizabeth Shackleton Webb ('Lizzie'), Webb's wife, is more difficult to measure. A member of the neighbouring Shackleton family and therefore part of the tight Quaker network in the Dublin area, Lizzie had known Webb since they were children. Webb admits that it was his mother who actually suggested the match, which he thought a sensible and novel idea; his father referred to Lizzie as 'a very good young woman of reputable family' whom Webb liked very much.[66] The two married in 1861.

Webb realized in retrospect that Lizzie must have found those first years of married life difficult. 'There is something awful in what most women give up in leaving their old home [to marry]', especially his wife who left a lovely country home for 'rooms in a four-storied townhouse where her only servant also had to look after the rooms of two other occupants'.[67] That servant was named Bridget, was employed by the Webbs for 29 years and earned only £6 a year (evidently on a part-time basis).[68] The Webbs eventually moved to a larger house on the Highfield Road, where they were able to plant a garden and keep goats for milking. Webb himself took care of pet hedgehogs and had a black dog named Lady, who he walked every morning before breakfast.[69] When Webb became an MP in 1890 he and Lizzie put their belongings into storage, rented a house in London and lived with Webb's sister, Deborah, in the summer recesses. In 1897, the Webbs moved a final time, building a large house which Webb named 'Shelmaliere', a reference to *The boys of Wexford*, a celebration of 1798.[70]

Lizzie's personality is somewhat of a mystery. She did not work outside the home or take part in public life; although Webb often attended public meetings with his sister, Deborah, his wife does not appear to have participated. When Webb was in Parliament, he recalled that she frequently watched from the Ladies' Gallery and remembered the procedures and speeches better than he did. Webb mentions her in a letter to his close friend J. F. X. O'Brien as having encouraged him to write letters to newspapers, remarking 'I suppose Mrs O'Brien sometimes makes you toe the mark of your duty.'[71] Webb also congratulated John Dillon on his marriage in 1895, noting that 'it is a gleam of brightness in much that appears so dark in our Irish politics at present – that you will have the support and sympathy of a true wife.'[72] From all evidence, the relationship between Webb and Lizzie seems to have been a warm one. The two enjoyed travelling together, visiting the United States in 1872 and again in 1895, when they also toured Australia and New Zealand. However, Webb worked long hours: even after he had sold his business, he was devoting 12- or 14-hour days to the Irish Party.[73] It is not known what Lizzie did with her time: if she had hobbies, friends or interests. After her death, Webb told his colleagues that 'none had clearer and more decided views on National questions than she,' and that without 'her steady clear sighted help and encouragement I would never have battled through the last 40 years'.[74] Sophie O'Brien recalled Webb and Lizzie as almost acting as one single unit, resembling each other and having almost identical voices and ways of speaking.[75] Lizzie seems to have lived in the shadow of her husband, but that may have been by her choice; from all the available evidence they thought similarly and enjoyed a close and happy marriage.

Webb seems to have been closest with his sister, Deborah. Deborah was a poet but,[76] like her sister Anne, devoted part of her adult life to caring for her parents. She joined some of the same societies as Webb and also frequently made small donations to the various funds of the Irish Party.[77] It is not clear how Deborah made her money and if she sustained herself through her poetry. Like Webb she left the Society of Friends, 'to pursue spiritualism and less known religious alternatives'.[78] She had learned about Spiritualism from William Lloyd Garrison.[79]

Deborah never married or had children. After her father's death in 1872, she travelled in Italy for nearly 2 years with Miss Dunn, who Webb described as her very close friend. Some 10 years later, Miss Dunn became seriously ill and sought respite with her brother in Italy (presumably because the climate was better suited to recuperation). A few years later, Deborah acquired a house with Miss Sarah Harris. She chose to share this information in a short autobiographical sketch submitted to a Quaker poetry anthology, explaining she had lived 'for the last eight years in my own snug little suburban home, which I am so fortunate as to have with a dear friend'.[80] Webb also mentions that Deborah shared a home with Miss Harris. There is nothing curious about two female friends sharing a house, except for the way in which Webb explains their situation in his autobiography: 'Such love matches as theirs are more common between women, at least living in the same house together, than they are between men.'[81] Webb's autobiography does not reveal answers to the many questions that then come to mind: is he describing a romantic relationship? If so, how did he and the Webb family feel about this? Webb's willingness to print Thomas Haslam's pamphlets on taboo subjects may have indicated that he had a frank and open attitude towards sexual relationships, although his pamphlet 'Private advice' seems to indicate otherwise. However, the fact that nineteenth-century people used a euphemistic vocabulary to describe same-sex relationships,[82] if they in fact recognised their existence, makes these comments difficult to interpret. It is interesting that Webb differentiates between male and female 'love matches'. Lesbian relationships may have been viewed as 'disgusting depravity' by Victorians, at least those who could believe that they existed. However, female same-sex relationships were not criminalised: whereas men engaging in same-sex relationships could be prosecuted for sexual assault, many people found the idea of the stereotypically passive female sexually assaulting another woman difficult to believe. Webb's attitudes towards his sister's living situation could reveal many of his beliefs about women, but the language he used is equally provocative and vague, so it is impossible to define the situation and his views.

Webb's younger sister, Anne Webb, known as 'Nannie', trained to be a teacher but instead became caretaker to their widowed father.[83] Webb acknowledged in his autobiography that she was not content with this position: 'Nannie had been anxious to strike out in some independent career. I could see none for her and was not sympathetic.'[84] Anne also left the Society of Friends after the death of her mother in 1862.[85] Eventually, Anne met and married Donald Steel, a Scottish Presbyterian who owned a tea plantation in Ceylon. On their first trip to Steel's plantation in Ceylon, around 1869, Anne became ill with cholera and died. Ironically, for a man who had a long interest in India and women's issues, Webb never mentions his sister's death in South Asia in his writings on the topic. The fact that she was the wife of a colonial plantation owner might have been a source of embarrassment for reform-minded Webb, although he liked Steel very much and kept in touch with the Steel family long after Anne's death. On the other hand, it is possible that Anne's death was an upsetting subject for Webb that he avoided discussing.

Finally, Webb's brother, Richard, seems to have led a bachelor lifestyle, picking up and moving every few years, in California and the Pacific South Seas; at one point he was researching and preparing a Samoan grammar.[86] He died in 1882 at the age of 46, in Dublin, having cut short a holiday in Italy when he became ill. Fairly little is known about his life; although he and Webb were closest in age and seem to have got along well, Webb has not provided many memories of his brother.

None of these four Webb siblings had children. The fact that Webb and Lizzie did not have children would not be particularly noteworthy except for the friendship they shared with Anna and Thomas Haslam. Quinlan explains how Thomas Haslam's pamphlet, 'The marriage problem', in which he advocated a form of rhythm method as birth control (unfortunately erroneous), was printed by Webb in 1868. Haslam revised his position only 4 years later in a pamphlet titled 'Duties of parents'. In it he argued that excessive sexual intercourse was both harmful to women, producing 'an endless catalogue of maladies',[87] and also harmful to the couple. He advocated a celibate marriage as the most pure and spiritual union possible, and he practised what he preached. Haslam's approach in 'Duties' was an inherently feminist one. Haslam, and other feminists such as Mill and Butler, worried that birth control gave too much control to men, as women could not refuse sexual intercourse on the basis that they were afraid of pregnancy.[88] A celibate marriage was therefore considered by some as the ultimate statement of respect for women. Ultimately, though, we can only speculate as to whether Webb was at all influenced by the work he printed for Haslam.

In spite of Webb's involvement in the DWSA and the NARCDA, and his vocal support of suffragism, we know little about his exact philosophies. He was certainly respectful of his feminist mother. His wife apparently did not lead a radically feminist or even independent life, and we do not even know how she felt about her husband's activism. Webb was encouraging of his sister, Deborah, who had an atypical personal life and was probably a self-supporting poet. Webb was insensitive to his other sister Anne's career ambitions, although he came to regret this later in life. There is perhaps no reason to doubt Webb's sincerity as a suffragist, since ultimately he did write a pioneering essay on the political rights of women, but it is important to recognise that Webb's beliefs might have been anywhere on the broad Victorian spectrum between paternalistic and feminist.

Representing and exhibiting in Dublin

While Webb was agitating for NARCDA or suffragism, he was also becoming involved in elected politics. His career in Irish nationalism began in 1870 and will be dealt with in the next chapter. However, Webb's first foray into politics as an elected official was at the local level, when he won a seat on Dublin City Council (usually referred to as Dublin Corporation) in 1882, representing the Inns-Quay Ward. The Council dealt with all matters of local politics, including carrying out public works, the upkeep of municipal property and the provision of social services such as libraries. Webb would have known many councillors already, and many were Quakers: Abraham Shackleton, Sir John Barrington and his cousin Thomas Henry Webb. Edward Dwyer Gray, son of his friend Sir John Gray, was one of the most active members and for a time the Lord Mayor. The printer Gill was a councilor, as were several of Webb's Irish Party colleagues.

Webb's tenure as a councilor appears steady but unremarkable in the limited sources that exist – principally Council minutes and reports copied into newspapers. His first meeting was in November 1882, and he had good attendance through 1883, attending 34 meetings and missing ten. The Council required 20 members for a quorum and often struggled to get this many attending a meeting, possibly since the councilors all seem to have had other major commitments (many were, for example, also MPs). The meetings were possibly quite long, since it was not unusual for the quorum to be lost during the meeting, and the meeting would then have to end because votes could not be taken.

The minutes of the Council do not include debates or arguments made in Council, only the motions made and votes cast, so we do not know how vocal Webb was. He made or seconded a few motions, most of them procedural. One of Webb's motions was 'for the greater economy in the printing of reports' – instead of making copies for all councilors, Webb suggested that they be made available in libraries.[89] Unless he was trying to harm his printing competition, Webb's motion, which failed to be seconded, shows that he was thinking as a fund-conscious public servant rather than as a printer. It was probably this perspective, however, for which Webb was elected to the Libraries Committee by his colleagues. He was also given the responsibility of representing the Council on the Dublin Port and Docks Board, which regulated the port of Dublin.

In 1884, however, Webb only attended six meetings, and had virtually stopped attending by March. He resigned in July.[90] Webb's explanation for leaving the Council was that he could not agree with the Irish Party's choice of Lord Mayor, but in fact (as will be seen in more detail in Chapter 4), he had several other problems with the Irish Party and was partly resigning in protest at other issues unrelated to the Council business. Webb either had such unfaltering loyalty to the Party that he could not vote in opposition to it, or such profundity of principle that he could not vote with it. Webb did take his self-imposed role as moral beacon quite seriously, so it is possible his resignation was based purely on principle. One wonders, however, whether he was finding his other commitments to business and national politics too demanding, or whether the Council's business – regulating abattoirs, governing sheep pens in markets and examining tenders for public urinals – was overly parochial and not adequately stimulating for Webb. He was sufficiently popular or effective on the Council to be the subject of a motion from Councillor Cummins that, breaking with tradition, Webb be allowed to retain his seat on the Port and Docks Board after his resignation. The motion failed by one vote.[91]

What Webb did enjoy was being involved in local matters that had a much wider influence. The Dublin Exhibition of August 1882 was one such event, designed to showcase Irish manufactures and replicate the success of exhibitions in London and Paris. The experiment had been tried before, in 1853, but later commentators concluded that it had not been entirely successful, possibly having been held too soon after the Famine when industry had not yet recuperated. Although it was claimed that one million people visited, this exhibition ran a deficit of £19,000, which was paid for by its unfortunate sponsor, William Dargan.[92] A second Dublin exhibition was held in 1865, and in addition regional exhibitions had been held in other cities, including Belfast in 1870.

The agricultural disaster of the late 1870s reinforced feelings of vulnerability in the Irish economy. The attention towards Irish industry was not new; opponents of the Act of Union had long argued that Irish manufactures had suffered as its result, and the Statistical Society considered ways in which trade laws would impact upon the Irish economy. Sir Robert Kane, medic, suffragist and educationalist, argued in his 1845 book *The Industrial Resources of Ireland* that Ireland was extremely rich in natural resources, though in need of further infrastructure, such as canals and railways.[93] There were several reactions to the depression of the 1870s: one, well-known, was the political movement of the Land League. For Webb, a committed nationalist, the Land League was correct in its aims but suspicious in its methods; he never officially joined because he feared that violent tactics might be used.[94] He did correspond with Davitt about the possibility of establishing industry in the village of Carraroe in the west of Ireland.[95]

A second reaction to the depression was the idea of an exhibition. The *Freeman's Journal* argued that an exhibition would not only be a giant step towards alleviating Ireland's problems, it would crucially be 'a movement so broad, so utilitarian, so free from all tinge of political or sectarian taint, that it unites...all Irishmen'.[96] An exhibition would be 'a great lever to raise Ireland in the scale of substantial prosperity and national rank', just as the French exhibitions had elevated French goods.[97] The *Irish Builder* agreed that home industry was 'a cause in which all classes, irrespective of sect or party in the nation, should feel deeply interested'. Ultimately, it argued that '[o]ur industries and their development is not a party political question, but a national one.'[98] Public meetings were called, and in October 1881 a committee was established, with the *Freeman's Journal* offering support through a fund-raising drive in its pages.

The trend towards buying Irish goods is evident in the advertisements in newspapers. In 1881, as the *Freeman's Journal* took up subscriptions for an exhibition, many advertisements prominently declared the Irish origin of their goods. In its editorial section the newspaper emphasised that letters in support of an exhibition must not be used as free advertisements, indicating that retailers had interpreted the popularity of a 'buy Irish' campaign as a marketing tool.[99] For example, one advertisement from the Quaker firm Jacob's read:

> W. R. Jacob & Co. have been induced to draw special attention to their manufacture now in consequence of the present most important movement in favour of promoting Irish industry; and they trust that those who have hitherto used IMPORTED Biscuits and Cakes will give the genuine Irish articles manufactured by W. & R. JACOB & CO. a fair trial, and thus assist in giving that employment to Irish workpeople, which all acknowledge to be so urgently needed. The use of imported biscuits, or other articles that can be made as well in Ireland, is as injurious to the general prosperity of the country as it is really unnecessary.[100]

Pro-Irish feelings inevitably spurred anti-foreign goods feelings. However, rumours that English businesses were planning to exhibit were put into economic perspective by the *Irish Builder*: 'We have no objection to Englishmen manufacturing for exhibition, through Irish labour, in Dublin or elsewhere in Ireland. We want employment for our native artisans, and the expenditure of money in Ireland is to be welcomed in the mean time.'[101] However, despite the press's efforts to keep the focus on the welfare of industry, politics was never far away. The opening on the Exhibition coincided, in a parade and string of celebrations, with the ceremonial unveiling of the new O'Connell monument as well as the centenary of the establishment of the short-lived Irish Parliament.[102] The Ceremonial Committee was chosen from representatives of the two committees that organised the Exhibition and the O'Connell statue, plus five of the trades exhibiting and the Home Rule League. Political identities also came into play, and the Exhibition was almost abandoned when the suggestion that royalty be invited to open the Exhibition was rejected by nationalists.[103] When the Exhibition was finally underway, the *Irish Builder* concluded that politics had marred but not ruined the event.[104]

According to Webb, 'I was one of the hardest workers in getting up the Exhibition...the labours and responsibilities nearly killed me.'[105] It is difficult to ascertain when Webb became involved in the Exhibition. He was not nominated to the organisational committee at the first meetings in autumn of 1881. Once organisation had got underway, newspaper coverage dropped off until the immediate run-up to the event in the summer of 1882. He next appears publicly in the month before the Exhibition, when he explained to the committee that demand for exhibition space had been phenomenal and that the event would 'exceed...expectations'.[106] At the opening of the Exhibition he was listed as a member of the 12-man Exhibition committee, and he introduced the Lord Mayor at the opening ceremonies. The Lord Mayor responded by finishing his address with special thanks that may confirm Webb's own claim:

> There is one name which comes up when I mention the staff, who, though not one of it in name, was its mainspring in all this involving hard work – I mean Mr Alfred Webb, our fellow-director. None of us on the board but will, I am sure, gratefully acknowledge the special services of Mr. Webb. Were Irish enterprise carried out in the spirit he displayed, then all would meet with the same marked success which shall, I trust, attend this undertaking.[107]

Webb was the only member named in this address. His efforts had mixed results. On the one hand, the Exhibition appears to have been a spectacular event. The *Freeman's Journal* wrote on the opening day of the

Exhibition that Dublin had been transformed and taken over by a festive atmosphere. The main hall of the Exhibition was decorated with a flag from each Irish county and statues of prominent Irishmen. The paper estimated that it would take more than a day to walk through all of the exhibits, which included everything from farming machinery to fine jewellery, bog-oak carvings to work boots. In addition there was a full musical programme and an exhibit of Irish paintings. And, of course, 'one feature too which gave the event much of its charm was the large and fashionable attendance of ladies'.[108] Typically, exhibitions published catalogues, but I have been unable to find one for 1881.[109]

However, despite the pride that Webb must have felt on the day, his memories of the event were bitter, since 'I saw so many poor people lose money in consequence of the manner in which that exhibition was boomed by the national press, that I determined never again to have to do with an undertaking of the kind.'[110] It is not clear why he felt so angry with the national press, with which he engaged on a regular basis, and whose support he was probably glad to have while he was organising the event. The loss of money may have been through subscriptions, or a result of other plans that never materialised – such as the idea to attract venture capital and form a corporation after the Exhibition to promote industry. Webb was, of course, exactly the type of person who would write to the national press and encourage his fellow citizens to support a worthy cause. For example, he gave a donation to the Gallery of Modern Art at the Royal Hibernian Academy, urged others to support it and wrote in the *Freeman's Journal* that 'it would not be too much to expect the Government to erect a Modern Art Gallery in Stephen's Green or elsewhere', as a suitable use for Irish taxes.[111]

Webb obviously felt that all of these campaigns were meant to have a real positive impact on individuals' lives and was disappointed when they failed. However, he also had a dramatic and even fatalistic memory. As will become more obvious through an examination of his career in national politics, Webb had a tendency to become quite despondent when he ran into difficulties with individuals or ideas; he inevitably encountered conflict in the public sphere but tended to withdraw and internalise that conflict. Webb resigned from the Society of Friends, Dublin City Council and nearly every political organisation he ever joined.

Certainly, Webb kept himself busy and did not give up on his activism. In addition to all these organisations, Webb was often giving his support to other smaller or less well-documented campaigns. He argued in favour of the disestablishment of the Church of Ireland in 1867, and later argued for increased funding to Catholic schools, especially those run by the Christian Brothers.[112] He hoped to see St Stephen's Green opened to the public in Dublin. Ironically, Webb's involvement in all these campaigns and activist projects, which undoubtedly must have consumed thousands of hours of his personal time, has been mostly forgotten. However, he has been remembered for another labour of love, a literary contribution.

Literary reputation

Webb developed a public persona by writing about many social causes in newspapers, in addition to papers given to specialist societies. However, Webb's major literary achievement was his *Compendium of Irish Biography: Comprising Sketches of Distinguished Irishmen, and of Eminent Persons Connected with Ireland by Office or by Their Writings*, published in 1878. Webb explains that his intention in writing such a volume was to fulfill a personal need: 'When reading Irish history I had found myself at a loss as to where easily to lay my hands upon more particular information as to the characters and actors named.'[113] Most of the research was done at the Royal Dublin Society and the libraries of Trinity College, the King's Inns and the Royal Irish Academy. Webb solicited assistance and advice from Irish scholars, most importantly Rev. Dr William Reeves, an antiquarian, Protestant bishop and president of the Royal Irish Academy. Webb's aim was to write a comprehensive biography, including over 1000 entries, in a 500-page volume. Only deceased notables were included, and although the title does not explicitly state this, Webb included Irishwomen of note as well, and communicated that in correspondence with Reeves.[114] Although Gill, the major Dublin printer and publisher and Webb's future co-councillor, is listed as the publisher, Webb printed and financed the book himself, at a printing cost of £150. His brother, Richard, arranged a visit to Dublin to assist with the printing. Webb does not say how many copies he printed, but claimed that he had not printed enough: around 1904, he wrote that it was 'long out of print and brings a high price at auctions'.[115]

Reviews of the book were mostly favourable. Typically, Webb clipped a large number of newspaper reviews, both positive and critical, and carefully pasted them in his scrapbook. The *Nation* called it a 'magnificent compilation',[116] the *Irish Times* felt that 'diligence, discretion, good taste and deep thought are exhibited in every item'[117] and the *Melbourne Advocate* thought it 'most interesting and valuable'.[118] Many of the papers pointed out omissions and errors, but admitted that the breadth of the volume made some such faults excusable. The *Express* noted many errors and omissions, but argued that 'after careful revision, the work will become one of general reference.' Webb took exception to this review and wrote to the paper in defence of his work; the *Express* printed his letter and responded by pointing out a few more errors.[119]

The *Express* was correct: the *Compendium* is still available in reference libraries, and was the major biographical source until Henry Boylan's reference book was published in 1978.[120] Anecdotal evidence suggests that it became a reference tool for Webb's contemporaries. Douglas Hyde and Charles Stuart Parnell[121] were known to have had copies and Davitt kept a copy with him in prison, a gift inscribed 'with the love and respect of the author'.[122] Webb's success with the *Compendium* seems to have brought him a small amount of fame. The *Freeman's Journal* showed some confidence in Webb's literary inclination when it asked him to contribute a personal list of 'the best hundred Irish books'. The titles were published in the paper with a letter from Webb. Forty-seven of his choices are historical, including historical biographies.[123] The *Nation* also relied on Webb for occasional book reviews.

Webb's gifts did not lie in creative writing – his correspondence occasionally contained snippets of dreadful poetry and jokes about his candidacy as poet laureate[124] – but he had a great belief in the need for literature. He enjoyed being active in 'the Moonlighters', later renamed the Ninety Club, an amateur literary society led by Anna Dunville Webb Shackleton[125] and also frequented by Thomas Haslam.[126] He endeavoured to read novels in French, Italian and German, though he found German to be a struggle.[127] He learned the 'manual alphabet' to communicate with his friend Charlotte Grace O'Brien, an activist for emigrants' welfare, who was deaf.[128] Webb was also prepared to share his beliefs. In an 1888 lecture draft, he defined his philosophy, arguing the necessity 'of cultivating our literary and artistic tastes, and of not allowing politics and desultory reading to absorb all our attention. Every side of our faculties and character should be regarded – men were never intended to be purely political any more than purely money-making machines.'[129] Literary message aside, the comment is moralistic and draws on ideas about self-improvement, appropriate use of leisure time and the harm of certain types of literature.

Webb's attitudes towards literature, publicly expressed, was possibly what prompted Charles Gavan Duffy to ask Webb to 'undertake to work on the directorate of the Irish Literary Society' in 1892.[130] This was perhaps part of Gavan Duffy's scheme to prevent Yeats from making the society into a radical, neo-Fenian organisation; Webb would have been an ultra-moderate counterweight.[131] Webb declined on the grounds that he was too busy with his political duties and argued that it was a society which should be organised by those who did not have the opportunity to serve Ireland through politics. He added that he hoped to produce a second edition of his *Compendium* 'as my contribution to the cause of Irish literature'.[132] For Webb, literature was as much a patriotic duty as the Irish Parliamentary Party; literature was not simply a means of improving one's own knowledge, but of improving Ireland's prospects.

Webb's tireless work for these campaigns – literary, political and moral – was not without reward: it brought him esteem in his community and a degree of name recognition. It also allowed him an intellectual life away from the business of printing. Social activism in Dublin was a widespread, varied and social pursuit. It had several distinct features. Logic and reason played a role: the suffragist movement, in particular, tried to make reasonable appeals rather than emotional, theological or moral ones. Webb and his colleagues in these various campaigns were, on the whole, not Utopians, Owenites or Saint-Simonians; they seem to have been influenced by a sense of civic duty that is not explicitly linked to a philosophical or religious tradition. Their activities overlap to a strong degree with Liberal social activism in Britain, and we have seen that in some cases there were clear connections with British Liberals, most notably the visit to Dublin of Henry and Milicent Fawcett. However, what is most striking about this social activist network in Dublin is how it cut across religious and political divides. This, perhaps, held the promise of cosmopolitan status, if campaigners could demonstrate that they had broad support across various identities.

As in Britain, Dublin social activism featured a large number of Quakers. A commitment to public good, self-confidence and an entrepreneurial spirit was probably instilled in many of these activists' lives through their upbringing in the Society of Friends. However, their religious convictions were variegated and variable (in fact many had left the Society of Friends) and, unlike many benevolent activists, they did not articulate coherent religious explanations for their social thoughts or actions.

On the whole, the individuals described in this chapter were not among the most privileged or wealthy: they were Dublin's middle class, often self-employed business people who had full-time jobs outside their activist projects, not a *gauche caviar* with independent means. Their lack of interest in hands-on benevolent social work did not mean that they were not dedicated. Social activism was apparently infectious: it is clear that most of these people knew each other through the overlap in their organisational affiliations. Public life in mid-Victorian Dublin was certainly not monopolised by national (or nationalistic) politics; these organisations often expressly avoided discussion of national politics because they were divisive. The ethos of the Statistical Society, for example, did not support national regime change as the first necessary step for the alleviation of social problems. Webb's involvement in groups such as the Statistical Society and various moral or reformist campaigns was not unusual for a middle-class Quaker in Dublin. What was more unusual was the fact that he also became involved, up to the highest level, in the Irish nationalist movement.

4
'Some curious characters floated on the surface'[1]: Webb's Entry into Nationalist Politics

In the late 1860s Webb became convinced that Ireland needed self-government and in 1870 he joined the young Irish home rule movement. This was an unusual political cause for an Irish Quaker to adopt, but it did not constitute a rupture with his friends, family or social circle or a bizarre and illogical departure from his beliefs. Webb's sense of social justice led him towards home rule, just as many British liberals and radicals eventually embraced Irish home rule alongside suffragism, temperance and Indian reform. Webb was, then, an Irish member of a much wider global trend in liberal social thought. However, it is also in examining his intense participation in the home rule movement that his character and values really start to emerge. The highs and lows of politics sometimes stretched Webb's personality to its limits, and he struggled with depression; he also clung to his own ethical code and resigned when he could not accept decisions that impinged on his conscience.

The goal of this chapter is not to pick and choose evidence to explain either the failure or the success of the Home Government Association and the Home Rule League, or to give a comprehensive history of the movement, but to examine Webb's experience in these two organisations and to observe how events unfolded through the eyes of the treasurer. Compared to the post-1878 period, few historians have devoted themselves to the era of the Home Government Association (1870–1873, hereafter 'Association') and the Home Rule League (1873–1880, hereafter 'League'), and of those who have, few have done so recently. The two classic biographies of Isaac Butt date from 1946 and 1962.[2] The latter, David Thornley's *Isaac Butt and Home Rule*, is still treated as the authoritative account of this era. More recent treatments of this era have tended to be articles or chapters in longer works on the phenomenon of home rule. What, therefore, can one chapter in a study of Alfred Webb tell about this era, which has been largely treated as a lull before the excitement of the 1880s?

Webb's position as a behind-the-scenes administrator, rather than a public spokesperson, reveals what individuals within the movement were really thinking and who was doing all the work. The main sources for the home rule era are the Isaac Butt and William O'Neill Daunt collections held in the National Library of Ireland. However, for the study of Webb's experience of this era, the Butt correspondence is less interesting than the Daunt correspondence: Daunt was a secretary of the League and, like Webb, was involved in the day-to-day administration of the League, and Butt, as becomes clear through reading the correspondence, was not. Both the Butt and Daunt collections have been intensively trawled by previous historians. However, Webb's insights into this era, through his autobiography, have not been studied in detail.[3] More importantly, the Public Record Office of Northern Ireland (PRONI) holds a damp-press copy book of the Association and League's outgoing correspondence, 1873–1878, the only officially consolidated record of these organisations.[4] Although this source is included in the Hayes catalogue[5] and was donated to PRONI in 1927, it has not been fully exploited in the studies of this era.[6] As a source, it provides insight into the institutional side of affairs, and will thus prevent the history of hundreds of individuals working towards home rule from being overshadowed by the personalities of Butt and Charles Stewart Parnell. It also provides evidence that the relationship with nationalists in England and Scotland was frequently strained and often relevant.

The road to the Home Government Association

This behind-the-scenes or institutional approach might reverse the impression that there was a slow and rather boring period in Irish political history between Young Ireland and the Repeal movement of the 1840s and the rise of Parnellite obstruction in the late 1870s, with only some intermittent comic relief from jumbled Fenian uprisings. On the nationalist front in the 1850s, Irish Catholic MPs formed an independent opposition in Parliament (meaning that they used bloc voting to oppose government measures), but they never fully organised as a political party.[7] This bloc of parliamentarians had the support of the Catholic clergy but their impact on Irish issues in parliament was limited. Their support was drawn from their loose alliance with the Irish Tenant League, which was dedicated to extending tenant right throughout Ireland.

The torpor created by the dispersal of the independent opposition was tackled by the National Association, established in 1864 by former Repealers, including William O'Neill Daunt and John Blake Dillon. The National Association was essentially a Repeal organisation, stating that its 'sole object is the restoration of a separate and independent Parliament to Ireland'.[8] Crucial to its rules was that 'no member of the Association shall be held responsible for any opinion of any other member, save only for the one fundamental principle of the Irish National League, viz.: that Ireland ought to have self-government.'[9] As such, the members could differ 'in religion, in politics, in tastes'.[10] Self-determination was then the only and ultimate political issue, but it did not prevent nationalists from having other political opinions. As an organisation, the National Association suffered deeply from lack of funds: it did not have a treasurer, and it did not even have receipts for the occasions when it received money.[11] Even its most active members were critical of its methods: John Martin was frustrated with the National Association, and he wrote to Daunt in 1866 that it 'serves for a convenient refuge for the middle class comfortable Repealers who don't like to expose themselves to the smallest risk either in body or goods'.[12]

In the late 1860s, a number of changes took place that galvanised public opinion and shook the Irish bourgeoisie out of its mid-Victorian comfort zone. Fenianism, although producing only two minor risings in the late 1860s, produced an amount of fear in the populace throughout the United Kingdom that was disproportionate to its real capabilities, and Gladstone's Liberal government answered the public call to 'pacify' Ireland when it was elected in 1868. In the northern part of the country, Orangeism was enjoying a revival led by the maverick MP William Johnston, who was imprisoned in 1867 for defying the Party Processions Act. In Parliament, two pieces of legislation jolted Irish society: the Disestablishment of the Church of Ireland and the Land Act.

The Disestablishment of the Church of Ireland was introduced in 1867 and became effective in 1869. In return for compensation, the Church of Ireland lost its protected position as a state church. The Disestablishment was a triumph for both the Catholic and the dissenter populations, and was a delight for Webb, who had seen the establishment as a 'grotesquely hideous wrong'.[13] It was, of course, a blow to the interest of the Church of Ireland and it both heightened fears that Protestant privilege was being eroded in Ireland and created resentment against Gladstone's government for some Irish Protestants. Some members of that community concluded that Protestants would need to lobby the London government to protect their minority rights, and others arrived at the opposite conclusion, that self-government would best protect their interests.

Within the Catholic community, the triumph of Disestablishment was followed by the disappointment of the 1870 Land Act. Given that tenant farming was the occupation of a large percentage of the population, the tenants' rights campaign was, for many individuals, the campaign that had the capacity to effect the most immediate change in quality of life for most Irish people. The failure of the Land Act to extend the 'Ulster custom'[14] throughout Ireland created disappointment among those who had had high hopes in Gladstone's desire to meet the demands of tenant right. The Land Act therefore heightened many tenant farmers' belief that, ultimately, only an Irish parliament would be willing and able to enact the kinds of changes that Ireland needed. Some responded to the new advanced nationalist call of Fenianism, and others looked back to O'Connell's Repeal movement.

Within the Dublin elite in 1870 there were representatives of all these political positions: Conservatives and Liberals, men of property and men of business, old Repealers and new converts to Fenianism, and revitalised Orangemen. Butt believed that home rule had the potential to unite these opposing factions and he embodied these contradictions. He was a Protestant from Donegal, a conservative by nature, a Freemason[15] and an imperialist. He was also a lawyer who defended rebels, both Young Irelanders and Fenians. From a member of 'Orange Young Ireland' in the 1830s, he evolved into an articulator of an Irish patriotism designed to make Ireland a better participant in the United Kingdom through devolved government. At the same time, Butt also drew the mass of Catholic Ireland on board by presiding over the Amnesty Association and supporting demands for tenant right. In this sense, home rule was envisioned as a compromise, not a revolution: a movement that hoped to bring together all those parties of influence who wanted to improve Ireland's welfare.

Alfred Webb was the type of individual that Butt wanted on his team: a relatively young Protestant businessman receptive to politics. Webb grew up in a home that espoused some forms of Irish nationalism, with its morbid relics of 1798 and the visits from his father's friend Daniel O'Connell. However, many of the people with whom he associated – who were just as committed to social justice as he was – did not believe that an independent parliament or repeal of the Act of Union would improve conditions in Ireland. The Quaker community, in particular, had a deep opposition to any estrangement from Great Britain, including repeal of the Act of Union.

Webb was not involved in organised nationalist activity prior to 1865, with the exception of his teenage fascination with 1848. He reflected that 'my churchism, my bachelor days, my marriage, mother's death, [and] the American War tended somewhat though not entirely to dim the National proclivities of my youth.'[16] By 'churchism' he probably meant his disagreements with the Society of Friends and his experimentation with the Church of Ireland. Certainly, Webb was deeply concerned with the American Civil War (1861–1865), and was devastated by the death of President Abraham Lincoln in April 1865; he recalled in his autobiography that he heard the news of the assassination and 'ran off to tell the US Consul and other friends. We wept in unison' and they organised a meeting of condolence to the Northern states.[17] It perhaps seems odd that Webb would have been informing consuls of events in their own countries, and he may have chosen his words to amplify his own involvement (perhaps to articulate the profundity of his emotion); but it may be correct, since the news arrived on a steamer in Cork, not via telegraph. A sensitive man ahead of his time, Webb saw nothing wrong with weeping in public.

Abolitionism and Fenianism both tested the pacifistic doctrine with which Webb had been brought up. He was sympathetic, for example, with John Brown's Harper's Ferry raid,[18] just as he believed that many 'abolitionists and peace lovers' were. The Fenians, whose revolutionary agenda was a reaction to (their belief in) the failure of the Repeal movement and the Independent Opposition of the 1850s, ironically inspired Webb to 'convert' to *constitutional* nationalism. Initially he had taken little interest in the Fenians and regarded them as 'a pestilent set of ruffians set upon murdering Protestants and landlords'.[19] However, that changed during the Fenian trials of 1865. His father was due for jury duty but was ill and Webb went to the courts to present a doctor's note. There, Webb saw three Fenians in the dock – Charles Joseph Kickham, Thomas Clarke Luby and John O'Leary. The three were convicted, and as he watched the sentence being delivered Webb became convinced that they were 'as great and pure intentioned men as were any of those of '98'.[20] Webb spared no drama in describing the moment when he recognised the spirit of his own nationalist heroes rekindled in these Fenian prisoners: 'Like Paul on his road to Damascus a sudden light shone on my mind and I left Green-Street Court House a changed man.'[21]

In the 1850s, according to Richard Vincent Comerford, many men 'underwent an experience that has been compared to religious conversion. Dedication to any humdrum profession was henceforth impossible.' That religious calling was a 'personal devotion to nationality'.[22]

Webb had such a conversion, although not until 1865. His profession as a printer did not become impossible, though; like many of his nationalist colleagues who were involved in the newspaper industry, he found ways to complement his nationalist vocation through the vehicle of the printed word. The first such outlet was through the Amnesty Association, which was established to lobby the British government to pardon Fenian prisoners. After the execution of the 'Manchester Martyrs' in 1867, popular support in favour of the Fenians grew and the Amnesty Association thus became a recipient of far-reaching sympathy, rather than a revolutionary fringe group. Butt became its president in 1869. Webb began attending meetings of the Amnesty Association and he also 'secretly printed a number of memorial cards and sold them' to benefit the families of the three Martyrs.[23]

Webb also shared his opinions in print through the letter to the editor. Fenianism, he wrote in the *Manchester Examiner and Times* in 1866, 'was no projected rising of the lowest orders for objects of murder and plunder'.[24] Webb was expressing publicly what others were writing privately, such as Martin, who argued that 'the Fenians seem to me crack-brained enough. But that is the worst that can be said of them.'[25] Rather than dwell on the violence of the Fenians, as many bourgeois businessmen might have done, Webb was deeply sympathetic and identified with the Fenians: 'I believe the movement is an expression of that longing after nationality – after some country to love, and some way of showing love for it – which is one of the strongest feelings of our nature.'[26] Yet Webb, for all his passionate love of Ireland, was not a separatist: his article also suggested that Irishmen would be more contented if the Queen had palaces in Ireland and if Irish regiments were formed in the army, with 'distinctive dress'.[27] Webb further tried to convince readers in the *Daily News* that it would be wrong 'to make us [the Irish] loyal to a united government by eradicating our nationality', and it would not be in Britain's best interest: 'it is difficult to understand what use a union would be to you with a wretched mass of jelly-fish without spirit.'[28] Webb's idea of union was based on a respectful and equal alliance between strong nations and a celebration of their national cultures.

Through his involvement in Amnesty and such public pronouncements on Irish affairs, Webb, in his own description, 'became well known in nationalist circles'.[29] Webb was already a busy man in 1870: running a business, printing pamphlets about birth control, sitting on the council of the Statistical Society, attending meetings about women's suffrage and visiting the wards of the Cork St Fever Hospital. It may have been these activities, rather than his clandestine Amnesty printing, that awarded him sufficient social status to be invited to join in forming the Home Government Association.

The Home Government Association

The first meeting of the Home Government Association, which Butt created to launch the home rule movement, was held at Bilton's Hotel in Dublin on 19 May 1870 and participation was only through invitation. In his memoir, *New Ireland*, participant A. M. Sullivan described it as a 'private meeting of some of the leading merchants and professional men of the metropolis, of various political and religious opinions, to exchange views upon the condition of Ireland'.[30] Sullivan lists 59 men who formed this 'strange assemblage' of founding members of the Association and he classifies each one according to religion and political leanings. Although his classifications seem to overlap (for example, it is unclear exactly how a Catholic nationalist repealer is distinct from a Catholic nationalist or a Catholic repealer), they are useful as the opinion of one participant. Sullivan classifies 25 as Catholic, mostly liberals, 26 as Protestant (presumably belonging to the Church of Ireland), and eight as neither of these religions. The lone Quaker nationalist was, of course, Alfred Webb. Although not a precise measure of the group, what is clear from Sullivan's classifications is that the largest group of individuals was Church of Ireland conservatives. The second largest group was Catholic liberals. There were more Orangemen than there were Fenians.[31]

The Home Government Association was established with both the purpose and desire to be a parliamentary lobbying group composed of upper-middle class men. It was not a mass movement, and it would be wrong to view this organisation with some kind of regret, as if it was obviously the manifest destiny of the Association members to lead a mass nationalist movement but that they were too myopic to realise their own potential. Some members of the Association were sitting MPs, but many had never been involved in national politics and had developed their public personae through business, local government or philanthropy.

The earliest public reaction from Webb after the meeting is a reminder of one of his greatest concerns in 1870. 'Now, surely I am not to tell my Irish lady-friends, anxious for equal rights with men, that when we get a parliament in College-green, any hopes of their obtaining these rights will be at an end,' he wrote in *New Ireland*. This would be a strategic mistake: 'Some of them *are* nationalists, would they *continue* so, if they thought such would be the nationality.'[32] In spite of these reservations, Webb's interest in home rule was not dampened and he claims that he quickly became 'in truth one of the most earnest and active members'.[33]

Over the summer of 1870 a constitution and set of rules for the new Association were drafted; Webb may have done the printing because copies of the proofs are in his personal collection.[34] The goal of the Association was to achieve 'a domestic parliament', and, as with the National Association, this was the only goal that members had to support:

> It is declared to be an essential principle of the Association, that while every member is understood by joining it to concur in its general object and plan of action, no person so joining is committed to any political opinion, except in the advisability of seeking for Ireland the amount of self-government contemplated in the objects of the Association.[35]

This clause was crucial to the operation of the Association: it reassured those who wanted to support home rule but retain their independence. It also, ultimately, limited the Association's ability to shape parliamentary politics.

The ideological lynchpin in the home rule plan was Butt's own pamphlet, *Irish Federalism*.[36] Butt was advocating a federal arrangement, in which Ireland would have a devolved parliament and still retain members at Westminster to take part in the discussion of imperial and foreign affairs. This was not simply the repeal of the Act of Union, which would have (in theory) returned Ireland to a pre-1800 Parliament.[37] Some Repealers happily adopted the new federalist plan, and others did so only grudgingly,[38] when they felt that Butt's movement was gaining sufficient momentum.

From its very beginning the organisation was concerned about money and propriety and therefore the treasurer had a critical role and had to be a reliable individual. The membership fee was set at the gentlemanly amount of £1 per annum, and associate members were admitted for 1 shilling per annum. The Association also anticipated that it might have the funding shortfalls that the National Association had experienced: it specifically stated in its constitution that it invited monetary donations towards achieving its goal. It also stipulated that an independent auditor should review the Finance Committee's accounts each month.[39] It appears that Webb became treasurer sometime in 1870 or 1871; certainly, by May 1871 he was communicating with colleagues about the state of the Association's finances.[40] At the same time, Webb professionalised his role in the Association when he decided in the autumn of 1870 that he would not take on any more printing for the Association, because of fears that he would be seen as profiting from home rule: 'I have so often felt my free action and opinions hampered in this matter by printing for the Association...I do not wish to leave it in anyone's power to say that anyone is upholding the Association for interested monies.'[41]

The Association was an exciting venture for Webb. He felt that there were 'many fine and loveable men connected with the agitation' in its early years.[42] His early correspondence to colleagues in the Association is enthusiastic and optimistic, and he reminds us that he was getting the opportunity to work with some individuals who had been heroes of his youth. Writing to Daunt, an honorary secretary of the Association, about some administrative matters, Webb includes a touching postscript: 'Long ago when I would see your name in connexion with national affairs, I little thought that I would ever have the honor and pleasure of corresponding with you.'[43] He later writes to Daunt, as if he were addressing a close friend or mentor, that whenever he thinks of Association business 'you come to my mind; and I only wish you were living near us'.[44] Likewise, Webb cherished his friendship with another secretary, Rev. Galbraith, reflecting later that 'almost a love grew up between Galbraith and myself...I have somewhat the feeling of love and reverence for him that I had for my Father. Their portraits hang near each other in my dining room.'[45] Home rule demanded much of Webb's time, and he became quite close with many of his colleagues. Webb's letters are often expressive of a very tender friendship.

However, all was not smooth sailing: Webb's correspondence reveals that he was riding a rollercoaster of emotions. An extremely panicky letter to Sullivan in September 1870 (when the Association was just being formally incorporated) deserves to be quoted at length, for it demonstrates the extent of Webb's concern:

> My anxiety about our Federal Movement is my excuse for writing you a line. Are we not too standstill? Ought we not to be getting up meetings in the country? Ought we not to be getting in subscriptions? Two meetings ago we passed 'an address' to be put in all the Irish papers. I cannot see that it has been put in any of them.
>
> I cannot shake off the feeling that there is a coldness creeping over our movement. I have not fears for the ultimate triumph of our

principles, but indeed it would be a bitter mortification to many if this movement did not proceed satisfactorily.

Can it be possible that the country is not at our back? It cannot be believed. The Committee selected is most excellent. Is there anything to prevent our pushing on?[46]

Webb's correspondence fell into a manic pattern over the next few years (or, really, next few decades): one day he was despairing that the movement was not gaining support fast enough, that funds were short, and that opportunities were being missed; a few weeks later he would be convinced that the movement was destined for success. Occasionally, he would express all these views in the same letter. Writing to Martin in March 1871, he argued that 'the cause... is making good way and is forcing itself on the attention of all.' He cited a Society of Friends literary society, previously opposed to any discussion of home rule, that 'is now spending two nights discussing the "Irish Question" – total separation – repeal or Federation'.[47] But as to the Association, he was less optimistic: 'We are doing our best. But somehow we have not attracted people or talent in the way I would have hoped.'[48] Six weeks later (i.e. just 1 year after the Bilton's Hotel meeting), he was telling Sullivan that the Association was in debt.[49] He also wrote an open letter 'To the Members of Council of the Home Government Association who usually attend Council Meetings' (a revealing address), warning that the Association was in 'crisis'. He encouraged his colleagues not to give up, but to press on with business and 'call upon the country members to form themselves into branch Associations'. There was room for optimism: 'We ought to have confidence in the country that it will not throw us over until its gets something better in our place. I think we feel more encouraged upon this point than we did a month ago.'[50]

One month later, Webb was feeling pessimistic again, this time concerned by and frustrated with Butt's leadership. It is difficult to prevent Butt's personality from overshadowing the home rule movement itself. Butt was a fascinating character: highly intelligent, entrepreneurial, gregarious, generous and a charismatic speaker. He was also something of a loose cannon: because he was disastrous with money and constantly in debt, Butt's spurts of energy in the national movement were carved up by his need to earn a living as a Queen's Counsel at the bar. His colleagues in the Association knew that Butt was the only figurehead who could lead such a mixed conglomerate, but they seem to have constantly feared that his behaviour could also have a disastrous effect on the movement. Furthermore, Butt was difficult to pin down, even for tasks in which the leader would obviously be expected to participate. Webb had to write to Butt, in a polite but firm letter, to inform him that a date had been set for the 1871 annual meeting, and specifically asked Butt to attend and to help draw up resolutions. In the same letter Webb also expressed regret that Butt had opposed a resolution to support a home rule candidate, and he worried what impression this might give: 'the case was so plain and clear that if we are ever to aid a home rule candidate I think we should do it on this occasion. ... People would I fear give us up as incompetent if we did not make some move on such an occasion.'[51]

The issue of how and whether to support parliamentary candidates was a thorny one: supporting candidates took money and organisation, and it was difficult to know whether candidates were sincere in their dedication to the cause. The first home rule candidates to successfully contest seats in 1871 – John Martin in January, Mitchell Henry in February, P. J. Smyth in June and Isaac Butt in September – either had significant reputations already established, or identified with other major political causes (such as tenant right) or both.[52] Thus, a major test of the movement came in February 1872, when a by-election in Kerry produced an unknown candidate for the home rule cause, receiving support from the Association in the form of the canvassing by its members. Sullivan, who travelled to Kerry to canvass, offers amusing anecdotes about how this young Protestant landlord, straight out of Oxford, defeated the preferred candidate of the Catholic establishment, including the local bishop and a well-loved landlord. Moreover, the candidate had a particularly difficult name, Roland Ponsonby Blennerhassett, which was abbreviated to 'Mr Hassett' for simplicity. Sullivan describes accompanying the candidate through remote villages in Kerry, and being mobbed by enthusiastic well-wishers who had heard the gospel of home rule and become believers. Sullivan was indeed a campaigner, a strategist and a journalist, and his description of the passionate response that 'Mr Hassett' elicited from the Kerry peasantry, in which he was offered rosaries as well as votes, may be exaggerated spin.[53] As a third party, the bipartisan multi-confessional gentlemen's club had serious problems to contend with, not least the gap between popular politics and Westminster politics. Sullivan's glorious tale of canvassing for Blennerhassett includes vignettes of peasants both young and old vocalising their support for home rule, but this is just as likely to have been their recognition that home rule was the latest 'Irish Catholic catch-cry', to borrow Comerford's description,[54] as a sign of their knowledge of and support for Butt's federalist scheme. As in every democratic election, the populace was probably hazy on the details of national politics. Thus, the Association was treading very carefully: according to Webb the Council fretted over changing one word in an address they were preparing for publication, 'to avoid frightening very timid people by any change of nomenclature'.[55]

Ultimately, Sullivan did not invent the election results, and his triumphant home rule candidate was sincerely devoted to the Association. However, he immediately found Butt's cautious approach and long absences from Parliament problematic. In February 1872, Blennerhassett wrote to Butt that he understood,

> ... that you have much business to occupy you and that a constant attendance in Parliament is not to be expected owing to the many other demands upon your time. 'The weaker brethren' may therefore hope to be of use – I am anxious to undertake a share of the work, of course I have no Parliamentary experience and must not venture on too much.[56]

Although Blennerhassett's tone is polite, there is a sense of the desperation he must have felt as he prepared to enter Parliament, on the back of a riotous watershed of an electoral campaign, and found himself not knowing what to do.

Questions arose about how much control the central leadership should have over branches outside of Dublin. Galbraith worried that the country was 'not so ready' for the type of national organisation it had experienced under O'Connell, and that it would be too difficult for a central office to handle all the membership money and governance of branches.[57] Galbraith lost this debate, apparently over money: the central organisation needed to take in membership money to meet its operational costs. And all was not chaos: the Association leadership had firm ideas about how branches should be founded and operated, and gave specific instructions to parties interested in establishing branches. A copy of the rules and regulations of the Association were sent out to those who made enquiries about establishing branches. One of the secretaries, Daunt, also offered practical advice. The first meeting of a new branch should only have temporary officers, so that the general public would not think that everything had been decided already by a small clique; there should be no permanent chair, but a chair nominated at each meeting since 'the permanent chair is ornamental and his election causes jealousy.'[58] Once officers were elected, they should serve a 6- to 12-month term: 'If elected for too short a time they never learn their duties properly, if for too long it often causes disputes.'[59] Two things are abundantly clear from such official correspondence from the Association. First, no one expected that home rule would be achieved overnight. Writing words of encouragement (perhaps to an individual in a fledgling branch) in the summer of 1873, Daunt assured his correspondent that 'a steady Association which works honestly for the cause can always accomplish good and by keeping up the spirit of the movement keeps people ready for the decisive time.'[60] Second, there was also the expectation that individuals would be thirsty for the opportunity to support home rule and to take on leadership roles in their communities.

Initially, the Association was the sole umbrella body for branches all over the world, and with a small administration and limited funds it struggled to develop its corporate image and protect itself from imposters. It was receiving correspondence from confused individuals about literature received, and giving replies such as 'we have no connection with the persons who sent you the circular. Kindly permit us to keep it.'[61] In the summer of 1873 it reacted to these false reports by resolving to publish statements of its principles in English and Scottish newspapers. This form of dissemination, it hoped, would stop 'our enemies' from dismissing the Association as disorganised and meaningless.[62]

The Association also had difficulty keeping track of branches, especially those in Great Britain. It first attempted to put advertisements in British newspapers, requesting that branches make contact with the Dublin office; it then decided that this was a waste of money (evidently it was ineffective) and wrote to its known contacts in England and Scotland to ascertain where branches were in existence.[63] The confusion should have been eradicated when the Home Rule Confederation of Great Britain (hereafter referred to as the Confederation) was established over the course of two conventions in 1872, 8 January in Manchester and 26 February in Birmingham. Two members of the Association Council also sat on the Council of the Confederation, and the two bodies remained in close contact. However, there seems to have been either dissatisfaction or confusion over this arrangement, judging by the number of letters sent from the Association (and, later, the League) to individuals in England in Scotland, insisting that under no circumstances would English or Scottish branches be allowed to circumvent the rules and affiliate with the Dublin body instead of the Confederation.[64]

Furthermore, the Association was still receiving correspondence directly from branches in England and Scotland, some of it suspicious. One 1873 letter from an Association secretary, Daunt, to a regional organiser in England demonstrates the level of confusion:

A Mr Martin Sheen reports himself a Sec. of the H. R. Assoc. of Bunlern, do you recognise him? In Walsall a W. P. McNaughton reports that he and not W. O'Halloran is the Sec., in Derby a Mr Peter Keenan of Walker Lane reports himself as a Sec. of an Assoc. is he in connection with you?[65]

Ironically, the Association had much better luck with its branches in New Zealand, Canada, the United States and Argentina.[66] Correspondence with these branches was frequent, and their membership dues were paid promptly and in full.

Alvin Jackson argues, 'For a time – in the early 1870s – home rule bound some Irish Catholics and Protestants in a shared, moderate, secular and conservative vision of a semi-independent Ireland. This bond was ephemeral, and was superseded by the increasing sectarian polarisation of Irish politics in the later 1870s and after.'[67] Certainly, many of the founding members of the Association did not become members of the League – particularly the conservative Protestant ones. Increasingly, as the League became a popular organisation, more Catholics joined and diluted the influence of the Protestants – with the noted exception of the leaders: Butt, William Shaw and Parnell. But to describe the Catholic–Protestant bond as 'ephemeral' perhaps overlooks the sincere and profound intentions of the Association leadership. Although their dreams of a non-sectarian movement might have been utopian, they were genuine; Protestant involvement in home rule was a cornerstone of the movement and almost an obsession for some members. Martin wanted to join the Association when it was founded, but waited: he argued that some Protestants felt he was 'extreme' and 'they might consider it an intrusion if I intermeddled in the preliminary groundings of their new movement.'[68] One member of the new Association even suggested that the membership cards bear an image of 'the Protestant and Catholic joining hand and hand...over the prostrate figure of Erin'.[69] This suggestion was not adopted; perhaps the Protestant and Catholic were too difficult to illustrate. Webb was thrilled that the Association's first delegates to Dublin Corporation formed what he described as 'a shamrock': a Catholic, a Protestant (presumably, a member of the Church of Ireland) and a Presbyterian.[70] However, as early as the summer of 1871 Webb was frustrated with Irish Protestants:

> I sometimes begin to think that...we must give up the hope of attracting any *large* number of our Protestant fellow countrymen. What traitors they are as a rule – willing to sell their country, bound

over hand and foot, so long as they are allowed to have gilded chains on.[71]

This horrified Webb's deep sense of responsible citizenship: 'the country is being emasculated and demoralised by being deprived of the right of self-government... It would be better to be poor and self-governed than *rich* and governed against our moral sense of what is just and fair.'[72]

If Jackson is correct in his assessment of Protestant involvement in home rule, what role did Webb have in an era of growing sectarianism? He did not leave the home rule movement, or feel pushed out because of his religious background; rather, it seems that he was encouraged by a movement that was eager to retain and attract Protestant members. Amid these debates about the character of home rule, Webb was devoting more and more time to its organisation. His disapproval of the movement's apathy towards women's suffragism, the departure of prominent Protestants and the frustrations he had felt as treasurer under the leadership of Butt did not dampen his interest in home rule. He remained optimistic about the success of the movement and proud of its attempts to be all-embracing. In 1873, his close colleague Daunt was also still confident that the Association's constitution was completely inclusive, and guaranteed that 'every section of politicians from the Tory of the most antique pattern to the red republican of the latest brand can support us, while still maintaining his own political ideas.'[73]

Evolution of the Home Rule League

Lawrence McCaffrey argues that the Association was 'an immediate success'.[74] On the other hand, Alan O'Day has emphasised that 'in retrospect it is astounding that the movement survived infancy.'[75] In a sense, it did not: after only three years the Association's leaders set out to transform home rule into a more popular political machine. A national conference to form the Home Rule League and disband the Association was called in November 1873. Butt had insisted on a national requisition to give more authority to the conference, and 25,000 signatures in support were gathered.

The conference was held at the Rotunda in Dublin over 4 days. Eight pre-prepared resolutions were distributed to the delegates and introduced by speakers from across the country. The speakers had been organised ahead of time, although not too far ahead: the Mayor of Cork began to speak with the words 'since I came into this room I have been asked to move the third resolution', claiming an Irish privilege to manage Irish affairs.[76] The conference organisers endeavoured to allow 'our friends from the country'[77] to speak, and to select 'gentlemen to speak who were representative men from the different districts'.[78]

However, the emphasis was on allowing people to speak, not to debate. When an amendment to the third resolution was offered by the polemical priest Rev. Thaddeus O'Malley,[79] the organisers worried that a long debate might ensue, and this would be time-consuming. Furthermore, Protestant home ruler Captain King-Harman believed that this would give the wrong impression to the outside world: 'let us put it forth to the world that we are not split up by any small matters of detail.'[80] This tension was at the heart of the Home Rule League in this era: wanting to become a formal and wide-reaching organisation, but fearful of making any moves that would alienate anyone or cause division.

Some dissenting voices were heard at the conference. One was an amendment, put forward by a Mr Cahill and supported by Joseph Biggar, that home rule MPs should 'always vote in a body, or abstain from voting on all party divisions'.[81] This amendment was rejected after a heated discussion: some participants felt that binding pledges were demeaning, some resented that MPs were being called into question and some were angry that MPs had not been present to support Butt's previous bills in Parliament. Second was the issue of repeal: some such as Martin gave their support to the League but argued that they would personally prefer simple repeal.[82] However, imperial policy was a cornerstone of Butt's federalism. He argued that simple Repeal would give Ireland no representation at the Imperial Parliament, and therefore Ireland would have no say in the future of the Empire. This would be disastrously unfair, Butt argued:

> The United Kingdom, of which Ireland is now a part, has vast foreign and colonial possessions. Many of these possessions have been acquired during the period of our disastrous partnership of seventy years. Heaven knows we have paid dearly enough for them. We are entitled to our share of them.[83]

Butt's view of imperialism has never been explained as anything other than a personal attraction or evidence of his 'Orange Young Ireland' roots.[84] However, given the obsession with recruiting Protestant bourgeois support for the home rule movement, it is possible that this idea was not simply a pet project of Butt's, but a strategic one aimed at reassuring those Irish who had a stake in the empire. Recent research into the level of Irish involvement in the British Empire has shown that it was high in certain areas and classes, especially during the mid-Victorian period in which Butt was formulating these ideas. There was ample coverage in Irish newspapers, including home rule newspapers, in the 1870s on discrimination against Irishmen in imperial military service and imperial examinations,[85] and less Irish control over Imperial affairs could have indicated fewer job opportunities for Irishmen. It is pure speculation, since we have little knowledge of Butt's strategic intentions, but given what we now know about Irish imperial participation it is entirely possible that Butt knew this point would appeal to the invaluable and elusive Protestant middle-class vote.

Furthermore, this issue was a major point of discussion at the 1873 Home Rule Conference. Galbraith presented his home rule arguments in terms of empire, arguing 'while I openly avow that I love that empire, I cannot conceal the opinion that its most serious source of future danger is Irish disaffection.'[86] Sir Joseph McKenna described the Act of Union as an anomaly in an era when Britain was resettling its terms with its colonies: 'All the chief colonies' since the Union 'had received constitutions and parliaments of their own, and it was during that notable seventy-three years that the East India Company had surrendered its dominions and India had been absorbed into the Empire'.[87] The implication is that Ireland was a colony and should be treated as a colony, with a new settlement and devolved government. McKenna was possibly thinking of the federation of Canada in 1867, although his arguments do not apply to many other British colonies. Whatever the flaws in McKenna's understanding of the empire, he was drawing strong parallels that he felt would be convincing to his audience.

Webb did not speak during the conference but was one of five secretaries who played an important role in organising the event. The words of thanks expressed to the secretaries at the termination of the conference indicate that Webb was the least-distinguished and well-known of the five. John Blunden was described as a man 'whose name was well known and revered in Dublin'; Captain King-Harman's 'public estimation was shown by the cheers which had greeted him'; Philip Callan was described as 'an unostentatious and laborious worker' who had kept the London Irish informed about home rule; and Daunt was referred to as 'a gentleman whose honesty and consistency were most distinguished'. Alfred Webb was thanked simply for the 'excellent arrangements' he had made for the Conference.[88] It was Webb, however, who accepted thanks on behalf of the secretaries and offered a mix of warning and encouragement to the delegates:

[The] real work was only beginning. It was easy to feel enthusiastic under the influence of this great gathering and those crowded galleries, and after having listened to such cogent reasoning, to such stirring bursts of eloquence. Long weary days of constant labour and untiring exertions were before all who meant to be true to the cause.[89]

Webb certainly knew what he was volunteering himself for when he committed himself to the movement, though one wonders whether his colleagues thought him something of a killjoy. At the end of the conference a 16-man committee was drawn up to prepare a constitution for the League. It is a rough indicator of who some of the major actors were at this time: Isaac Butt MP, Joseph Biggar MP, John Barry (a Manchester organiser), Kenelm Digby, John Ferguson (of Glasgow), Mitchell Henry MP, Rev. William Malone, Joseph Ronayne MP, and the six men associated with the Conference organisation: William Shaw, John Blunden, William O'Neill Daunt, Philip Callan, E. R. King-Harman and Alfred Webb.

The League, despite the backing it had received through the national requisition, was still Dublin-based and somewhat elitist through the mid-1870s. It was governed by a Council of 100 members: 50 who were elected by all the members of the League, and 50 others who were 'co-opted' by the first 50. This co-option system was based on the fact that the Council had weekly meetings, and 'very many of the first fifty councilors might be resident so far from Dublin that they could not conveniently give frequent attendance.'[90] Therefore, to ensure adequate attendance, most of the co-opted members were Dublin residents. Martin wrote as League secretary that 'the Dublin members have but few shopkeepers or grocers among them, while there are many professional men. But the important question is the fitness of the men chosen, whatever their social circumstances.'[91]

The fitness of those men was tested sooner than they had expected, when Gladstone's government was dissolved and an election called in January 1874. The League had less than 1 month to find MPs to contest seats and it struggled to do so. The Association had already successfully contested several by-elections, but the League was still in its infancy. There were plenty of reasons why any new organisation in a multi-party election system might have difficulty finding potential MPs from its constituent base, and some of them have nothing to do with those constituents' dedication to the cause. It is useful to remember Sullivan's account of his own reaction on being asked to run for Parliament in 1867, and how he responded to the accusation that he had urged political action through his newspaper, the *Nation*, but had never run for election himself: 'the *Nation* has never said that a hard-working journalist is bound to spend a thousand pounds for the honour and glory of rendering laborious service at Westminster. Men of ambition, men of fortune, or men with personal advantages in view, may do so. I will not.'[92]

However, the home rulers had achieved something: their organisation was still shaky, but their philosophy had become well-known. Thornley has argued that 90 per cent of non-Conservative candidates in the 1874 election referred to home rule in their campaigns. The League's efforts to incorporate conservatives were partly stymied by the electorate: some Conservative party home rulers, including King-Harman, lost their seats in favour of more liberal candidates.[93] The new Irish Parliamentary Party entered Parliament with 60 members.[94] This party was also referred to as the Irish Party and the National Party, and these terms will be used interchangeably in this text.

In spite of the electoral success, the League was having other problems: chiefly, it did not have enough money. A National Roll had been established to allow those who could not, or would not, join League branches to publicly express their support for home rule: for 1 shilling each their names could be added to the list. The National Roll was meant to raise both the funds and profile of the League, but it was evidently failing on the first goal. As treasurer, Webb naturally concerned himself with the financial health of the organisation, but he had a more personal cause for concern. Writing to Captain Dunne in 1874, he explained with regret that action would have to be taken to cut costs:

> We are in extremes for funds, and it is absolutely necessary for the Council of the League to give up the [National] Roll offices. I think bad of it – but it is absolutely necessary indeed. ... I could not afford it, for hitherto *I have held myself personally responsible for all debts*.[95]

Indeed, anyone owing payment to the Home Rule League at this time was requested to make their cheque out to Alfred Webb.[96] Webb had admitted in his correspondence with Henry a few months earlier that, with regard to funds, 'I am completely in despair. (Bear in mind, however, that I generally look at the black side of things).'[97] The sharp increase in membership that he had anticipated after the Conference had not occurred. Over the summer of 1874, Webb poured out his heart to Daunt. He worried that the members were progressing well, but the country was apathetic. The low number of Protestants joining was particularly upsetting: 'Oh how it wrings one's heart to see nearly all the Protestants of Ireland settled down in stony apathy on this question and resting satisfied under such a degrading system of government and destruction of their country's liberties!'[98]

Comerford has written: 'It is difficult to assess the degree of seriousness with which anyone regarded the call for home rule in 1874, more particularly after the general election had placed Disraeli and the Tories in power with a comfortable majority.'[99] Yet Webb, in spite of his frequent bouts of depression, was serious about home rule: in his own words, 'home rule affairs appear to me very dead at present though in my breast the feeling of the necessity of the change burns as strong as ever.'[100] His tendency towards pessimism is outweighed by the fact that he was willing to bankroll the Home Rule League. Was Webb naïve, foolish, or an unsung nationalist hero?

Webb was certainly serious about home rule in 1874, when he published a 30-page pamphlet titled *Why I Desire Home Rule*. The pamphlet is written from a decidedly middle-class point of view (as opposed to an Ascendancy or a tenant farmer position), one inspired by Grattan and convinced that home rule was a practical constitutional solution to a political, not an ethnic or a religious, problem. There are several themes in the pamphlet – of international responsibility, liberty and the lack of a 'Catholic threat' – that he would return to in writings throughout his political career. Webb begins by quoting Grattan, then explains his thesis: 'My most ardent desire is that I should live to see the solid foundations laid of a hearty union between the Nations forming the United Kingdom', and the attainment of an 'ideal state of liberty' that would fulfil '[Abraham] Lincoln's noble definition of a true government, "Of the people, by the people, for the people".'[101] Webb believed that there was an international responsibility to improve Irish governance, since 'we are citizens of the world as well as citizens of Ireland,' and Ireland was doing the United States a particular disservice by sending it huge numbers of 'immigrants utterly unused to political power'.[102] Moreover, Webb also addressed the position of Ireland in the Empire. Ireland, he wrote,

> has it in her power to influence for good the fortunes of so many millions who have come within the influence of the United Kingdom in her foreign possessions; and she should be peculiarly fitted, by her past connexion with Empire, to take a fairer and more unbiased view of our relations with foreign states.[103]

He appealed to his audience and echoed Butt's view that Ireland could not be satisfied 'at being shut out from her fair share of the administration and control of the Empire', although he admitted that personally 'I regard our foreign influence with humiliation, considering how it has been acquired, and for what selfish motives it is maintained.'[104]

Webb also addressed and dismissed Protestant fears about home rule. His argument is an unusual one, and one that could probably only have been articulated by a Protestant author. Rather than simply trying to demonstrate the unreasonableness of Protestant fears, he opted for a psychoanalytical explanation: ' "Catholic Ascendancy" and "Ultramontanism" are in the main phantoms of the Irish Protestant conscience, engendered by the guilt of past oppressions and past ascendancy.'[105] Ultimately, he encouraged Protestants to see religion as a private matter of conscience (which, theologically speaking, was consistent with many Protestant views), and to participate in the home rule scheme. If Ulster Protestants refused to support home rule, Webb was ultimately not bothered: 'I deny the right of 936,000 to dictate for 5,400,000.'[106]

Webb summarised the options. Complete identification with Britain 'would appear to me impossible'. Complete separation was an option, but international responsibility suggested it was not wise. Although Webb had already established that Ireland was distinct from Britain, perhaps having observed the nationalistic military activity in continental Europe he argued that it would not 'advance the peace and happiness of the world to have another distinct nationality adding to the warring interests that hitherto have cursed the earth'.[107] Simple repeal was 'impractical and undesirable', he believed, as an eighteenth-century answer would not suit nineteenth-century problems. There was, Webb concluded, one remaining viable option: Butt's plan for federal home rule, which would secure 'Imperial Unity with National Freedom', a solution 'based on reason, on truth, on justice, and on common sense'.[108]

Webb's pamphlet on home rule shows the degree to which he fully embraced Butt's programme, but also reflects his Quaker sense of justice and his logical, step-by-step style of argument. This suggests he was not foolish and, although he might have been slightly naïve about the progress of the movement, he had a concrete vision of Ireland's place in the world system and a faith in classic democratic principles.

Viable alternatives

While Webb and a few other administrators were loyally manning the ship in Dublin, the Irish Parliamentary Party was charting a new course in Parliament. Butt was prepared to proceed cautiously with his demands for home rule, but other members were impatient and saw little hope of compromise with Disraeli's Conservative government. Joseph Biggar pioneered a new phase of obstructionism: a commitment to filibustering, disrupting and generally prolonging debates in Parliament as a means of drawing attention to Irish issues and to disable the government. Biggar irritated Butt, who condemned his actions in the House of Commons,[109] but he amassed a small band of adherents, including Charles Stewart Parnell and Frank Hugh O'Donnell. Webb's words in 1871 to his colleagues[110] proved prophetic for Butt: that the country would not give up on him until something could be found to replace him. The obstructionists were now presenting that viable alternative in parliamentary strategy.

Furthermore, problems reemerged with the Confederation in 1875, in part due to the lack of funds on the other side of the Irish Sea. The Confederation was acting like the League's stroppy teenage offspring: rebelling, jealously guarding its independence, but always turning to the League when it was low on money. In 1875, the Confederation voted in support of Biggar's obstructionism.[111] That did not stop one of its secretaries from writing to Butt in July of 1876, asking for £100 without which, he warned, 'the Confederation will receive a blow from which it will not easily recover.' He asked that Butt personally intervene: 'the Council [of the League] will decide next Monday. A word from you would meanwhile settle the matter.'[112] The grant was opposed by some members of the League 'taking into consideration the fact that the Home Rule Confederation is at present indebted to the League in the sum of £350 and upwards'.[113] Problems persisted in 1876, and the League was receiving letters complaining of mismanagement that was causing 'a number of Irishmen to abstain from joining' the Confederation.[114] The League had no jurisdiction to deal with these complaints, and referred correspondents to the Council of the Confederation.

The Confederation has been described as 'a largely moribund organisation' when it elected Parnell as its President in August 1877 with only 40 delegates present, placing Butt in a vulnerable leadership position.[115] This description does not seem accurate in light of the correspondence relating to the Confederation in PRONI. The Confederation had been a headache for the League since its inception, and was far from moribund just 1 month after Parnell's election, when Butt called a national convention and wanted to limit the numbers of Confederation members attending. The resolution eventually passed by the League on this matter was that 'fifty members of the Home Rule Confederation of Great

Britain [are] to be chosen one by and from each branch of the fifty most numerous branches.'[116]

The Council of the League stood by Butt to the end, but Butt himself was under few illusions, except perhaps of his own effectiveness in Parliament. 'The home rule party is broken up and the national cause thrown back for twenty years,' he wrote to George Delaney, 'However I must stick to my post to the last and try and save the ship but... the question of my retirement will before long settle itself.'[117] He remained convinced that, under his leadership, home rule could have been won with 'a few years patient working'.[118] Others were less confident, so long as Butt's MPs were allowed to privilege their independence over Irish issues. Although MPs were not bound to vote on all Irish issues, many home rulers were horrified at the lack of discipline among MPs. Henry was infuriated in 1877 that only 32 of his colleagues in Parliament could be found to vote that Ireland was overtaxed, and his response was that 'I will no longer keep terms with the systematic violation of duty which is fast-rendering the home rule party impotent and ridiculous.'[119]

Internal dissent was also crippling the League. In the summer of 1876 Sullivan admitted to have written a series of 'Eye-Witness' letters, critiquing Butt's leadership, in the *New York Catholic World*. Jackson describes Sullivan as 'one of the most loyal' of Butt's supporters, but Terence de Vere White argues that Butt did not trust Sullivan, and that Disraeli was convinced that Sullivan hoped to replace Butt as leader.[120] Sullivan denied this in several newspapers, but many were unconvinced: the *Irishman* argued that 'Mr A. M. Sullivan's insidious attempt to supersede Mr Butt in the leadership of the home rule party has failed ignominiously.'[121] Even if Sullivan had not intended to challenge Butt for the leadership, the damage was done if it appeared to the public that even the most loyal supporters could be turning on their leader.

Webb himself had grown tired with Butt and with the League politics. In December 1876, he resigned as treasurer of the League. His resignation was accepted 'with great reluctance'.[122] Webb's resignation seems to have been genuinely regretted: he was evidently a hard worker. His melancholy had no adverse affect on his work, as far as it possible to tell, since it is rare that anyone comments on a treasurer doing the job properly: normally mistakes are all that is noticed. Webb did not completely resign from the League: he appears to have remained a member of the Council, until he resigned for a second time in March 1878.[123] Webb was not the only frustrated one. Galbraith and Blunden stated their resignations as secretaries of the League in December 1877.[124] Sullivan resigned his parliamentary seat in February 1878,[125] followed by O'Donnell in

March.[126] However, despite high-profile members resigning, there were still 174 individuals competing for 50 seats on the Council of the League in January 1877.[127]

Furthermore, money was, as always, causing its own problems. Part of this was a result of non-payment of dues.[128] The League was resorting to private solicitations for funds from wealthy members.[129] In mid-1878 the League had to discharge its clerk, James Collins, with apologies and the promise of excellent references, because it could not afford to pay his salary.[130] A few weeks later McAllister, the secretary, resigned with deep sadness because the League had too little money to pay his own salary.[131] McAllister remained, in effect, an unpaid secretary: after 6 years of devotion to the League, he hated to see it fall apart. In November, he wrote to the League's landlord to say that it would be giving up some of its rented offices in order to cut costs.[132]

It is clear why Webb titled the section of his autobiography dealing with this era 'Rise of home rule to my despair in 1878'. Funds were dangerously low, prominent members were resigning, not enough subscriptions were coming in, the Confederation was supporting very different policies and a leadership contest was dividing League members. However, his despondency did not render him inactive. Webb was busy doing other things: in 1876, he printed and published his *Compendium of Irish Biography*. He was not the only one who juggled a literary life with a work life – Butt himself had published a two-volume history of Italy in 1860.[133] He remained deeply committed to home rule and he vented his frustration in Dublin's newspapers. Just weeks after his first resignation, he lashed out in the *Nation* against the policy of 'taking our part in government matters exactly as if the question of home rule did not exist – of trying to get all we can, personally and publicly – of accepting titles, and places, and influence – of joining the constabulary, and fighting the battles of the United Kingdom'.[134]

After he resigned a second time, Webb wrote three articles in the *Freeman's Journal* criticising the direction of the home rule movement: 'The home rule movement', 'The present position of the home rule movement' and 'Public opinion in Ireland'.[135] These three letters urged decisive action and lamented the fact that Irish public enthusiasm for home rule was waning. Intriguingly, Webb blamed apathy not on internal schisms or lack of progress in the League, but on several international trends: the depression in the United States, the Franco–Prussian War, a failed revolution in Spain and the perception that the United Kingdom was more tolerant of Roman Catholicism than many countries in Continental Europe. Minor improvements in Ireland had also placated public opinion.¹³⁶ Webb argued that a 'really patriotic public opinion should be established in the country' before home rule had any chance of success. Webb summed up his argument with patriotic flourish: 'I advocate no craven submission – no paltry West-Britonism. Irish we are, and Irish we shall remain. Home rule or no home rule, we shall never cease to assert our rights until we have every constitutional privilege that they have in Great Britain.'¹³⁷

Webb later regretted having written these pieces, and found that some of his friends misinterpreted these articles as a sign that Webb was rejecting home rule itself.¹³⁸ However, Webb also claimed his opinion pieces got a very positive reception from a young MP: like so many others, Webb has indulged himself in reconstructing the rise of Parnell, with himself as an important supporting actor. In his autobiography Webb described how, soon after Parnell's election to Parliament, he and Parnell sat together at a banquet, and Parnell 'very earnestly expounded to me a plan of Parliamentary action by which, if he could persuade others to join, he hoped they could force attention to Irish questions'.¹³⁹ After these 1878 letters were published in the *Freeman's Journal*, Webb described (in an anecdote that cannot be substantiated in another source) how Parnell came to his printing office, and said the following to him: 'Mr Webb you are perhaps a dangerous man to speak to, honest as you are. I have read your letters. I now mean to try with the help of others to bring about a different state of affairs to that which you deplore – we shall see the outcome.'¹⁴⁰

To describe Webb as 'dangerous' seems slightly far-fetched, unless perhaps he had such a reputation for moral rectitude that his opinions were taken quite seriously. 'Dangerous' Webb waited to see the outcome. Butt ultimately lost his position as leader, and was replaced by William Shaw (who had chaired the 1873 Conference), who was later replaced by Parnell. Butt died in 1879. In the meantime, Webb maintained a correspondence with Parnell,¹⁴¹ and by 1880 he was ready to rejoin the revitalised nationalist cause.

5
'I am willing to take any dangerous part'[1]: Webb in the World of Parnell and Gladstone

The 1880s and the ascent of Charles Stewart Parnell into the home rule leadership marked a change of mood and a change of strategy. Chiefly, Parnell was a master of the politics of ambiguity, a style of politics to which Alfred Webb was spectacularly unsuited. Webb's almost pathological honesty caused conflict on several occasions: when he felt compelled to speak out against party policy and when others deceived him. However, Webb also found new usefulness for himself as a Protestant home ruler, and continued his campaign of letters to the editors of newspapers in Britain and Ireland. He served as treasurer several times and was always an active member of the nationalist community during this era. Whatever push factors led him to resign, there were always stronger pull factors that kept him from straying from the home rule movement.

Land, the law and the National League

Parnell assumed leadership of the Home Rule League in 1880, replacing the rather forgettable William Shaw. He had gained the leadership of the Home Rule Confederation of Great Britain in 1877, and now new developments in domestic issues gave Parnell an opportunity to expand and solidify his leadership in Ireland. Agrarian depression and grass roots agitation in Mayo led to the foundation of the Land League in 1879, and this became a national organisation through the energy of Michael Davitt, a former Fenian prisoner. Parnell assumed the leadership of the Land League in 1879.[2] Like Isaac Butt, Parnell appreciated that he had at least to pay lip service to Fenianism and land agitation. Parnell, however, was the master of ambiguity, and his connection with Fenianism was purposefully vague: he never explicitly responded to John Devoy's suggestions of cooperation between Fenians and home rulers.

The difficulty home rulers faced in sharing their leader with the Land League was the suspicion, especially in Britain, that the Land League sometimes turned a blind eye to violent confrontations. These allegations were formally made in a Special Commission ordered by the Conservative government in 1888. Webb also shared these fears, and explained that his abhorrence of violence prevented him from actually joining the Land League. However, because he and Davitt were personal friends, he did assist the movement: he spoke at the 1880 Land Convention, organised by Davitt,[3] and at the request of Parnell he collected information for himself and Parnell to use in speeches.[4] Webb's claims of pacifism may not have been the only thing that prevented him from joining: it is not clear how much he knew or cared about land issues.

Webb was, however, an earnest comrade. When coercive legislation led to the arrest of many of the leaders of the land agitation, Webb endeavoured to support his colleagues by sending them Christmas cards in prison and writing encouraging poetry about their plight: 'Bear up true hearts, the winter storms blow round us / But spring with flowers is near.'[5] When he learned that William Forster, the Chief Secretary for Ireland, was using the Statute of Edward III to justify the legality of coercion in Ireland, Webb wrote to the *Freeman's Journal*, supplying a copy of the statute in the original French, with an English translation. The newspaper thanked Webb for providing 'a timely service' to thousands of readers who would not have had access to the statute books.[6] Webb also created a pamphlet for MPs to demonstrate that the agitation in Ireland was not unique, but rather that many countries had experienced such instability 'in times preceding... the amelioration of the conditions of the people'.[7]

The imprisonment of many (male) leaders of the movement led to the establishment of the Ladies' Land League under the leadership of Anna and Fanny Parnell, sisters of Charles Stewart. Although there is no official record of Webb's position in 1881, Anna's correspondence to Webb indicates that he had slipped back into a treasury role for the Home Rule League ('do you wish to have the caterer charged?').[8] He had also resumed printing for the nationalist cause, apparently having lost his concerns that he might be seen as profiting from the movement. On the release of Parnell from prison in 1882, Webb worked overnight to print 10,000 copies of a manifesto.[9] Anna Parnell had too much printing for Webb to handle on his own,[10] but she also employed his printing shop as a safe house. Webb claimed that she 'was once nearly getting me into prison' for asking him to keep hold of some 'books' of which Webb did not approve.[11] However, her letters to Webb seem fairly straightforward: 'I want you to take all the matter which I should prefer to keep from the knowledge of the Castle until it is ready for use, and I think your establishment is the safest in the respect.'[12]

Parnell's assessment of Webb's home as a safe one echoes a comment he made himself about being overlooked by the authorities. Webb divulged in his autobiography that during this era when many nationalist politicians were being arrested, he had 'attended meetings where I felt I was so likely to be arrested that I brought biscuits in pocket to eat in the police cell'.[13] He claims that the police never arrested him because he was a Protestant, and that therefore his arrest would have backfired politically for the authorities. It is also possible that he was not seen as a decision-maker within the Home Rule League, but as someone who was not really aware of what was going on; certainly, Anna Parnell seems to have deceived him. On the other hand, Webb was not a total political innocent, and his romantic nationalism was tempered by his refusal to aggrandise the reputations of his colleagues. One of the most amusing anecdotes in his autobiography concerns a visit he made to the Ladies' Land League offices, at a time when these women were viewed 'as Joans of Arc', to find the clerks, 'a long row of them sitting one behind the other, each engaged in combing out the hair of the girl before her'.[14] Webb was both a home ruler and a suffragist, but he was not willing to fabricate hagiographies about his colleagues to suit the movement.

The Land War came to end in 1882 and Parnell turned his attention back to home rule. The movement was given new momentum when the Home Rule League was disbanded and a new organisation, the National League of Ireland, was established in the autumn of 1882. The National League's constitution had five principal goals: national self-government, land law reform, local self-government, the extension of both parliamentary and municipal franchises and 'the development and encouragement of the Labour and Industrial Interests of Ireland'.[15] It was a purely national body; it did not adopt Devoy's argument that Irish nationalism should fight for the rights of oppressed nationalities throughout the world.[16] It pledged to support educational initiatives for working people, such as reading rooms and Mechanics' Institutes, and to obtain information and provide support for the extension of industry and manufacturing in Ireland. It is very easy to conclude that the National League had little sincere interest in such matters and was simply trying to bring on board the working people of the Land League. However, Davitt and Webb's interest in building Irish industry may have rubbed off on Parnell: he wrote to Webb in 1883 to release funds so that Parnell might 'send an agent to Germany to investigate the peat industry there and afterwards in Ireland'.[17] Webb had taken a lead role in organising the Dublin exhibition of August 1882 for the purpose of promoting Irish trades and manufactures, which had the blessing of the Home Rule League (see Chapter 3). He and Davitt also corresponded about improving technical education in Ireland and building industry in Connemara.[18]

Nominations for the National League's organizing committee were received in October 1882 from affiliated organisations. The Home Rule League nominated George Delaney, Joseph Biggar, T. D. Sullivan, Judge Little and Webb's old friend Abraham Shackleton. The Irish Labour and Industrial Union nominated J. J. Clancy, Daniel Hishon, Thomas Sexton, Timothy Healy and Parnell himself. The Mansion House Evicted Tenants Fund nominated Charles Dawson (the Lord Mayor), Edward Dwyer Gray (the High Sheriff), John Redmond, Edward Leamy and Webb.[19] This organising committee created an executive with Parnell as chairman, Timothy Healy, Timothy Harrington and T. Brennan as secretaries, and Biggar and Webb as treasurers.[20]

Webb and Biggar had an important role, as the National League was not only providing funds for the home rule campaign, but handling requests from dispossessed tenants on behalf of the Land League. The exception was the so-called Paris Funds, a considerable sum of Land League funds that Parnell transferred to an account in Paris. Webb must have been aware of this fund, which acquired a mythical status in the 1890s. Although the demands for money grew, nationalists now had an unprecedented level of funding from Irish-Americans, and fundraising lecture tours in the United States – by Parnell, Dillon, Healy and Davitt – raised large sums. The National League was not in as precarious a financial situation as the Home Rule League had been, although it was still fielding requests for funds from its counterpart in Great Britain. Parnell wrote to Webb on this matter, explaining that he always had expected that the National League of Great Britain would be financed by the Irish one, to the tune of £500 a year. The organisation of home rule in Britain was part of Parnell's strategy, and already in 1883 he believed it was effective: 'Controlling as the League here does the seats of 97 English and Scotch members, it forms a power the importance of which is incalculable and which cannot be over-estimated. ... the great results expected from it are on the point of being obtained.'[21]

Acting as treasurers brought Webb and Biggar into correspondence with nationalists across Ireland, Britain and the United States. However,

Webb's return to the nationalist fold after his 1878 resignation was not easy. His determination to fight for justice, regardless of the greater political implications, had serious implications during the 1880s. Two events gave Webb notoriety in nationalist circles and possibly contributed to his decision to resign as a nationalist city councillor in Dublin (as discussed in Chapter 3). His actions could superficially be seen as inconsistent, since he 'could not always toe the party line',[22] but Webb was consistent in his desire to approach each political event separately and judge it on its own merit. He sometimes came to regret his tendency to reach decisions and act on them immediately, admitting that 'a dislike to occupy an undecided indefinite position is one of the faults of my character.'[23] His colleague Timothy Harrington explained Webb's tendency to buck the majority trend in another way: 'the only fault that he [Harrington] could find in Mr Webb's political career was that he was a little too tolerant of the opinions and feelings of those who had no regard whatever for the opinion and feelings of the majority of the people.'[24]

Both incidents in which Webb sided with the minority concerned trials and the ostracism faced by those who cooperated in prosecutions. The first episode, in 1883, concerned Mr D. J. Field, 'who so narrowly escaped assassination as a result of having acted as a Special Juror in one of the trials under the Crimes Act'.[25] Webb recognised that Field 'had played a peculiarly obnoxious part in convicting some of our friends',[26] but he nevertheless could not condone assassination attempts on jurors. A fund, the Field Testimonial, was established to collect donations in support of Field's family, and Webb became its treasurer. Webb's colleagues on the Testimonial committee included prominent Conservatives and unionists, including Lord Ardilaun (Arthur Guinness). Webb thought that he was supporting justice, but his actions were clearly seen as giving support to the National League's political enemies.

Webb's actions drew outrage from his home rule colleagues and his constituents for the Dublin City Council. The Inns-Quay Registration Association met and resolved that Webb's support of the Field Testimonial 'stultified the National League and National interests generally'.[27] In response Webb wrote to the *Freeman's Journal* and offered to resign his position: he argued that his support of the Testimonial and the League were not incompatible, but he recognised that his actions went against the general nationalist feeling. Webb eventually resigned in the summer of 1884, claiming he could not accept the nationalist candidate for Lord Mayor.[28]

The second event in which Webb took a position against the majority of nationalists was concerning the Curtin Affair in 1885. In late 1885 Mr Curtin, a National League member in Kerry, was shot on his farm – apparently after he refused to give up arms in a raid. Those accused of the shooting were locals, and when the Curtin family testified against them they were boycotted by the local community and received no assistance from the National League. Margaret O'Callaghan has suggested that the murders were not about land, and that the Curtin case demonstrates 'that the offences for which Irish Nationalist politicians were to be held answerable encompassed every private vendetta of a peasant society'.[29] But Webb, who might not have known the specifics of the case, believed that the National League was siding with the wrong individuals, and he took it upon himself to fight the Curtin family's corner. He visited the family and was shocked by the violent behaviour of their neighbours, especially when a group of girls destroyed the pew in which the Curtin family had been sitting at mass.[30] He recognised that his observations of such violent behaviour 'might be used as arguments for coercion' if he made them public. He did feel it was 'the duty of all Nationalists openly, unequivocally, and effectually to stand by the family',[31] which had suffered the loss of Mr Curtin and was being persecuted for cooperating with the legal system. Webb was deeply disappointed when his colleagues did not join him.

Furthermore, Webb was troubled by the leadership of the party. Although he had favoured a more disciplined structure over that created by Butt, he was stifled by Parnell's management. In the summer of 1884, he expressed his wish to resign his post of treasurer of the National League. This was possibly not the first time he had suggested that he might resign to Parnell. He later claimed resignation on account of 'not being able to stand Parnell's autocratic arrangement about funds'.[32] This autocratic attitude can perhaps be glimpsed in Parnell's correspondence with Webb; in one letter, Parnell requested that a situation concerning catering fees 'which is to be brought before the committee at their next meeting had better be attended to by me and not by the committee'.[33] Webb had by now established a track record of resignations in his 14 years in nationalist politics. He had resigned as treasurer of the Home Rule League, then from the League itself then from his elected City Council post. Parnell's reaction to his decision probably reflects this: he expressed his regret, urged Webb to 'have a talk with me on the subject before you finally make up your mind' and not to act hastily, but he was not surprised by Webb's decision, 'as it is not the first time that you have felt that, for one reason or another, you are not sufficiently in sympathy with the management of the movement... I do not now feel myself entirely at liberty to press you to remain.'[34] Webb's friend Davitt urged him to reconsider, but also applauded him for his 'dignified protest by way of resignation'.[35]

Without much other explicit commentary from individuals inside the movement, it is only possible to speculate as to whether Webb's position as self-appointed moral compass was becoming tedious to his colleagues. Sophie O'Brien has one recollection of how Webb's honesty became an irritant. She wrote that in the early 1880s he was responsible for sending press clippings about the national movement to the diasporic branches, and 'so great was his sense of fair play that when sending the papers representing the Irish side, he thought it his duty to add to the parcel anti-Irish papers, so that the readers should have both sides of the controversy.' The party leadership thought it absurd to use its funds to pay for the dissemination of anti-Irish material.[36] The qualities that made Webb an excellent treasurer – honesty, fairness – also made him a complete failure as a publicity officer for the party of ambiguity. Healy apparently told Webb that his resignation as treasurer cost the movement thousands of pounds. Biggar remained in his position and drew little complaint as treasurer, but Webb observed that there was a 'looseness of management' of funds.[37] This appears to have come from the top down: Biggar explained to Harrington on one occasion that 'Mr Parnell has something over £1000 of remittances which he will give me first time he remembers to bring them from his lodgings.'[38]

After his resignation as treasurer Webb continued to be involved in Irish nationalism in an unofficial capacity: attending and sometimes chairing meetings of the National League, and writing and printing. He described himself as 'business advisor of the Parnellite Party' in 1890,[39] although it is unclear what this job entailed and under what circumstances he held it. He also wrote a regular column for the *New York Nation* under the pseudonymous initials 'D. B.', taking the last letter in each of his names. Some of these articles were reprinted as pamphlets for Irish audiences. One, titled 'The Irish Question', used some of the language of his 1874 defence of home rule: he argued, for example, that 'since the French Revolution it has not be possible permanently to crush national aspirations,' but that the threat of separation could be quelled by the extension of equal right: 'Were rights granted [to Ireland] and aspirations respected, it would appear reasonable to expect that Ireland would soon respect and love a flag and power under which were guaranteed peace, security and honour.'[40] Webb also maintained his belief that Irish governance affected the welfare of the colonies. In particular, he argued that Parliament had a responsibility to the welfare of millions of Indian people, yet Indian issues were 'shuffled through in a few hours' after Irish questions had wasted Parliament's time. Webb promised that a separate Irish parliament would therefore benefit India.[41]

'Phantoms of the Irish Protestant conscience'[42]

In 1886, Webb began to write his autobiography, but then decided to destroy his draft. He felt disheartened by the recent political events: although Gladstone had converted to home rule and an alliance had been struck between the home rulers and the Liberals, the home rule bill had failed in Parliament. Webb reverted to type: his intense elation at the prospect of a home rule bill was replaced by despondency about its failure. At the age of 52, he felt old and worn. About this time, a young Protestant, Charles Oldham, wrote to Webb for advice about joining the home rule movement. Oldham was only 26, half Webb's age; he was active in the Statistical Society, his sister Alice Oldham was a suffragist active in the DWSA, and later in life he would become a prominent professor at University College Dublin.[43] He was also one of the 'brilliant young men' who graduated from Trinity in the early 1880s, founded the *Dublin University Review* and, according to F. S. L. Lyons, 'were not congealed within the austere Anglican-unionist ethos...their minds were open and hopeful for the future'.[44]

Webb's frank advice to Oldham reveals his characteristic mixed feelings of hope and disillusionment:

> I need not say how deeply I feel interested in the awakening of people like you to politics. You will enter upon them with hope. I am old compared to you and have had much of the hope knocked out of me. And I have made so many mistakes...that I have not the same confidence in myself I used to have.

He encouraged Oldham to become involved in the home rule movement, but also advised him to bear in mind that, as a Protestant, he would meet specific challenges:

> Regretfully self-abnegation will be demanded from any Protestant (who means to keep to be a real Protestant) who enters in Irish politics. For a long time – perhaps a generation or two – until the flicker of politics wears off the present excessive clerical spirit of Irish nationality – Catholics will fairly and naturally be preferred in every position

the challenge to the Protestant...

of trust representative or otherwise. But it is our duty to try and set about reversing the hateful attitude some Protestants have heretofore assumed in the affairs of our country – and show that we are for liberty and freedom and justice.[45]

Webb's candid letter hints at frustrations he might have felt with his own role within the movement; it also shows that he was convinced that Protestants themselves could bring about change. Presumably, his logic was that the clerical nature of nationalism would wear off if Protestants could reassure Catholics of their support for home rule. Protestants becoming nationalists would not prevent Catholic priests from also being nationalists, but Webb might have hoped that increased Protestant representation would temper the influence of those priests. Although he played a crucial role as a treasurer, he perhaps felt that he had been passed over for well-deserved positions because he was a Protestant. It is unclear why Webb, who had been active in the nationalist movement since 1870, did not become an MP until 1890. This letter also reveals Webb's true thoughts about the influence of the Catholic clergy on the nationalist movement, since his cordial dealings with clergy and his Catholic colleagues never suggested his discomfort with this influence.

Webb and Oldham both found a sense of purpose in this mission of converting Protestants to home rule, realised in Webb's pamphlet, *The Opinions of Some Protestants Regarding Their Catholic Fellow Countrymen*, and the Irish Protestant Home Rule Association.[46] The organisation and the pamphlet were both vehicles for mobilising Protestants in support of the home rule movement. Webb's pamphlet, self-published in 1886, sought to tackle head-on the Protestant fear that home rule would lead to Catholic persecution of Protestants. His pamphlet provided 54 testimonies from Protestants around Ireland, including many clergymen of both Anglican and Presbyterian denominations. Webb's cousin and close friend, Thomas Henry Webb, contributed the statement, 'I belong to the most Protestant of the Protestant religious bodies – the Society of Friends – and I believe, under a constitution such as Mr Gladstone's Bill would give to Ireland, the civil and religious liberty of every individual would be as secure as in any other country.'[47] The individuals who offered testimonies all expressed the belief that they had nothing to fear from home rule or from Catholics in political power, and that they had had only positive experiences of working with their Catholic friends and neighbours. The pamphlet apparently proved successful; although the number of copies produced in each edition is unknown, only 3 weeks after its publication date a third edition was brought out, enlarged and including the resolutions of the newly formed Irish Protestant Home Rule Association (IPHRA).[48]

The IPHRA has perhaps been accorded an importance that is not proportional to its size; the minute books of the Dublin executive reveal monthly meetings attended by 60 or 70 people, as well as struggles even to get the executive committee to attend weekly meetings.[49] The organisation is important to historians not so much for the impact that it made as for what it reveals about the Irish Parliamentary Party and the mood of the nationalist movement after the defeat of the first home rule bill. The IPHRA was entirely created by independent Protestants who supported home rule; the only relationship it had with the National League was some overlap in membership.

Webb was inescapably a Protestant home ruler and therefore something of a novelty. He identified himself as such, and others referred to him in this way: T. M. Healy's short book *A Word for Ireland* was printed by Webb in June 1886, and in the dedication Healy wrote, 'To the printer of this book – my friend Alfred Webb, one of the oldest Protestant Nationalists – my best thanks are due for much pains in preparing this Index, and for many suggestions.'[50] The IPHRA was organised with the purpose of being a distinctly Protestant organisation.[51] Evidently, the founders felt a need to distance themselves from the Irish Party and function as a sort of safe haven for Protestants who supported home rule but might have felt alienated by what they perceived as the overtly Catholic character of the Irish Party. Men such as Oldham, one of the founders of the Dublin branch, may have also been taking heed of Webb's argument that Protestants would be overlooked within the Irish party. Those Protestants in the IPHRA seemed deeply bothered by the fact that their co-religionists did not support home rule, and seem to have felt a sense of guilt that Protestants had been historically advantaged in Ireland. An early resolution of the Dublin branch, declaring that 'the attitude of large numbers of Irish Protestants in blindly resisting the cause of Self-Government for Ireland places Protestantism in an anomalous and humiliating position in this country,'[52] echoes Webb's sense of duty in reforming Protestant opinion. The IPHRA also convinced those in the nationalist party of what they wanted to believe: that Irish Protestants would eventually support home rule. As James Loughlin has explained, while the IPHRA 'undoubtedly failed to convert the Irish Protestant community to home rule, it did impress both nationalists and Liberals anxious to believe that Irish Protestants would come to accept it'.[53]

From the outset, the IPHRA flirted with division. The Belfast branch was formed first on 21 May 1886 under the leadership of David Briggs as secretary and Thomas Shillington as president. Some Dublin Protestants, including Webb (who sent his apologies), had been invited to the first meeting in a Belfast hotel. The members included a mix of businessmen, clergy and solicitors. The Dublin branch followed only a week later, and declared itself willing to be a second executive in a national organisation. The Belfast branch responded that it would recognise Dublin as only a subsidiary branch. The debate over the status of the Dublin branch dragged on for several weeks, with the final conclusion that Belfast was the district for 'Ulster' and Dublin for 'outside Ulster'.[54] Belfast retained the right to consider itself the executive, although the Dublin branch often pushed for a right to have national meetings in Dublin as well. The amount of time and effort put into the organisation of the Dublin branch – with provisions for annual elections – suggests that the IPHRA did not consider itself an ad hoc, quick-fix organisation. In other words, the organisers anticipated that the home rule issue would not be resolved within a year.

The language and strategy used by the IPHRA differed from that of the Irish Party. Principally, the Dublin branch tried to appeal to the interest of Protestant businesses, and to also emphasise the links between the Irish Party and the British Liberal Party. This strategy is evident in public lectures on topics such as 'The material benefits which self-government would bring to Ireland'. The Dublin committee also decided to invite a prominent English Liberal over to give a public lecture in Dublin on the merits of home rule; after considering inviting Shaw-Lefevre or Gladstone himself, it settled on inviting Lord Rosebery.[55] Other public lectures appealed to a Protestant's Imperial pride, such as the lecture 'How the British colonies govern themselves', by Professor J. G. Swift MacNeill MP.[56] Although the text of this lecture has not been located, it presumably made comparison between Ireland and those colonies which had negotiated a degree of self-government. The organisation also steered clear of divisive issues and was sensitive to Protestant proprieties, making decisions such as that 'it would be unwise for [IPHRA] representatives to attend and address political meetings held on Sundays.'[57]

Webb occasionally chaired the Dublin meetings, both executive and public, although his role seems to have been largely ceremonial. Loughlin's observation that the Dublin branch 'included well-known Protestant home-rulers such as Alfred Webb'[58] must be a testament to Loughlin's knowledge of the organisation and era, since Webb certainly is not well-known today. However, the minutes of the Dublin branch do support Loughlin's point. Oldham's solicitation of Webb's advice in the early days of the IPHRA, combined with the fact that Webb was an ex-officio vice-president of the organisation despite missing a good number of meetings, shows that Webb brought much-desired clout and experience to the organisation.

However, the IPHRA's activities – hosting speeches, offering its members up as speakers at events, and challenging the Irish Loyal and Patriotic Union to a debate (an invitation never accepted) – were not sufficient to mobilise the Protestant vote. Loughlin believes the failure of the organisation lay in its refusal to engage in the land question. Other possibilities could be that the individual members seem to have led busy and active public and private lives; one gets the impression, judging from the attendance records of the Dublin branch, that the IPHRA was the top priority of few of its members. Ultimately, the IPHRA's nuanced strategy – to work exclusively with Protestants to prove that one day they could live peacefully with Catholics under a Catholic majority – may have been too complex.

The IPHRA continued its work through the 1880s, although its official records after 1887 have not been found. In the meantime, Webb enjoyed the fruits of the Liberal alliance. He occasionally was asked to lecture in England on Irish and home rule issues, and he hosted English visitors, many of them prominent Liberals, who were eager to understand the situation in Ireland. One event that epitomised the excitement that was created around the Liberal alliance was the invitation of two of the most prominent English Liberal home rulers, John Morley and the Marquess of Ripon, to a convention in Dublin in February 1888. Morley was Gladstone's Irish secretary in 1886, a sincere advocate of Irish home rule, and one of the draftsmen of the first home rule bill.[59] Ripon had been viceroy of India and returned to England in 1885; he had a close working relationship with Charles Gavan Duffy, both of them applying ideas from their experiences in British colonies to Irish home rule.[60]

Webb kept a low profile during this convention – his name appears little in the proceedings – although he explained that the job of writing up the proceedings from press reports fell to him.[61] Although ostensibly organised by Dublin Corporation the convention served the National League in several ways: it capitalised on Liberal support, it created a jubilant atmosphere for home rulers and it sent a message of enthusiasm and solidarity. The convention claimed a reception committee of over 3000 individuals, including Webb, all of the home rule MPs and 19 Catholic bishops.[62] The event coincided with the release of T. D. Sullivan from prison and he was honoured with chairing many of the events. Morley and Ripon arrived in Monkstown by boat and were met with a crowd and procession to Dublin, led by a temperance society band and members of the local National League and Gaelic Athletic Association (GAA) branches.[63] In Dublin, a larger parade featured representatives of 51 Dublin trades, including the Coal Labourers' Society, the Fire Brigade with nine of its fire engines, the Hairdressers' Assistants (who marched with their very own fife and drum band) and branches of the National League. The GAA produced a strong show of Irish culture and masculinity: 'About a thousand strapping young men clad in distinctive jerseys and bearing their *camans* on their shoulders marched along under the banners of their respective branches.'[64]

On the second day of the convention Morley and Ripon were both given the freedom of the city of Dublin. The Freedom had been first awarded only in 1876, to Isaac Butt, and other recipients had included Gladstone in 1877, Ulysses S. Grant in 1878, Parnell in 1882 and William O'Brien in 1887.[65] The rest of the programme included pro-home rule speeches from the invited guests, statements of thanks and support for Morley and Ripon from a range of home rulers, and a concert of patriotic music.

In attending to such events as the Convention, Webb remained active in the nationalist cause. In fact, he was earnestly offering his services in 1887, when he wrote to Harrington, 'I am willing to take any dangerous part that would be thought desirable (printing notices, putting my name to calls for meetings of local League, attending meetings etc).' As noted before, Webb was never arrested when many others connected with the movement had been, and he was eager to pay his dues: 'I would feel bad (very bad) if others are to suffer and risk in this business and if I have not a chance of bearing my share – I have not had yet my share of suffering in politics, and I feel rather mean about it.'[66]

Webb's opportunity to suffer came unexpectedly in 1890 when, after 20 years of service to the nationalist cause, he was asked to stand for an Irish Westminster constituency, West Waterford. The seat became open after the death of the nationalist MP, J. D. Pyne. Webb's selection as an unopposed candidate for Waterford was a last-minute affair. J. J. Clancy wrote to Timothy Harrington in February 1890 to explain that there had been an eleventh-hour change of plans:

> I don't know whether you are aware, but it is a fact, that Foley who was selected by Mr Parnell has written to Corbett to say he won't stand after all. Under these circumstances and seeing that there is

only tomorrow and after to see about the nomination papers and the other necessary arrangements, the members mentioned met this evening and not being able to see or communicate with Mr P. or with Campbell decided on Alfred Webb.[67]

'Of course', Clancy continued, 'everything is done subject to approval or disapproval by Mr P.': further evidence, if any were needed after the Captain O'Shea election in Galway, that Parnell's choice of candidate was the most important one. Evidently Parnell did not object to the change of candidate, if he in fact found out about it before the deadline.

Why did Webb not become an MP earlier? He may not have wanted to, or may not have felt capable of making the time commitment: acting as a treasurer and running a business in Dublin was a huge task without also representing an Irish constituency in Westminster. As an MP Webb gave up his house in Dublin to cut personal expenses, but when the House was not sitting he and Lizzie stayed in Dublin with his sister Deborah. Soon after he was elected, he began to think about retiring from the print business. Furthermore, the League needed a reliable person to remain in Dublin and take care of business matters, a fact that Webb sometimes complained about once he was an MP and was expected to return to Dublin to keep financial affairs under control.[68] Webb's personality, and his lack of confidence in his public speaking abilities, may have been another factor: it is possible that he was considered too weak to be nominated in a constituency that would be fiercely contested.[69] Webb also had many other interests that took up time and energy: printing, writing and membership of societies. In fact, on the eve of his nomination to Parliament, no issue affecting the quality of Irish life was too insignificant to escape Webb's notice. As he wrote to the *Freeman's Journal*, 'Does anyone agree with me in thinking that the sentry boxes being erected before the new Museum Library are deficient in taste? They appear to me ugly in themselves and obstructive of the view of Leinster House from Molesworth St. and of Molesworth St. from Leinster House.'[70]

It could not have been easy for Webb to find the time – already he was a moral compass, full-time printer and self-appointed ombudsman for taste in public architecture – but his election as MP suited him and the party. Webb's mother was from Waterford and he had friends and relatives in the area, so he felt a genuine affinity with the people of his constituency. Webb's election was a boon for a party that was trying, as always, to increase Protestant representation. His Unitarian colleague (and fellow temperance activist) John Pinkerton, MP for Galway City, commented in an interview in 1888 that only ten of the 86 nationalist MPs were not Catholic. He argued, though, that he felt at home in the party because most of his Catholic colleagues were 'men of very broad views'.[71] As a Protestant, he believed that he held the ultimate defence of Irish intentions: since he represented an overwhelmingly Catholic constituency, 'if any man comes forward and says the Irish Catholics are bigoted I can appear upon any platform and flatly contradict them in my own person.'[72] Webb also worked this argument to his own advantage and argued that if a Protestant could be elected from such a Catholic constituency, there was further proof of the goodwill Catholics felt towards Protestants – an indicator that home rule could indeed be a success. In 1895, Webb was nominated to represent the Irish Parliamentary Party at the jubilee marking Dr Thomas Croke's twentieth anniversary as Catholic archbishop of Cashel.[73] Webb would have been very sympathetic to Croke's political record – like Webb, he supported the home rule movement and became an anti-Parnellite – but significantly, the committee was happy to be represented by a Protestant at the jubilee.

Webb was in Parliament as a home rule MP – not as a Quaker MP. Elizabeth Isichei notes that Quaker MPs, though rarely voting en bloc, were perceived as rather eccentric for their 'faddish' philanthropic concerns.[74] Although Webb also voiced some such concerns in Parliament – particularly opium trafficking – he identified himself as a member of the Irish Party, and his views on these subjects reflected those of some of his fellow home rulers, not his co-religionists (although all ten Quaker MPs in 1886 were Liberals, and seven of them voted for home rule in 1886).[75] As an MP Webb spoke occasionally on a variety of issues, including education in Ireland, the Irish judicial system and the Irish constabulary.[76] His speeches were not known for rhetorical flourish, but were logical and well-researched. The only resolution he proposed was a condemnation of the opium trade in India.[77] Webb was not confident in his speaking abilities and was urged to allow the stronger speakers to raise issues about home rule.[78]

Webb entered Parliament an enthusiastic and optimistic man, although he frequently became despondent about the failure of the movement to progress as quickly as he would wish. He took great pleasure in the friendships he shared with his colleagues. In hindsight Webb argued that the Irish Party on the eve of the Split was living through a 'golden' time, and that 'our unity and brotherhood were the envy of other parties.'[79]

'Led to our doom with Machiavellian ingenuity'[80]

The balance of power within the home rule movement was shaken when the news of Parnell's divorce case was made public. Certainly, Webb had clashed with his colleagues when he felt that his core values and morals were being ignored in the pursuit of nationalism, as in the case of the Curtin affair and Field Testimonial. Webb's belief in the accuracy of his own moral compass made him simultaneously an asset and a liability to the nationalist movement. Yet despite his frustrations with home rule, Webb felt exhilarated by the sense of camaraderie between home rulers and their English allies. Therefore, the events of the Parnell Split created a deep sense of vulnerability, as individuals who had invested so much personally in nationalism, not least of all trust in other people, felt that those investments might have been lost.

Unlike most other nationalist MPs, Webb seems to have been unaware that Parnell had been carrying on an affair with Katherine O'Shea, and that the couple had children together. This was something of an open secret in the hierarchy of the Irish Party: Biggar had written to Healy in 1886 that 'the Parnell-O'Shea connection is a disgusting one and unless the former ends it his ruin and that of his leadership must follow. I wish the party to be ruled by Mr Parnell but not by Mrs Shea.'[81] Betrayed, Webb was less shocked by the affair than by the dishonesty of Parnell, that Parnell had lied to him and the country. He had also been dissatisfied with Parnell's autocratic leadership. Webb was one of the individuals present in Committee Room 15 when the party took a vote on Parnell's leadership, and he quickly declared himself opposed to Parnell's continued leadership.[82]

For Webb, the Parnell Split was traumatic for the impact it had upon his relationships with colleagues, family and friends. He took the split personally. Writing to his close friend J. F. X. O'Brien, he explained how he needed to visit his Waterford constituency, but 'I shrink from it – there live my nearest relatives beyond my wife and sister – and it would be horrible to me to go there and not be able to put up at the house as usual – they are all, but one, on the wrong side.'[83] In Webb's ever-dramatic way, he wrote to J. F. X. O'Brien, who was in London, and described Dublin as a ghost town: 'It is very unhappy here in many respects. Nearly all our close friends and relations have gone Parnell worse than ever, and our circle is quite broken up. Walking the streets is like walking a city of the dead.'[84] Webb also resigned his post of Vice-President of the IPHRA when it voted in favour of Parnell.[85]

The outcome of these events was the division of the Irish Party into two: the minority were Parnell's supporters, and the majority were anti-Parnellites, led by Justin McCarthy. Webb was optimistic that 'if any rapprochement appears possible... I might be of use in preventing friction between men',[86] but reconciliation appeared unlikely: the two groups were vigorously contesting elections against each other, and the anti-Parnellites had a security guard stationed at the *Irish National Press* newspaper offices.[87]

Webb correctly prophesied that 'money... [will] be our great crux.'[88] A second outcome of the Split was that Webb reemerged as a treasurer, this time in partnership with J. F. X. O'Brien, Webb handling funds in Dublin and O'Brien in London.[89] Webb's cousin and friend Thomas Henry Webb remained with Parnell and took over Webb's 'business adviser' position for the Parnellites.[90] Through the treasury, O'Brien became a close personal friend who Webb trusted completely. 'You are exactly of my opinion with regard to blank cheques,'[91] Webb wrote to O'Brien, probably with a sense of relief. The treasury system under Parnell had made Webb anxious: 'I am glad the days of "going it blind" in accordance with Mr Parnell's directions or messages, are over. It appears to me that even at fifty-six years of age I have had many lessons of prudence to learn.'[92]

The anti-Parnellites needed a new organisation to replace the now-Parnellite National League, and decided to launch the Irish National Federation (in the meantime, they had quickly produced new stationery declaring themselves the 'National Committee in Sustainment of the Irish Parliamentary Party').[93] The Federation was created with a 15-man executive committee and three treasurers: Joseph Mooney, William Martin Murphy and Webb.[94] Webb's talents were again used in drafting and creating proofs of the constitution. This constitution included a pledge for MPs and vows of 'maintaining a position of absolute independence of all British parties'.[95] The power of the executive to force unity was strengthened in revisions to the constitution in 1892, when it was agreed that every member of either the Council (composed of MPs) or the Executive Committee (a combination of MPs and non-MPs) 'shall be bound to accept the decision of a majority of the Council or of the Executive Committee, as the case may be, and to act with such a majority'.[96] Previously, this had not been Webb's strongpoint.

However, new treasury matters became pressing and drew on all Webb's fairness and diplomacy. As a treasurer, Webb was responsible for keeping the accounts in balance and well-maintained, but he seems to have had little political power to decide how funds should be spent. In the beginning of January 1891 the Federation's bank account was overdrawn by £6302, which Webb believed could be paid off by donations from Americans. Webb was taking instructions from John Dillon, and Webb explained to J. F. X. that 'Dillon's directions are so explicit that it will be impossible for Kenny and myself to otherwise allocate one penny of American money until his overdraw [sic] is cleared off.' Webb was also answering to Healy: or, at least, he agreed to meet Healy to discuss money matters, but when he arrived at the meeting place at the designated time, he revealed to J. F. X. that 'All were out and no message left for me. At which, between ourselves, I feel a little hurt, as I am stopping on these days at Mr Healy's desire.'[97]

The greatest financial problem after the Split was the fate of the Paris funds. Parnell had been diverting money to a bank account in Paris under the management of Monroe and Co. to escape the scrutiny and control of the British government. By 1891, there was something in the region of £40,000 in Paris.[98] Much of this money had been pledged to help dispossessed tenants – or, at least, many tenants believed that they were owed something from the fund. The fund became a source of controversy because Parnell was one of the signatories on the account, and he refused to release the funds for disbursement by the anti-Parnellites. The other trustees were Dr Kenny (who remained a Parnellite) and Justin McCarthy, now leader of the anti-Parnellites. By autumn of 1891 Dillon was furious with Parnell, who was not responding to letters in a timely manner and was thus, Dillon felt, preventing a resolution to the funding issue. At Parnell's instructions Dillon had written him at his estate, Avondale, but Parnell had gone to England and not received Dillon's letter. Dillon argued that Parnell was forgetting their priorities: 'I marked my letter urgent because the condition of the tenants is such as to make it vitally important that there should be the least possible delay in making the arrangements necessary from the Paris fund.'[99] Dillon was irate that Parnell refused to sign off on the funds and therefore, Dillon believed, he was personally responsible for preventing dispossessed tenants from receiving aid.

Tempers and expectations both ran high and the dispute over the funds dragged on for years. After Parnell's death the Parnellites maintained their claim to have control over the funds. Archbishop Croke tried to mediate between pro- and anti-Parnellite camps; Davitt, Dillon and Harrington were selected to consider 'prior claims' (i.e. pre-Split) to funding, though by late 1894 they still had not reached a resolution.[100] In 1896 Davitt was still receiving letters from former tenants, referring to 'their "implicit reliances upon my sense of justice" etc. etc.' but he was unable to settle their claims.[101] Demands for funds were overwhelming, and Davitt explained to one applicant that 'if *all* the claimants are to be satisfied in their demands we would require power to squeeze another £40,000 out of Monroe and Co.'.[102]

Webb had no control over the funds because he was not one of the trustees, but this wrangling over funds for evicted tenants was the backdrop to his own treasury responsibilities. Webb was dealing with funds on both sides of the Irish Sea, pertaining to Irish MPs in Westminster, regular operations in Dublin and tenants in rural Ireland. With the decision to inaugurate an Irish National Federation as the new anti-Parnellite replacement for the League, Webb was busy organising the fiscal records.[103] As when he was treasurer of the Home Rule League, Webb was willing to take a personal risk when the movement was desperate from funds: his list of incoming funds for March 1891 includes one labeled 'Self (loan) – I hope Mrs Webb won't hear of it – £200'.[104] When the Federation was established, Webb and J. F. X. O'Brien were the acting treasurers: Webb dealing with Federation funds, sometimes in Dublin, and O'Brien specialising in the funds of the Party, based in London.[105] Richard Barry O'Brien assisted in London, and William Martin Murphy in Dublin, and ultimately Webb, J. F. X. O'Brien and Justin McCarthy were responsible for Party payments (including the sometimes controversial issue of payments and reimbursements for MPs).

Although Webb had begun as a Federation treasurer, when the constitution of the Federation was revised in 1893 Dillon took over as treasurer. Webb took on the new responsibility of managing the Parliamentary Fund with J. F. X. O'Brien and John Barry. As Lyons has observed, the years 1895–1900 were financially the most difficult years for the Irish Parliamentary Party and its various sister organisations.[106] Webb's correspondence to his colleagues, especially to J. F. X., reveal the personal toll this financial hardship had on executives in the Party, as well as would-be beneficiaries of the Party's financial help. Webb had little discretion with funds and usually had to obtain permission from the Party committee to make payments. The Party also maintained several different bank accounts, and used to shuffle around money from account to account to obscure its debts, sometimes even borrowing from its fund for evicted tenants to meet its operating costs.[107]

The lack of funds threatened to curtail the Party's activities in Parliament. The Party had pioneered payments for its MPs, according to individual needs. In the 1880s there were sufficient remittances to allow these payments – indeed, some contributors explicitly asked if their donations could be used to pay MPs.[108] In 1893 Webb wrote to Dillon that 'now that money is coming in it is earnestly to be desired that if at all possible a sufficient sum should be laid aside, ear-marked to pay the members for a couple of years to come.'[109] However, the overall financial state was poor: the split in the Party combined with economic uncertainty led to a drop in donations. In 1894, this had reached crisis point, and the Party put an urgent request for funds in the *Freeman's Journal*. It also wrote to its MPs, 'that owing to the cessation of remittances, they [the Committee] see no prospect of being able to provide the Treasurers with the means to pay the balance of the current installment of the Parliamentary allowances within the present quarter'.[110] Webb's fiscal prudence was tempered by his sympathy on these occasions: although he was keen to balance the books, his letters also suggest his frustration when individuals who he felt were loyal home rulers and deeply in needs of funds, were denied grants.[111] He personally intervened in 1895 when funds were temporarily unavailable to provide MPs with a stipend to return home to Ireland for the summer recess, 'so as to enable them to leave town, that I have drawn cheques on my private account (overdrawing it) for some'.[112]

By 1895 Webb was in a new quandary: T. M. Healy, a member of the Federation executive (though, as Frank Callanan points out, Healy was not recognised as one of the 'troika' leading the Federation: Dillon, McCarthy and Sexton).[113] Healy was the master of brutal (but often hilarious) invective, and had metamorphised from Parnell's protégé into his most vicious critic.[114] Healy had ambitions towards leadership and had been amassing supporters over the early 1890s, including Arthur O'Connor and William Martin Murphy. The minutes of the committee of the Irish Party in the early 1890s show that Healy had been occupying a frictional role for some time: he nearly always voted against the majority in decisions, some of them seemingly trivial or procedural.[115] In 1895, Healy spoke out against the party's decision to ask its informal ally, the Liberal Party, to put up candidates in place of home rulers in some northern Irish seats. The rationale was purely financial: some of these seats were expensive to contest and the party struggled to find the necessary funding. Healy publicly attacked this plan as a treachery to the home rule cause. The constitution of the Irish National Federation had vowed 'advancing the cause of Irish nationality and maintaining a position of absolute independence of all British parties'.[116] However, it also demanded a pledge of its MPs, that they would follow the will of the party. Webb believed that Healy was, therefore, flouting this pledge publicly. Healy was, however, keeping true to the other pledge of the Federation, of independence from other political parties.

Webb has been described by Callanan, in his biography of T. M. Healy, as a 'naïve' and 'gentle Quaker', a 'mild and decent' man who had once been friends with Healy.[117] Webb described Healy at the time of the Split as 'my closest political friend', but the events of the mid-1890s convinced him instead that 'not patriotism, but personal spite, and a hatred of all placed above him, was the moving spirit of Mr Healy'.[118] While many others were angry with Healy's behaviour, Webb considered Healy's actions a personal betrayal and a betrayal of the Party. Famously, at one meeting in 1895 Healy reduced Webb to tears.[119] The *Irish Weekly Independent* ran a front-page cartoon of Webb, flanked by Healy and McCarthy and wiping away his tears with a handkerchief, with the caption 'Good bye, Sweet Heart, Good bye!'[120] Healy evidently recognised Webb's skills as a treasurer, but he had no patience with Webb's sensitive side.

The dispute between Webb and Healy reached a climax in 1895. This clash can also be viewed as a microcosm of some of the major themes in Irish nationalism in this era: the role of personalities, friendships between nationalists, the relationship with liberalism and the Liberal Party, and the nature of Irishness within the British parliamentary system. The next two chapters will explore these themes, and in particular how they relate to Webb's major achievement of presiding at the Indian National Congress in 1894.

6
'A union of hearts firmly based on love of Ireland'[1]: Cosmopolitan Friendship in the Imperial Metropolis

In the previous two chapters Webb's inside role in Irish nationalism has been described through his duties as a treasurer, his leadership as a Protestant and his personal anguish over the Parnell Split and its aftermath. However, when Webb joined the Irish nationalist movement he did not renounce his radical upbringing or abandon the range of progressive causes he had joined in the Dublin of the 1860s. Rather, his interests came full circle through his political and social contacts in London. Nor did he live a lonely life in the Irish Party, or cut a strange figure as a progressive Quaker: as well as enduring several high-profile feuds, the Irish Party fostered deep friendships that have received comparatively less attention. With hindsight, Webb recalled that on the eve of the Parnell Split 'our unity and brotherhood were the envy of other parties.'[2]

Friendship and social activism moved with Webb to London when he became an MP. Just as mid-Victorian Dublin had a vibrant civic life that surmounted religious or political divides, the capital of the British Empire was home to multicultural activism and socialising. The contacts that Webb and some of his colleagues made with Indians living in London directly led to Webb's selection as president of the Indian National Congress, which will be explained in detail in Chapter 7. In order to understand how that happened, this chapter will explore three issues: the integration of Irish MPs into London society (especially via the Liberal alliance), the spaces and ways in which Irish and Indians interacted in cosmopolitan London and the ideas about friendships and social relations within the Irish Party that underpinned these interactions.

The liberal face of Irish nationalism

The alliance between the Irish Party and the British Liberal Party (1886–1893) was an ambiguous one. For many Irish nationalists it was a matter of convenience, a vague agreement that should be tolerated as long as it led to the quicker attainment of Home Rule. For Alfred Webb and some of his colleagues, it was the marriage of their own liberal beliefs with those of a much wider social circle based in London. This circle included members of the Liberal Party, but also campaigners, activists and intellectuals from across the Empire. Irish MPs were not simply limiting to socialising with each other: they knew their colleagues in the House of Commons, they met non-Irish individuals in clubs and societies in extra-political London and they were on the receiving end of attention from those who embraced their cause. These were most often English or American individuals, but Timothy Harrington and Justin Huntley McCarthy also had French contacts eager to learn about the state of Ireland.[3]

In his autobiography Webb names a large number of liberal and radical individuals who formed part of his London social circle: these included Sir Charles Schwann, Ida Wells, Henry J. Wilson, Alfred Marks and the Russell family (relatives of the former prime minister).[4] In general, Webb's autobiographical hindsight needs to be treated with some wariness, but in this case his views of his life in 1904 can probably be trusted better than some of his correspondence at the time. He wrote to Dillon in 1894 complaining that 'I make no way socially or otherwise in the House or London – I have none of the qualities for it,' but this is belied by the evidence of his social activities that will be described in this chapter.[5] It seems more likely that Webb was writing to Dillon during one of his many short periods of depression, and that he was projecting some of his frustration with his political talents onto his overall experience in London. Webb did struggle because he was not confident as a public speaker; he was convinced that his talents lay only in administration and that he was not an asset to the Party in London.[6] The invitation to preside at the Indian National Congress, and his success there, surprised Webb more than anyone else and helped him to see that others did not doubt his abilities.

In reality, the Irish Party offered Webb the opportunity to travel throughout Britain and Ireland and to make many friends and acquaintances along the way. Both Anna and Charles Stewart Parnell asked Webb to host guests who were visiting Ireland to learn about the state of the country.[7] These included John Morley, George Shaw-Lefevre, James

Bryce and Henry Norman. In addition he invited Henry George, Michael Davitt's American friend with advanced ideas about land, to his Dublin home.[8] The constant stream of intellectuals and activists from Britain and America was similar to what Webb's parents had promoted when he was a child. He brought foreign guests to see evictions, not unlike how he had travelled through famine-ravaged Ireland with English Quakers in his youth. As well as the evictions, Webb recalled that he played tour guide and there were many 'delightful excursions with parties of English sympathisers to Glendalough, the Dargle, the Vartry Waterworks and elsewhere', which frequently involved singing patriotic ballads. Webb writes about this era in his autobiography as if it were one great day out, especially recalling 'the excitement at evictions' and how he kept a crowbar as a souvenir of one such event.[9] Having visited famine-afflicted areas in his youth and having read the extensive literature, Webb could not have been blind to suffering in rural areas and the delight with which he describes these visits is somewhat jarring. He may have been remembering the excitement with the hindsight of writing an autobiography, but his comment reveals a truth, that all of the individuals involved in home rule undoubtedly found it exciting that they were part of a period of political upheaval, and perhaps that they were helping to enact change.

Within London, one meeting place where liberals and nationalists could interact in this era was the National Liberal Club in London, a short walk from the Houses of Parliament. For Irish MPs, membership of the Club was a symbol of commitment to the Liberal–Nationalist alliance. The Club was formed in 1882 to promote liberalism and to provide a 'central, convenient, and inexpensive Club in London for Liberals throughout the kingdom'.[10] It was therefore intended to be less elitist than other private members' clubs in the capital. Founding members included MPs Jacob Bright, Henry Campbell Bannerman, Charles Dilke and Henry Labouchere. Irish membership of the Club was always a small percentage of the total membership because joining the Club only made sense to individuals who spent time in London. In 1884 only 59 members out of 3791 were Irish, of whom 25 were from Dublin and 19 from Belfast. In 1885 there were 50 members from Dublin, and just 24 from Antrim. In 1886 there were 82 members from Dublin, and 32 from Antrim. Although Irish membership was tiny, the individuals who joined between 1882 and 1885 were typically Belfast- and Dublin-based merchants; after 1885, the Irish membership was overwhelmingly Dublin-based and included prominent nationalists.[11] Alan O'Day has noted the absorption of Irish politicians into British politics through club memberships pre-1886;[12] the number of them who joined the National Liberal Club post-1886 is further evidence that could support his argument and carry it into the later-Parnellite period. Timothy and Maurice Healy both joined in 1887, as did T. P. O'Connor and Donal Sullivan. Justin McCarthy joined in 1889. Joseph Biggar, John O'Connor Power, Rev. Galbraith, George Delaney, John Deasy, David Sheehy and Swift McNeill were also all members by 1891.[13]

Records for 1889–1900 are available which indicate who proposed new members; individuals had to be proposed and seconded by existing members of the Club and existing members were allowed to express, in writing, their disapproval of prospective members, although the minutes indicate that this rarely happened. It is possible to see how Irish members formed a chain, using their membership to co-opt other Irish members. For example, T. D. Sullivan, listing his occupations as MP and 'Dublin journalist', was nominated in February 1890 by William M. Murphy and W. J. Corbett.[14] Charles Stewart Parnell was created an honourary member of the Club, a considerable accolade for that organisation, in the spring of 1889.[15]

It is impossible to quantify the type of socialising that took place in the Club, or to know how much the Irish MPs integrated with other MPs. T. D. Sullivan offered a talk in the Club's lecture series 'On the Irish Question' in 1889.[16] In the late 1890s, O'Connor Power became an active member of the Club's Political Sub-committee, which was responsible for organising functions and inviting speakers.[17] O'Connor Power was a practicing journalist, and many of the individuals he nominated for membership were also London-based journalists.

One individual who did not join the Club was Webb, which seems somewhat out of character. It was not out of any antagonism with Liberalism: the alliance suited Webb perfectly, complementing his radical upbringing and generally progressive outlook. He described himself 'as a Nonconformist, perhaps as fully in sympathy with the general aspirations of English Liberals as any Irishman that ever sat in Parliament'.[18] One reason may have been that he was not an MP for very long, and because he involved himself in many other social campaigns while in London. Webb's wife Lizzie also accompanied him to London while he was an MP and enjoyed following the proceedings in Parliament;[19] Sophie O'Brien has remarked that Alfred and Lizzie were a couple who spent a great deal of time together and shared ideas on political questions.[20] Lizzie Webb was apparently not content to stay at home while her husband played at politics, and she had no children. The National Liberal Club did not allow women to join or even enter as guests, and this may have discouraged Webb from joining; Webb has remarked that they socialised together on the terrace of the House of Commons.[21] He also admitted that 'it is no small satisfaction to look back upon intercourse with such men as Gladstone, Morley, Bradlaugh – to remember pleasant talks in the Tea Room with Labouchere and Sir W. Lawson.'[22]

There is no indication that Webb had any personal objection to joining the Club, unlike his friend J. F. X. O'Brien (who, despite living much of his life in England, was profoundly Anglophobic). As O'Brien wrote in his autobiography, 'I always thought it wrong for members of the Irish Party to identify themselves with an English party, to the extent of becoming members of the National Liberal Club, the centre and focus of the Liberal Party.'[23] O'Brien did favour closer social interaction between members of the Irish Party. Whereas Webb wrote that on his entry to Parliament 'I at once felt at home. Already I knew personally nearly all of our Party and very many of the English and Scotch members,'[24] O'Brien lamented that the Irish members did not meet often enough. 'Some of us subsequent to 1890 endeavoured to put into effect the old idea of bringing the men and their families together in social gatherings', he explained in his 1898 autobiography, but the idea did not take off and 'while a few are accustomed to foregather in the smoke-room over a glass and a pipe or cigar the most of us have been practically strangers to each other all those years.'[25] O'Brien did make a great personal sacrifice for his close friend Webb: he attended the luncheon honouring Webb's success at the Indian National Congress, held at the National Liberal Club in 1895.[26]

Irish absorption into multicultural London society can be described as cosmopolitan. Cosmopolitanism can be defined, with potential for contradiction, as both 'free from national limitations or attachments' and 'composed of people from many different countries'.[27] It is seemingly impossible, then, for nationalists to be cosmopolitan, as cosmopolitanism would require renouncing national ties. But Webb and his colleagues who embraced multiculturalism tended to see nationalism as a step towards more just government in the world, and especially in the British Empire. Webb's activities and ideas embody what Georgios Varouxakis has termed 'cosmopolitan patriotism'[28]: love of country that was not chauvinistic, but that was rooted in a respect for all humankind. As a religious minority, Webb had always spurned exclusively Catholic ideas of Irishness, and his cosmopolitanism was consistent with his inclusive, civic Irish nationalism.

However, cosmopolitanism was a double-edged sword in Ireland. On the one hand, until 1894 most voters seem to have understood that Ireland's best chances for home rule lay with the Liberals; F. S. L. Lyons even argues that the 1892 general election, in which the pro-Liberal anti-Parnellites gained an overwhelming majority, was 'a verdict in favour of the Liberal alliance'.[29] However, these cosmopolitan nationalists, who comfortably moved between Dublin and London, were at odds with another strain of thought in Ireland. This was the idea that British-ness and Irishness were incompatible, and that those Irish who admired or imitated British ideas or fashions were 'West Britons'. Senia Paseta has described in detail the difficult position in this era of the Irish Catholic middle classes, who were self-consciously preparing themselves for leadership positions in the expectation of a domestic parliament in Dublin. This class was ridiculed by those seeking to 'de-Anglicise' Ireland, particularly D. P. Moran, who saw this professional advancement as incompatible with nationalism.[30] Arthur Griffith even condemned cosmopolitanism by name.[31]

Membership of the Club could bear out Richard Vincent Comerford's argument that during the late Victorian era 'the striving for respectability in all its forms undoubtedly absorbed more Irish time and energy than all the famous politics and conspiracy of the era'.[32] However, there were several competing visions of respectability in late-Victorian Ireland; specifically, the respectability surrounding the House of Commons was no longer revered by these Irish cultural nationalists such as Griffith and Moran. Those Irish who joined the National Liberal Club were not necessarily Anglophiles or sycophants desperate to be accepted in English society, although they were aware that their domestic audience might interpret them this way. O'Day has argued that Irish MPs were aware that their English alliances could be met with suspicion, and these alliances had to be downplayed, justified or denied in the nationalist press.[33] Irish MPs even tried to convey 'the picture of lonely, isolated Irishmen shunned by and shunning the foreign community within which they lived' in memoirs of their time in Parliament, although this was often far from the truth.[34] Certainly, if it was important to downplay these social relationships in 1890, it was even more important to do so when some of these politicians were writing their memoirs in the Irish Free State in the 1920s. The two sides of this issue are demonstrated by Donal Sullivan, who wrote to Webb in 1894 refusing to accept reimbursement for his expenses out of donations made to the Irish Party by Gladstone and Lord Tweedmouth. His principled stand

112 *Cosmopolitan Nationalism in the Victorian Empire*

against accepting money from the Liberals was, however, written at the National Liberal Club using Club stationery.[35] And John Pinkerton's wife received invitations to socialise with Lady Tweedmouth, although Pinkerton seems a surprising figure to have been on the receiving end of such invitations. A tenant farmer in Ballymoney who became politicised during the Land War, he represented a particular radical, Presbyterian agrarian political tradition. As a supporter of Davitt and an MP for Galway City he was an unusual person to have been invited to dine with the Queen. Yet, in the 1890s, because of his party's links with the Liberal Party, he did that, and also was regularly invited to exclusive London addresses for social events with leading liberals. His wife was evidently also accepted by the English Liberal establishment and invited to events held by the Women's National Liberal Association.[36]

The price Webb paid for his cosmopolitanism was the accusation of mimicry and the indictment that he was less than fully Irish. Webb did not see being an Irish nationalist as incompatible with having English friends; his conception of Irish nationalism was necessarily constitutional and inclusive, since he himself would have no role in a Catholic nation-state. However, the Irish press could mistake – or purposefully misrepresent – Webb's lack of Anglophobia as sycophantism. In a lengthy, satirical poem titled 'The flight of the Webbs', Webb is lampooned for selling his Dublin business and relocating to London. The poem suggests that he is unable to bear the atmosphere of Dublin, although in fact he made these decisions for purely financial reasons (he found it too costly and time-consuming to maintain a house and business in Dublin while serving as an MP in London).[37] The poem plays on the *Aeneid* and features Webb comparing his departure from Dublin with Aeneas's flight from Troy.

The poem opens with references Webb's anti-Parnellite stance, his temperance and abhorrence of drink, and his fixation with the development of Irish industry:

> I, Alfred, too take flight, Home Rule impends,
> Which once I hoped for; now I vastly fear
> The Parnellites rule Dublin, dear to me
> As Troy was to Aeneas. 'Rapscallions', says
> The Fortnightly Reviewer, multiply,
> And 'Corner-boys' abound, and 'urban riff-raff'
> Swarm in the towns of Erin, haunt the pubs,
> Giving a base example to our youth
> And poisoning the springs of industry.

The poem continues with a dialogue between Webb and his hapless servant, Pat, who fails to catch the classical references in Webb's words. The poem concludes with a final speech from Webb:

> And, now, let Healy snarl, and Dillon rave,
> And Will O'Brien, from wild Connaught's depth,
> Break now and then the silence of despair,
> And lash himself to the foam, like the long wave
> That burst in useless rage on cliffs of Moher
> Let the fierce Redmonds raise their banner high,
> And bully Asquith, and denounce meek Morley!
> Let Harrington his flaming falchion wave,
> And Leamy load his pen in Abbey Street,
> To rake the Government: I will array,
> And by the Silvery Thames a new house rear,
> Where gentle Justin at my tea-parties
> Shall smilingly attend, and grave T. P.
> With roguish laugh, make fun of the dull Saxons,
> There 'neath the shadow of Westminster's tower,
> Shall I and mine enjoy unanxious peace:
> This our best guarantee no other needed.
> Erin farewell!
> (Seizes bat and umbrella and exit to mail-boat).[38]

Webb is thus presented as too intellectual, too weak or too meek for Irish politics; as one who was better suited to hosting tea parties than facing Irish problems. The poet also suggests that these MPs had a twisted relationship with Englishness, simultaneously trying to imitate and mock it.

The problem with explaining Irish politicians' ease within the British political system is that it often carries a value judgement. Ultimately, that Irish nationalists found common cause with colleagues of different nationalities is a fact, and to state that fact is neither to celebrate it nor to condemn it. Revealing the friendships between these politicians – Irish and non-Irish, nationalist and non-nationalist – exposes them as human beings who were able to look beyond rigid national boundaries. In fact, it exposes these boundaries as not so rigid after all. Nationalism, in the Irish case, did not always lead to chauvinism or provincialism. For Webb, and many others in the Irish Party who have hitherto not been identified as a group, it led to a respect for other people's nationalism and to an espousal of cosmopolitanism. Living in London, participating in Parliament and socialising with Englishmen (or Indians, or anyone else) did not make Webb less Irish or less nationalistic, but the reactions towards Webb do reveal the many different understandings of Irish nationalism that coexisted within the Irish Party. In fact, it is perhaps because they interacted with nationalists from other countries that Webb and others understood that participating in British institutions did not have to dilute their Irish nationalism. This phenomenon could be termed cosmopolitan nationalism.

For some members of the home rule movement, the 1880s and 1890s were the height of Irish nationalist absorption into the British parliamentary system. J. F. X. O'Brien believed that nationalist unity suffered through this absorption, but for individuals like Webb, who had grown up in a liberal (even radical) environment, this was a comfortable friendship. Webb's parents had committed themselves to social issues as a priority, and had international connections with other liberals, including many in Britain. Webb also knew many English people through the Society of Friends (even the future Chief Secretary for Ireland, Forster). Webb had none of the Anglophobia of some of his colleagues: while remaining an ardent nationalist, he enjoyed the visits of English sympathisers in Ireland. Some of Webb's colleagues had similar upbringings, or were involved in careers that enabled (or allowed) them to cross boundaries of class and nationality, such as practicing London journalists Justin McCarthy and T. P. O'Connor and English-raised Michael Davitt, who had extensive political contacts in England, Scotland[39] and the United States. These individuals also learned, through their activities in liberal London, that there were many Indians who embraced a similar cosmopolitan nationalism.[40]

Cosmopolitan London

In the same era that Irish MPs were attaining respectability in British politics, and British politics was dominated by debate over the ethics and purpose of Empire, Britain was home to a growing community of Indians.[41] Both Indians and Irish flocked to the imperial capital, sometimes driven by penury and sometimes (as in the case of most of the individuals studied in this chapter) by the desire to pursue more elite professions such as law, journalism and politics.[42] The unofficial leader of this Indian community in late-Victorian Britain was Dadabhai Naoroji. Naoroji was a Parsee from Bombay who had grown up in poverty but earned a scholarship at Elphinstone Institute, where he excelled and went on to become the first 'native' professor in 1852. He then emigrated to England and set up in business as a merchant, first in Liverpool then in London. Naoroji continued his political career in India and was one of the founders of the Indian National Congress, while immersing himself in liberal London. He acquired a status of father-figure for many of the Indian students migrating to Britain and a huge reputation in India, where he is affectionately known as the 'grand old man of India'. Naoroji's political career will be dealt with in the next chapter, but it ought to be prefaced with an explanation of his extensive involvement in the clubs and societies of London. His club membership in general, and his membership of a number of Irish clubs in particular, has not featured in some of the biographical studies of his political life.[43]

The National Liberal Club was also a meeting point – physical and intellectual – for Indians with liberal interests. Naoroji joined the National Liberal Club in 1886, in the same month that he was selected as a Liberal candidate for Holborn. Indian membership was, like Irish, small but significant. Indian members, as with Irish members, are difficult to track in the records if they gave a London address and joined as town members (rather than giving an address in India); many of the members who listed Indian addresses were actually of British extraction. As the Irish club members did, Naoroji co-opted Indians into the club. For the years 1889–1900, it is possible to trace the individuals who joined with the nomination of Naoroji and other individuals working for the Indian cause – frequently William Digby and William Martin Wood. Digby was the Club's first secretary, and joined as a member when he left that post in 1887. Digby had been a journalist in India in the 1870s and had organised massive famine relief schemes. He and Naoroji clearly found a common purpose in the Club. Between 1889 and 1898, Naoroji proposed or seconded 38 individuals for membership. These included George Yule (in 1889), 14 Indian students studying in England, usually in law, four Indian lawyers, five Indian businessmen, four bureaucrats in Indian-related departments, three Indian newspaper owners, and a Bombay High Court judge. Naoroji was therefore ensuring that Indians in London were absorbed into his Liberal network.

Also like the Irish MPs who joined, Naoroji and the Indians he nominated gained respectability through their club membership, and they gained a physical space through which to network with prominent Liberals. Naoroji wrote many of his letters from the Club, and usually used its stationery, and thus in his correspondence made obvious his Liberal connection. There is also evidence that Irish and Indian nationalists were employing the Club as a space to meet and exchange ideas. In early 1888, Naoroji's friend and fellow suffragist Josephine Butler wrote to him with good news. Her friend T. P. O'Connor had recently visited her home for a long weekend, and Butler had told him all about Naoroji and the cause of Indian reform. According to Butler, O'Connor responded by saying, 'that is the next question that you and our friends must take up, and we must get Mr Naoroji into Parliament'.[44] O'Connor then requested that Naoroji meet him at the National Liberal Club in London for a serious discussion of the matter.

Naoroji already had Irish contacts by 1888, but it is important to note this connection because it was forged through the friendship he had with Butler through progressive societies. In London Naoroji joined Butler's British, Continental and General Federation for the Abolition of Government Regulation of Prostitution.[45] This organisation was similar to the National Association for the Repeal of the Contagious Diseases Acts (NARCDA) and the Ladies' National Association which Webb joined and supported in Dublin. Webb's awareness of these efforts, especially of the campaign to end the Cantonment Acts in India after the CDAs were repealed in Britain and Ireland, is evident in references in his Congress presidential speech.[46] Other individuals who opposed the CDAs and had a connection with the Indian reform movement included Ursula and Jacob Bright MP and Eva McLaren (wife of Walter Stowe Bright McLaren MP). Like Webb, Naoroji also supported women's suffrage societies and NARCDA. Naoroji supported or spoke at the Women's Liberal Federation, the Women's Franchise League and the National Union of Women's Suffrage Societies.[47] People who supported Indian reform and also women's suffrage included Webb, the Fawcetts, the Brights, the MacLarens, G. B. Clark, and later the Labour leader James Keir Hardie.

Naoroji also shared a preoccupation with drugs and alcohol with Webb, MacLaren, Digby, Clark and Hardie. Naoroji had refused to stock opium or alcohol when he had been a merchant in Liverpool, and in 1888 he set up the Anglo-Indian Temperance Association with Samuel Smith and W. C. Caine. He also received circulars from the creatively named United Committee for the Prevention of the Demoralization of Native Races by the Liquor Traffic.[48] When Webb went to India as Congress president he addressed temperance groups, speaking alongside Annie Besant.[49] Webb's Congress speech also lamented that 'there is scarcely a family in the United Kingdom that has not suffered from the ravages of drink', and warned his audience to be 'upon your guard against its insidious advances'.[50]

Both Webb and Naoroji were associated with the various humanist societies under the leadership of Catherine Empey, an English Quaker, and Celestine Edwards, a West Indian preacher.[51] As Varouxakis points out, some Victorians eschewed the term 'cosmopolitan' in favour of discussion of humanity or universality.[52] This parlance is reflected in the organisation, 'Society for the Recognition of the Universal Brotherhood of Man' (SRUBM), which produced a publication called *Fraternity*, edited by Edwards. *Fraternity* was radically anti-racist and committed to 'the cause of struggling helpless races in America, India, Africa, and Australia'.[53] It also pledged 'to try and awaken the Christian conscience of England to the vast influences and *responsibilities*, religious, political, moral, commercial, of that tremendous thing called the BRITISH EMPIRE'.[54] The religiosity of the publication probably did not sit well with Webb who, while being privately religious and publicly recognised as a Quaker, fits in better with a secular radical tradition in public life,[55] but Naoroji sat on the Council for some time. The Brotherhood launched branches across Britain, many of them run by women, but never established branches in Ireland. *Fraternity* embraced the Congress, women's suffrage and the plight of freed slaves (which it referred to as 'Afro-Americans') in the United States. It did not tackle the question of Irish political status, although it did allow its one Irish writer, Miss St Clair Knox of Dublin, to print a poem condemning coercive British rule in Ireland.[56]

Jonathan Schneer has rightly argued that there were links between Irish cultural societies and other 'anti-imperial' societies in late-Victorian London, but Naoroji's papers in Indian archives reveal the surprisingly high level of his personal Irish connections. London branches of the Irish National League invited him to many events, including St Patrick's Day balls in London in 1890, 1892, 1894 and 1906, to which he sometimes also made donations.[57] He was invited to speak at several London branches of the Irish National League of Great Britain including the Dulwich branch in February 1892[58] and the St Pancras branch in March 1894 (as part of a demonstration against the House of Lords).[59] On his election to Parliament in 1892 he received letters of congratulations from the Clerkenwell and East Finsbury branches.[60] He was elected a member of the London Metropolitan Branch of the Irish National League of Great Britain in May 1894,[61] and he made a donation to the Irish Parliamentary Fund in the same year.[62] In 1901 he made a donation to the Metropolitan Branch of the United Irish League of Great Britain (UILGB), and in 1904 he paid an annual membership subscription to that same branch.[63]

Apart from Naoroji's friendship with Webb, Davitt and Swift MacNeill, he also was frequently badgered by ex-Indian Civil Servant and

Irish Party MP C. J. O'Donnell. Brother of Frank Hugh O'Donnell, he frequently pestered Naoroji in the early 1900s, explaining in 1902 that he was 'anxious to form your acquaintance' because they 'work for the same excellent end' of Indian reform.[64] O'Donnell seems to have taken more interest in Naoroji than Naoroji did in him, complaining once that he saw Naoroji at a political event but Naoroji did not recognise him. He also employed a degree of moral blackmail in his letters, such as when he asked Naoroji to help promote his new book by writing letters of support to newspapers: 'Do – *for India's sake* – write to the Editors.'[65]

In 1906 Naoroji was asked for a donation from the Holborn branch of the UILGB, partly in recognition for the voluntary canvassing members of that branch had carried out for Naoroji during a parliamentary campaign; he immediately gave a 'generous' donation.[66] He was also induced, with the urging of C. J. O'Donnell, to join the Irish Club in London in 1906 as an honourary member, for which he did not pay fees. The secretary of the Club, Samuel Geddes, believed Naoroji's membership would be mutually beneficial. Geddes boasted that although the Club 'is non-political and non-sectarian, amongst our members there are a great many who are most sympathetically inclined towards your country',[67] whereas at the same time Geddes acknowledged that 'you have numerous friends who might very possibly join the Club, if they knew you were a member.'[68]

This is the context and background to Irish–Indian political collaboration. As the capital of a vast empire, London was a multicultural city with myriad opportunities for people from across the Empire to interact with one another. The activities that Webb and Naoroji in particular embraced were those that were associated with liberal and progressive politics, and in the case of *Fraternity* with an anti-racist agenda. Naoroji and many Irish MPs joined the National Liberal Club as a formal way of cultivating Liberal social and political contacts. By studying the records of organisations like the National Liberal Club, spaces are revealed through which Irish and Indians met at the imperial core and found an international context to their nationalism.

Friendship and nationalism

Any political party is merely a collection of social relationships created through a belief in a particular political ideal, and support for the political ideal can create feelings of friendliness, kinship or belonging among individuals who might otherwise share little in common. As a nationalist organisation, the Irish Party took this to an extreme, enshrining the predominance of the nationalist cause above all others. In that regard, it united individuals from across a wide spectrum of political beliefs: individuals who, had they lived in a different polity, may have pursued disparate political strategies as, for example, liberals and conservatives. Some historians have emphasised the divisions this caused within the Irish Party: Jackson, for example, has observed that Fenians like Joseph Biggar (Webb's co-treasurer in the National League) 'hated their "Whig" colleagues with a passion which, if anything, exceeded their detestation of Orange Toryism'.[69] James McConnel has instead examined the social aspects of the Irish Party in this time period.[70] Without ignoring the friction that existed between some factions within the Irish Party – so evident whenever Timothy Healy was involved – Webb's experiences highlight the second aspect of the movement. Most striking in Webb's experience is that friendships could be forged across seemingly impassable boundaries, based on either personality or individuals' other social interests.

Webb's experience in social activism in Dublin prepared him for this. As a sometime member of the Society of Friends and an active member of the Statistical Society, he emerged as a nationalist from a largely unionist circle. As a member of the temperance movement and a suffragist, he was accustomed to interacting affably with his political opposites. At temperance meetings Webb and fellow home rulers Jeremiah Jordan and John Pinkerton happily put aside political differences to share a stage with Orangeman William Johnston and unionist T. W. Russell. As suffragists Webb and Johnston also worked closely with moderate unionists Isabella Tod and Anna and Thomas Haslam. If Webb and his fellow nationalists could put aside political differences for such campaigns, it makes sense that they could also form friendships across national divides as well.

Webb's two closest friends in the Party were probably Michael Davitt and J. F. X. O'Brien. Webb and Davitt had much in common: they both considered themselves to be printers, they loved travel, languages and literature, they were passionate about international affairs and they were well-versed in history and new social movements (their correspondence includes references to the legacy of the Roman Empire and the relevance of socialism).[71] Webb and J. F. X. O'Brien, though, were friends in spite of their ideological differences; they knew each other through sharing treasury duties. When O'Brien (hardly a literary man) drafted his autobiography in the late 1890s, he asked Webb alone to read the draft; Webb referred to it as 'a labour of love'.[72] However, Webb was bothered by O'Brien's overt racism in his descriptions of living in Louisiana during the American Civil War, and asked that O'Brien include a footnote explaining Webb's abolitionist position.[73]

What O'Brien and Davitt had in common, and Webb did not, was that they had both been members of the IRB and spent time in prison.[74] Their 'advanced' pasts had not blunted their sensitivities, and both corresponded with Webb about a delicate subject: his moods. Webb's frequent vacillation between great excitement and deep disappointment over the progress of the home rule cause was not tempered by over 30 years of experience. His moods, and his sensitivity, seem to have been well-known to his friends and colleagues (especially after they were caricatured in a newspaper cartoon), and appear to be a part of his personality that was exacerbated by the intensity of politics. In twenty-first-century terms, Webb showed signs of being clinically depressed. He may have inherited this trait from his father. In his study of Irish anti-slavery, Douglas Riach notes the same persistent behaviour in R. D., that he was 'given to self-deprecation and periodic bouts of despair at the likely outcome of the anti-slavery movement'.[75]

Webb was feeling particularly despondent after a lengthy vacation in 1895, when he returned to Ireland and believed the country had become politically apathetic. O'Brien responded to Webb's frustrations; although O'Brien's letter has not been found, Webb's response reveals the content, and also Webb's awareness of how his temperament put limitations on him:

> Your advice to me regarding my tendency to depression is good and will do me good. Your spirit is the noblest and the best – the right one. Well, if I am often depressed, if I find it so difficult to see things otherwise than they are, do I not strive on personally to the best of my strength and ability?[76]

Davitt had a similar message for Webb. In a very long letter, he explained to Webb that it was normal to worry about political developments, but that Webb must not 'lose sleep' over Parnellism or the Catholic University question. He acknowledged that he and Webb had different approaches to politics: 'You are, I fear, a pessimist in politics while I am an optimist. You feel too keenly the want of progress in our cause and get somewhat discouraged because you don't see our unfortunate country reaping more fully and readily the fruits of past services and sacrifices.' He encouraged Webb not to belittle his efforts in the national cause, and to be proud of his achievements:

I learned 'to hope on' despite *every* discouragement during my times in prison and the lesson has done me good. …When a man has striven honestly, persistently and unselfishly as you have for thirty or forty years to win Ireland's liberty, there is in the thought of that record (irrespective of results) enough to compensate you for most of the evils which today give you pain and cause discouragement.[77]

Sophie O'Brien disagreed: she described Davitt as a depressive type, who relied heavily on his American wife to stay positive.[78] Either way, these individuals had the ability to speak frankly about depression (though probably not with all of the medical implications the term would have in the twenty-first century). Webb went on to explain that his depression was mostly motivated by his frustration with the nationalist movement, and was not a major cause for concern. Looking back over his papers, he considered all his efforts for the cause, and wondered what good had come of his hard work. He felt himself to be anomalous: 'So few Protestants really feel as I do.'[79] In examining Webb's writing over his lifetime, J. F. X.'s belief in Webb's 'tendency to depression' does not seem to be an overreaction. Webb's admission that 'I generally look at the black side of things'[80] and his emotional reactions to political events do suggest a man who struggled with depression throughout his adult life.

Webb may have been prone to depression, and he had also found himself in a number of trying positions by 1896. For over 25 years he had been fighting for a cause that had twice been defeated in Parliament; he had the unenviable duty of being treasurer to a number of organisations that were frequently bordering on bankruptcy; and he had felt betrayed by colleagues, most notably Parnell and Healy. Webb also had a strict adhesion to his own moral code and this added complications to his political life. Writing shortly before his death, Davitt gently suggested that Webb's reactions to political events were disproportionate, or unusually intense: 'It is indeed very hard on you that your willingness to do what is right and good always should entail so much labour and impossibility. It is a testimony to one's worth, but it ought not to carry so heavy a penalty as it generally inflicts upon you.'[81]

But undoubtedly, Webb was also a happy person: he enjoyed his home life and his travels, and he found many aspects of his work satisfying (and the thought of doing nothing for Ireland unbearable). Painting a psychological portrait of Webb shows an individual who worked to keep his depression in remission much of the time, but who lost that fight under moments of stress. For individuals like T. M. Healy, Webb's vulnerability was pathetic and even comical. Interestingly, however, the issue of depression was not completely taboo in nineteenth-century Ireland. John Martin wrote to O'Neill Daunt in 1870 to explain he often suffered from debilitating anxiety, which spiralled into guilt about his inability to serve the nationalist cause. He self-medicated through exercise:

> When for a little time I fail to try to do any good, I then become dyspeptic and nervous and subject to blue devils; and experience has shown me that the best remedy is a mountain walk. ... the blue devils fly away from me, I suppose into the blue sky above.[82]

Depression apparently carried little stigma in masculine Irish nationalist circles, even among former advanced men such as J. F. X. O'Brien.

Webb did enjoy politics, and his friendships with other politicians meant a great deal to him. His warm expressions of love and friendship to his colleagues in the 1870s – the 'love and reverence' he had for Galbraith and the 'fine and loveable men' in the home rule movement – have already been noted.[83] Such expressions were not unusual. John Tosh has described the overwhelming trend in masculinity in the late nineteenth century as one of manliness, characterised by stoicism, courage and a strict division between men and women's roles.[84] However, the correspondence between some (male) Irish nationalists, Webb included, in this era uses language that was highly emotional, affectionate and even slightly erotic. The stoicism that may have characterised public interaction between these politicians is in total contrast with the free-flowing emotions in their letters.

Webb continued to love in the Parnellite and post-Parnellite eras, and was loved in return by some of his colleagues. Charles O'Reilly, the treasurer of the Irish National League in America, wrote to Dr Kenny in Dublin about Ireland in romantic language, and referred to fundraising 'for the poor old land and the brave young lads I love so well'. It was not a large linguistic leap to talk about his friendship with men in the movement in these words (on the occasion of the closure of the INL American office):

> I take this occasion to say that the thing that comes nearest a regret in the premises comes to me with a pungency, like smoke in the eyes – it is winding up official relations with you. Alfred Webb I still love, Moloney is gone, Biggar is dead – they were all honourable men – admirable men to do business with – but somehow your disposition –

so Celtic, so anti-Saxon – attracted, warmed and delighted me. We are about the same age and I dare to hope to live to see the consummation of our hearts' desire; and in that case, it will make little difference to me who heads the procession or who presides at the first solemn sitting of your restored parliament, if only Doctor Kenny is there to squeeze my hand with the old grasp and flash the friendly eye full upon me.[85]

There is no suggestion that any of these relationships were homosexual, even if the language (of consumption, desire and attraction) is suggestive. The extent of the friendships was sometimes even epistolary: Kenny and O'Reilly saw little of each other since they lived on different continents.

William O'Brien MP also had a close friendship with Joe Quinn, one of the youngest members of the Irish Party; his youth is reflected in the fact that several members of the Party addressed him as 'Joe' in letters, when surnames were most commonly used. O'Brien was only around 30 himself when the two were both imprisoned, separately, and corresponded with each other. O'Brien's surviving letters to Quinn thank him for 'your affectionate little note, which is in one respect as pleasant to me as a love-letter', and wrote that while in prison 'I miss your own affectionate ways the most intimately of all.'[86] In a letter that deserves lengthy quotation to capture the style, O'Brien encouraged Quinn not to look up to him, but to see him as an equal:

> You must not picture me to yourself in the least as a hero, dear Joe – I have not the least pretension to be anything of the kind, but simply one full of all sorts of faults and weaknesses, who has a greater passion for love than admiration, ardent enough in my own affections and craving intensely the affection of those who are dear to me. But here am I again falling into a passionate love-letter style – I shall have your pretty little correspondents cursing me for cutting them out. I don't know anyone else living to whom I can write my inmost thoughts so freely, so warmly, and with so much pleasure. ... Write me as long letters as ever you like and as careless. Believe me nothing you can write about yourself or your thoughts or hopes can be too small to be delightful.[87]

Quinn and William O'Brien both went on to marry; Quinn had a son named Michael Davitt Quinn, and O'Brien's wife Sophie was the chronicler of social life among Irish nationalists. As with the other MPs described here, there is no indication that O'Brien and Quinn were anything more than close friends and both O'Brien and Andrew Kettle make references to Quinn's interest in women.[88]

By the turn of the century, Webb and some of his colleagues who had been home rulers since the 1870s felt an era was ending: they were getting older, younger MPs were being elected and some cherished colleagues were retiring or dying. For those that removed themselves from politics, leaving behind public life also meant leaving behind the frequent companionship of colleagues. Webb wrote to J. F. X. that although he was very happy having retired from Parliament, 'after so many years living in close intimacy and almost daily (during the season) companionship – it is a great change suddenly to find myself away from them [his colleagues].'[89] John Pinkerton and Jeremiah Jordan, both Protestant Home Rulers, became close friends through the Irish Party. When Pinkerton left the House of Commons, Jordan wrote to him that 'London and the House are both lonely to me without you. ... Do you be lonely any time, being excluded from public life? Or are you happy without it in your domestic comforts?'[90] Jordan believed that John Redmond was doing well as Irish Party leader, and that 'a good many of the young fellows that came in are not bad', but for all the politeness of his younger colleagues, he felt that he was 'treated now by the cabinet and the new blood as a fossil'.[91] He enjoyed his independence within the Party, though, since Pinkerton 'was the only man I felt I had slavishly to be subject to'.[92] Timothy Healy felt that the death of Joseph Biggar was 'the greatest blow I have ever received' and regretted his absence in the House, remembering his 'unspeakable' kindness.[93] For Webb, the greatest blow came with the death of Davitt in May 1906.[94]

The sentimentality of much of this correspondence seems more similar to the romanticism of the early nineteenth century than the trend towards stoicism identified by Tosh in the Victorian period. Tosh has argued that industrialisation produced strongly defined gender roles and a predominant type of masculinity that valued stoicism, courage and self-control. This masculinity was 'manliness', and generally it did not involve writing romantic letters to one's colleagues. But because it was primarily a male space, the political party can be compared with other male spaces – elite boys' schools, the civil service, prisons and the military – where the appreciation of 'manly' characteristics sometimes bordered on the homoerotic.[95]

Romantic nationalism is usually associated with Young Ireland and the 1840s, but the romantic language still in use after Irish nationalists had turned into a constitutional and parliamentary force suggests that nationalism retained a strong emotional pull for its adherents. As these Irish MPs were quite familiar with the language of romantic nationalism, it may be that they are adopting the rhetoric of the national struggle to describe their personal roles and relationships. Furthermore, nationalism extends the idea of kinship from beyond the extended biological family onto the members of the imagined nation as a whole, and nationalist organisations can create strong bonds among their members; indeed, the Fenians called their organisation a brotherhood.

Another explanation for the emotive language used in this select correspondence could be the absorption of Victorian ideas about race, in which ethnic groups were variously considered to have different characteristics, with Ango-Saxons displaying the most 'manly' attributes.[96] Perhaps Irish politicians had more licence to be 'unmanly' because they chose to celebrate, rather than be offended by, an identity as Celts. For Matthew Arnold, the Celt had so-called feminine characteristics – such as sensitivity, an emotional disposition, and creativity. Beyond O'Reilly's letter to Kenny, there is other evidence that Irish nationalists embraced the so-called feminine characteristics of the Arnoldian Celt.[97]

Just as the Irish nationalists who worked together, sometimes across continents, adopted racial stereotypes to express their affection for each other, there is evidence that club and political memberships formed deep bonds among Indian nationalists. Motilal Ghose, founder of the influential Indian newspaper *Amrita Bazar Patrika*, wrote to William Digby that the two shared a kindred spirit in spite of their different ethnicities: 'I found something in you when we met which leads me now and then to fancy that you, tho an Englishman, are somewhat constituted like ourselves; so I can't help now and then giving you a bit of my inner mind.'[98] In this case, the Indian finds that the Saxon shares some of his constitution. William Wedderburn also described Congress founder Allan Octavian Hume as being of the 'true Aryan breed', 'a dauntless lover of freedom', who was 'thus in full brotherly accord with the Aryan of the East, the meditative and saintly type'.[99] Again, racial stereotyping could be used to rationalise brotherliness and to justify or reinforce close male relationships.

The relationship between masculinity and nationalism has been studied before, but often to the conclusion that nationalism reinforced traditional gender divides by promulgating ideals of gendered beauty, militarism and women's roles as homemakers.[100] Militaristic nationalism, it has been argued, allowed men to regain feelings of masculinity when it has been threatened – such as by loss of social status or land.[101] George Mosse has argued that certain forms of nationalism compromised autonomous personal relationships by subjugating them to a greater national ideal.[102] Also implicit in many studies of traditional masculinity is the assumption that this masculinity is stifling, and that men are forced to find strategies to reveal the emotions that this type of masculinity discourages. The romantic language of the Irish nationalist struggle provided a vocabulary and a format in which to reveal these emotions.

The concept of an 'affective revolution', as argued by Lynn Hunt and Margaret Jacob, is also useful. Looking at the correspondence of youthful British intellectuals in the post-French Revolutionary period, they comment on the bawdy and explicit nature of many letters and argue that 'the young radicals and romantics of the 1790s explicitly challenged authoritarianism in politics and personal life and did not stop short of experimenting with outrageous forms of expression.'[103] Although there is nearly a century between Webb's colleagues and Hunt and Jacob's intellectuals, all experienced major political upheaval. While the correspondence of Webb and his colleagues is not particularly outrageous, it does perhaps attest to the profundity of their emotional involvement in their political cause, and the extent to which they were at times emotionally overcome with the importance of what they believed they were doing. As Webb exclaimed, 'I felt the cup of my happiness overflowing. To think that in my time the cause of Ireland was about to succeed and that I was permitted to take a part in it!'[104]

What do these letters reveal about Irish masculinity in the nineteenth century, and of the character of home rule politics? Within the Irish Party the intensity of the nationalist movement, combined with the romantic imagery and vocabulary of nationalism, allowed men of varying backgrounds to form deep friendships and express their affection for each other. Most importantly, they reveal the human side of home rule politics, and the extent to which political battles had the potential to become personal when such important relationships were involved (and this possibly explains some of the despair created by the various splits in the Irish Party in this era). There is a need for further research on the wider implications of these writings between late-Victorian nationalists, but I believe that to draw broad conclusions about masculinity or Irish society without a richer, broader archival basis would be mere speculation at this stage; with more supportive research, these letters may contribute to our understanding of friendship and affect in general.[105]

This analysis is also crucial in order to make sense of Webb's personality. Webb is acquitted as not simply as a feeble Quaker, who was reduced to tears by Healy and depressed by political upsets, but as one of many nationalists who felt comfortable expressing his emotions, and who had the friendship and respect of important nationalist colleagues. These letters also serve as reminders that politics is not simply about policies, but about a particular type of human interaction.

7
'I stand beside you as a comrade'[1]: Irish and Indian Political Collaboration

It is clear that Irish and Indian politicians had ample opportunities to interact in Victorian London. This chapter will present the political process through which they collaborated, culminating in Webb's selection as president of the Indian National Congress. His presidency was not an isolated event, nor a chance invitation: it was the result of the sociopolitical interaction described in the previous chapter, through a particular set of political strategies and processes that will be explained below. Several factors enabled this to happen: Webb's personal background, the place of Ireland in the British Empire, the role of international affairs within the Irish Party and the political strategies of Indians in Britain. Webb's Indian nationalism brings into focus many of the ambiguities of Irish nationalism, particularly the relationship between nationalism and Empire. In this chapter these factors, and the resulting selection of Webb to lead the Indian National Congress, will be analysed.

Webb the internationalist in the Irish Party

Webb's interest in affairs outside of Ireland was partially formed by his parent's particular brand of Quaker social justice. The earliest evidence of the Webb family's interest in India is found in the British Hibernian India Society, co-founded by R. D. Webb in the 1840s. R. D.'s interest in India complemented his abhorrence of both slavery and drugs, and he was recognised by his contemporaries as a critic of British rule in India.[2] R. D. also kept up correspondence with some early British supporters of Indian reform, most notably John Bright,[3] although his main interest was in the abolition of American slavery.

Webb spoke and wrote about international affairs long before he was elected to Parliament, but undoubtedly being an MP in London exposed him to many individuals of different backgrounds and allowed him to learn about new international causes. Gradually, his ideas about imperialism and western intervention also changed. Recalling one of Webb's earliest public pronouncements on imperialism, in the 1850s, he allowed for a certain acceptance of European material superiority but condemned colonisation.[4]

In his autobiography, Webb was eager to present his life as one focused on international responsibility. He wrote that the social movements 'which most roused my enthusiasm were those concerning people oppressed that could not help themselves – such as slaves, women deprived of the franchise, the Indian people, practically without a voice in the government of their own country – the Chinese with the use of opium almost forced on them'.[5] That opium was often farmed in India, and Webb's disgust with the opium trade is reflected in his June 1893 parliamentary bill on the subject and his collaboration with the Quaker liberal Sir Joseph Pease.[6]

When he joined the home rule movement Webb was espousing some form of federation for Britain and Ireland, perhaps because he was optimistic about cordial relations between the two countries. He became associated with the argument that 'it is Irishmen who guide the destinies of the colonies of the United Kingdom' by the strong Irish presence in military and civil service, and even the political careers of Charles Gavan Duffy in Australia and Thomas D'Arcy Magee in Canada.[7]

By the mid-1880s, Webb was arguing in favour of federalist models of Empire because he now believed that Ireland had a responsibility to consider the fate of British colonies. Ireland had a special position in the Empire, and it should use that position for good: 'From our own experience we ought to be peculiarly qualified to sympathise with and understand subject peoples, to stand by them against imperial tyranny. It would perhaps be easier to wash our hands of such responsibilities – should we be justified in doing so?'[8] This was not an apology for imperialism, which Webb vigorously opposed: 'I hate the idea of Empire; I hate the means by which the Empire has been built up; whilst I believe the formation of such an Empire is proof of the possession of some of the very highest qualities of the British people.'[9] Webb struck a positive note, writing just weeks after Gladstone's public conversion to home rule, and his ideas fit into reformist liberal ideas of his time. Webb recognised that the British Empire would not instantly vanish, and he supported reform within the Empire to improve the lives of its inhabitants. This position is easy to understand in light of his domestic political ideas. Webb was an ardent Irish nationalist but did not fear 'killing home rule with kindness': he was committed not simply to a change in government, but to a change in Irish people's lives. Thus, he felt quite comfortable in the Statistical Society, which pledged to study social questions without the complications of national politics, and he did not feel that such ventures diluted his nationalism. He also argued in the *British Friend* in 1890 that a Quaker tradition supported political responsibility and that Quakers 'are bound... to inform ourselves' of the true welfare of those in British colonies, particularly in India.[10] He also argued in the House of Commons that his own Irish nationality prompted his interest in India, but he hoped that Irish home government would also create more of an interest in the Empire for the sake of its inhabitants. He appealed to his parliamentary colleagues to accept their 'responsibility' for the colonies: 'however we may have attained power, we are bound, where we possess it, to exercise it to the best of our ability, for the good of all, and especially not to use it for our own advantage, but for the advantage of the countries which we govern.'[11]

Webb's political consciousness extended beyond the British Empire, although his musings on Russia reveal some of his inconsistencies. Both he and his friend Michael Davitt became interested in Russian affairs in the late-1880s. Webb again expressed his ideas of international responsibility in the *Freeman's Journal*, this time referring to Russia:

> All absorbing interest in our own Irish affairs should not blind us to what is going on in other countries, should not lessen our sympathies towards men and women in other countries who are striving for free institutions as we are, and who are undergoing treatment such as in our days happily no Irishman is called upon to endure for the advancement of liberty.[12]

Webb believed that the governance of Russia was despotic, and compared it to Ireland as an example of prosperity produced by tyranny.[13] Davitt and Webb hoped to convince an Irish audience that Russian despotism deserved their attention, as Davitt wrote to Webb in 1889:

> Prince Krapotkin, whom I know intimately, will lecture in Dublin before the winter is over on the Prison system of Russia. He is poor; having made over all his property to the Nihilist cause, and we must try and get him up a *paying* lecture. I am sure it will be a success.[14]

Their friend, Sophie Raffalovich O'Brien, the Russian emigrée wife of their colleague William O'Brien, was highly critical of their support of the Russian nihilists, writing of Webb and his wife that 'these eminently peace-loving people had taken up the cause of the Russian terrorists with youthful enthusiasm... they had not a word of blame about bombs and blowings up – which, if carried out in Ireland or England would have excited their indignation.'[15] As with his romantic support of Fenianism in 1867, Webb pushed aside his pacifistic doctrines in a romantic case of the ends justifying the means in the fight against tyranny.

Imperialism, to Webb, was a universal concern, because he espoused a belief in universal social responsibility. He presented this argument in different ways for different audiences; to a Belfast audience in 1896, he argued that the Irish nationalist cause 'was not the cause of Irishmen or Englishmen; it was the cause of the Empire... because the Empire could never enjoy peace until Ireland was satisfied and at rest.'[16] This statement echoes the statement of Rev. Galbraith in 1873,[17] but Webb gives a humanist twist: nationality should be a means towards a more peaceful world.

Humanity was not the only reason behind Webb's interest in imperial affairs, and his preoccupation with the Empire was neither obscure nor unusual. Imperial issues did have relevance to Ireland because Ireland was part of the British Empire and participated in that Empire on several levels. Constitutionally, the Act of Union created Ireland's role as a partner in Empire. This is most recognisable in the fact that Ireland had representatives at what was then referred to as the Imperial Parliament (Westminster). However, Ireland retained an unusual colonial feature: a lord lieutenant, or chief secretary, somewhat comparable to a colonial viceroy. The ambiguity of Ireland's position prompted different political approaches. For many Irish people, the fact of 'British rule' was an all-consuming political problem and the fate of Britain's overseas colonies was irrelevant; for others, the fact that Ireland was both part of the Union and part of the Empire posed different problems and questions. Isaac Butt worried that Ireland was not extracting its fair share out of the Empire, whereas Alfred Webb was consumed with the guilt that Ireland had imperial blood on its hands. Both recognised the disproportionately high level of Irish involvement in India during the home rule era, producing two Indian viceroys, Lord Mayo (1868–1872) and the Marquess of Dufferin (1884–1888), up to one-third of the recruits to the Indian Civil Service at the time of the Indian 'mutiny' of 1857,[18] and perhaps 40 per cent of British Army troops in India.[19] Indian administrator Sir Antony MacDonnell, a Connacht-born Catholic, even joked that in the 1890s, 'Ireland had temporarily relieved England of the task of governing India.'[20]

Irish nationalist newspapers were loaded with information about the Empire, especially in the years just preceding the establishment of the Home Rule League. The Indian 'Mutiny' of 1857, the assassination of Lord Mayo (the Kildare-born Indian viceroy) in 1872 and Indian famines received particular attention in the Irish press, and such dramatic events in India created a general interest in the colony: the *Freeman's Journal* and the *Nation* responded with articles about the history, literature and religions of India. Advertisements in the *Freeman's Journal* also targeted members of the imperial armed services, particularly soldiers bound for India. The *Flag of Ireland* (later purchased by Parnell and transformed into *United Ireland*) and the *Nation* were much more critical of imperialism than the *Freeman's Journal*, although by the 1880s the *Freeman's Journal* was adopting the language of the British Liberal Party's imperial critiques. In all of these newspapers two facts are most evident: first, that there was no unified 'nationalist' Irish response to Empire, and second that Empire was omnipresent. Even the *Nation*, which perhaps wavered the least in its profession of hatred of Britain and its Empire, recognised the importance of the Empire as a global fact.[21] All of these newspapers participated in some form of imperial culture: whether positive or negative in their approach to the Empire, they all engaged with and used the language and events of British imperial history. The result would have been that an Irish newspaper reader would have been exposed to plentiful information and opinions about Empire and India.[22]

Four international approaches in the Irish Party

In spite of this large Irish stake in Empire, the Irish Party never had a policy on Empire or on international affairs. The various home rule vehicles committed MPs to a national parliament, and encouraged reform of local government, Irish land, and taxation. That does not mean that international affairs were not discussed. At the Home Rule Conference of 1873, Rev. Galbraith professed his love for the British Empire and argued that home rule was necessary 'not only for the purpose of increasing the future prosperity of this country, but also with the view of ensuring the future safety of the British Empire'.[23] His comments were followed by those from several others, drawing parallels between the British–Irish situation and the Austro–Hungarian and Swedish–Norwegian ones.[24] In the 1880s, it is clear that international affairs played a vital role in the Irish nationalist imagination. Dozens of pamphlets, newspaper articles and speeches, from both pro- and anti-home rule camps, relied on examples from international affairs. These included the status of self-government in Canada, Australia, Poland, Austria-Hungary, South Africa, Italy, France and the United States.[25] Many of these arguments were advanced solely to promote the Irish cause, not to express solidarity with other nationalists; they denote sympathy for foreign causes but do not indicate that Irish nationalists were prepared to take action on behalf of others. Irish writers were usually examining the relevance of foreign affairs to Irish politics, rather than assessing the importance of Ireland in the world system. For example, when addressing a meeting composed mostly of tenant farmers in Ballycastle, County Antrim, the future Irish Party MP John Pinkerton compared the position of Irish landlords in 1880 with that of Clive in India and slaveholders in the West Indies, rousing his crowd with the claim that his 'object now should be to free the white slaves of Ireland, who had been more trodden down than the worst of the West Indians'.[26] He did not, however, advocate freeing anyone else; his examples of oppression in India and the Caribbean were rhetorical devices that showed little sense of proportion between slavery and tenant farming. However, his choice of examples shows an anticipated awareness of such oppression on the part of his audience.

In the absence of an Irish Party platform, but in the presence of a vivid debate about the relevance of foreign affairs, it is possible to identify some individuals who represent major strands of thought within Irish nationalism. Butt displayed a superficial fondness for the Empire that likely represents the deference towards British institutions, and the desire to integrate Protestants into the home rule movements, that characterised his leadership in the 1870s. The Home Rule League of the 1870s was not interested in international issues: individual members cared, but as a body the League strictly avoided such questions as deviations from the League's mission. For example, it refused to formulate a policy on the Eastern Question in spite of requests from constituents.[27]

Charles Stewart Parnell represents the second, and probably the largest, variety of thought: he was interested in extra-Irish affairs only to the extent that they furthered Irish nationalist goals. Again, this represented his political leadership, which was strategic and purposely ambiguous. Parnell's attitudes are neatly illustrated through his dealings with Cecil Rhodes. After conversations with Swift MacNeill on a voyage from the Cape Colony to Britain, the diamond magnate and imperialist Rhodes wrote a lengthy letter to Parnell. Rhodes expressed his support for Irish nationalism and was candid about his intentions: 'I will frankly add that my interest in the Irish question has been heightened by the fact that in it I see the possibility of the commencement of changes which will eventually mould and weld together all parts of the British Empire.' He argued that under home rule the Irish should maintain representation at Westminster, paying a proportional amount of tax revenue towards imperial defence. He also told Parnell what Parnell probably wanted to hear: 'My experience in the Cape Colony leads me to believe that the Ulster question is one which would soon settle itself.'[28] He then offered £10,000 for the Irish Party, if 'you and your party could be prepared to give your hearty support and approval to a Home Rule Bill containing provisions for the continuance of Irish representation at Westminster'.[29]

Parnell's response is a classic example of his skill at dodging commitments. It also demonstrates how he neither saw imperial issues as ones which Irish MPs should pursue themselves, nor had any political or ethical objections to accepting money from an imperialist. He replied,

> My own feeling upon the matter is that if Mr Gladstone includes in his next home rule measures provisions for such situation, we should cheerfully concur in them, and accept them with good-will and good-faith with the intention of taking our share in the imperial partnership. ... It does not come so much within my province to express a full opinion upon the larger question of Imperial Federation but I quite agree with you that the continued Irish representation at Westminster will immensely facilitate such a step, which the contrary provision in the Bill of '86 would have been a bar.[30]

This was far short of committing the Irish Party to imperial federalism, but Rhodes read into this letter what he wanted to read: that Parnell was offering his 'cordial approval of the retention of Irish representation at Westminster'. This, Rhodes believed, was a crucial step 'to a closer union of the Empire making it an Empire in reality and not in name only'.[31] He forwarded Parnell £10,000, plus an additional £1000 from another supporter in South Africa. Thus, Parnell secured a large donation without actually having committed anything to Rhodes or towards the cause of imperial federation.

Parnell's attitudes and actions can be contrasted with those of one of his more notorious MPs, Frank Hugh O'Donnell. O'Donnell sat as MP for Dungarvan from 1877 to 1885 (until his seat was lost through redistribution; Dungarvan became part of Webb's future West Waterford constituency). Educated at Queen's College Galway and working as a freelance journalist in London, O'Donnell was extremely intelligent and knowledgeable, plus his brother C. J. O'Donnell in the Indian Civil

Service supplied him with information about Indian affairs. He was also an eccentric, known as 'Crank' Hugh O'Donnell to his colleagues, who was not shy about promoting himself or publicly criticising his rivals. O'Donnell apparently believed himself to be a threat to Parnell as leader of the Party,[32] although such suggestions are conspicuously absent from his colleagues' memoirs.

O'Donnell has loomed large in previous studies of Irish–Indian political connections. In 1910 he published a two-volume *History of the Irish Parliamentary Party* in which he made several claims about his own role in Indian politics.[33] There is independent evidence to substantiate his interest in India – he certainly addressed the House of Commons on Indian subjects and wrote to Irish newspapers with his opinions. His *History* stands out as one of the few sources for evidence of Indian–Irish collaboration before the 1890s. However, some of his claims seem fantastic and cannot be confirmed in other sources. Most notably he claims that he personally established the foundations for the Indian National Congress through his connections with wealthy Indians in London. This would not be problematic had not his ideas formed the basis for foundational works on this political collaboration.[34]

O'Donnell's creative ideas about Ireland and Empire are still worth noting. He believed that it was his personal mission in life to be 'Professor of Organisation to men and nations who, for one reason or another, had a quarrel with the British constitution'.[35] He referred to himself as 'an imperialist and a Nationalist', and he reserved the right to intervene in non-Irish issues in Parliament. O'Donnell argued emphatically that the good of Ireland was inextricably linked with the good of the Empire, that 'the decrease of the Colonial power of England in no way implies the better security of Ireland' (conversely, he argued that the demise of Empire could lead to increased English 'land-hunger' in Ireland). O'Donnell, describing Ireland as a partner in Empire, even went so far as to argue that 'a time indeed may come when Ireland, possessed of her national independence and enjoying her full share, political and commercial, in all the benefits of the common Empire, may resolve to go a step further and *to oust the British people entirely from all co-partnership.*'[36]

O'Donnell's vision of a British Empire ruled by Ireland is not created by his abhorrence of the nature of British imperialism, but by the dream of Irish profit. Thus, it is doubtful if he truly represents a 'humanitarian or internationalist strand in Irish nationalism',[37] or whether O'Donnell was taking Butt's attitude towards the Empire to a whole new extreme. As with Butt or Parnell it is difficult to assess how many Irish MPs, or

Irish people, would have adopted O'Donnell's ideas, but the emphasis on pragmatism and self-interest may have had some appeal.

Butt was deferential, Parnell was tactical and O'Donnell was slightly maniacal when it came to international affairs. After the fall of Parnell the party was led by Justin McCarthy, a Cork-born journalist and prolific novelist. McCarthy had emigrated to Liverpool in 1855 and had created a successful career as a journalist there and then in London. Like Webb, and like his fellow journalist T. P. O'Connor, McCarthy moved easily throughout London and did not have the Anglophobia of some other Irish nationalists. As his biographer summarised, McCarthy saw 'no dichotomy between wishing to see a self-governing Ireland and personally aiming to make a living as a scribe in London'.[38] McCarthy took an interest in international affairs and moved in some of the same circles as Webb did in London. However, McCarthy's mild personality, combined with the devastation of the Irish nationalist movement in the 1890s, meant that his worldly views did not become party policy.

Alfred Webb fits into this fourth strand of Irish nationalist thought. Like McCarthy, Davitt and Swift MacNeill, Webb took a profound interest in foreign policy for its own sake. His interest in foreign affairs was not primarily driven by beliefs about what would be most expedient for home rule, or by his own wish for personal fulfillment. These men pursued international affairs separately and together; they frequently tried to convince their colleagues to open their minds to what was happening outside Ireland, although their commitment to home rule never wavered. They did not simply recognise that Ireland had shared experiences with other nations; they went further and advocated global responsibility.

Internationalism in practice: Irish and Indian political strategies

For those home rulers like Webb who took an avid interest in international affairs, the lack of interest on the part of their colleagues was a source of frustration. Yet at the same time, participation in Parliament and residence in London created an opportunity for Webb and others to put responsible internationalism into practice. Webb's most important foray into international affairs was his involvement in Indian nationalism, facilitated by his election to Parliament. Webb's involvement in Indian affairs was possible because, following the establishment of the Indian National Congress in 1885, moderate Indian nationalists were developing a new political strategy. This strategy had two lines of attack: one was to ensure that Indian affairs were represented in Parliament and the second was to publicise the work of the Congress and raise awareness of India.

There has been some research into Irish–Indian parliamentary work before 1885. The best known is Mary Cumpston's 1961 article, 'Some early Indian nationalists and their allies in the British Parliament, 1851–1906'.[39] Cumpston practically could have inserted the adjective Irish in her title, for most of the allies she describes were Irish MPs, including Frank Hugh O'Donnell, Joseph Biggar and Justin McCarthy. Unfortunately, much of her information is drawn from an uncritical reading of O'Donnell's *History*. Cumpston incorporates virtually no manuscript sources, and many of her assertions are not footnoted. Her article is frustrating and tantalising; it suggests some fascinating ideas that it fails to back up. Likewise Howard V. Brasted, in an unpublished thesis, explains that a group including F. H. O'Donnell, T. O'Connor Power and Joseph Ronayne 'had taken the first tentative steps to establish an Indian Home Rule Association' in the 1870s, but he gives no citation.[40] Brasted's published material is important but does not clarify all the ways in which the Irish–Indian connection evolved.[41]

There are also some records left by the early pro-Indian groups in Britain. R. D. Webb's British Hibernian India Society has left little trace, but it was possibly one of the earliest of such groups in the United Kingdom.[42] Dadabhai Naoroji took several steps towards bringing Indian issues before the general public in Britain. In 1865 he established the London Indian Society with Womesh Chandra Bonnerjee with the intention of educating British people about problems in India.[43] This society operated intermittently throughout the next four decades under Naoroji's leadership, holding meetings with speakers on Indian issues.

Naoroji also became convinced in the 1870s that Parliament alone had the power to create legislative change and that, if India wanted reform, it would need representation in the Imperial Parliament. The India Reform Society, founded in 1853 by John Dickinson, is recognised as laying the foundations for Indian agitation in Parliament. In 1885 an Indian committee in Parliament was formed, but the dissolution of the House soon after led to its disintegration. Naoroji, however, wanted to secure representation through MPs: one option was to convince a British MP to act as a 'friend of India' and the second was to elect an Indian from a parliamentary constituency with the understanding that he would represent both his constituency and India.

The first option was initially more successful. The celebrated Quaker radical MP John Bright had long been recognised as friendly towards India, and the suffragist Henry Fawcett was a 'Friend of India' from the 1860s until his death in 1884. In the late 1880s Charles Bradlaugh agreed to represent Indian interests in Parliament. Bradlaugh had a difficult relationship with the Irish Party: although he was sympathetic to Irish nationalist grievances, and had supported the Fenians,[44] his atheism offended Catholic Ireland and his refusal to take the parliamentary oath annoyed some Irish MPs, who felt he was wasting parliamentary time. Most vicious among the public attacks on Bradlaugh were those from O'Donnell. Frank Callanan writes that O'Donnell wanted 'to posture as a high-spirited Catholic gentleman' in opposing Bradlaugh's admission to the House.[45] An additional reason for O'Donnell's venomous attack may have been that he wanted to monopolise the role of parliamentary hero of the Indian people. The bitterness with which he referred to Fawcett is revealing: he denies that Fawcett deserved any recognition for his work for India, which O'Donnell believed was 'entirely superficial' compared to his own.[46] O'Donnell saw himself as a friend of India, and indeed perhaps he was unfairly overlooked because he did not have a high profile.

O'Donnell did involve himself in the second option open to India, that of electing an Indian to a parliamentary seat. O'Donnell writes that in the 1870s he began socialising with some of the Indians who were law students in London, and that there he became friendly with a group of wealthy Bengalis. In around 1878, O'Donnell claims that they hatched a plan:

> four natives of India, to be selected by the Indians themselves, men of university attainments and considerable power of oratory, should be elected for Irish constituencies, to be Irish home rulers on all Irish questions, and to be members for India, and to be backed by the Irish party, on Indian affairs.[47]

O'Donnell explains that he first presented the idea to the outgoing leader Butt who responded 'warmly' but worried that it would lead to 'additional hostility from English conservative quarters'. O'Donnell claims that he later floated the idea with Butt's successor, Parnell, who saw little point to the plan. The plan never materialised, although Naoroji's name has become associated with it.[48] Naoroji had been looking for a potential parliamentary seat for some time.

O'Donnell's assertions can be trusted here because Davitt has continued the story in his *Fall of Feudalism*, explaining that the plan to elect Naoroji was briefly revived in 1883, but again failed to impress the Irish leadership.[49] Within a few years, though, Naoroji had decided that it would not be wise to seek an Irish seat: a keen follower of Irish affairs, he was thrilled by Gladstone's introduction of an Irish Home Rule bill, was convinced that it would be an eventual success and prepared himself to give speeches on the topic.[50] Therefore, when he approached Liberal politicians in the spring of 1886 he explained to them that 'an Irish constituency would be no use to me even if I got it, as in case the [Home Rule] Bills passed afterwards and the Irish members were wholly or partially removed from Parliament, I must go too.'[51] Naoroji finally won the chance to stand for an English constituency as a Liberal candidate in June of 1886 for the London Holborn division. He enthusiastically made Irish home rule the cornerstone of his platform, writing to electors that a vote for him would 'support Mr Gladstone's noble and conciliatory policy towards Ireland, and at the same time be able to respond to the appeal of the two hundred and fifty millions of your fellow subjects in India to have a voice in the imperial parliament'.[52] He also enjoyed the support of Davitt, who attended and spoke at an election rally for Naoroji.[53]

Naoroji lost the 1886 election but was not discouraged. The year 1885 had witnessed several major political watersheds in Irish, Indian and British politics: the introduction of the Home Rule Bill, the birth of an Irish–Liberal alliance and the establishment of the Indian National Congress. As in Ireland, nationalism in India was on the rise in the mid-nineteenth century, spurred on by increasing educational opportunities, the growth of the press and by the experiences of educated migrants to Britain. By the end of his Indian viceroyalty Lord Ripon had begun to worry that well-educated Indians were not being incorporated into the governance of India.[54] Ripon's successor, the Ulsterman Lord Dufferin, was not of Ripon's liberal persuasion, and in the first year of his viceroyalty (1885) he established an antagonistic relationship with Allan Octavian Hume, who presented him with plans for a type of consultative body with links to the government, composed of educated native Indians. Hume was a retired Indian Civil Servant from Scotland (in fact, he was a failed civil servant).[55] His efforts to pull together a national Indian movement, drawing ideas being discussed in 'native' Indian newspapers and a brief 'Indian National Congress' in 1883, were met with suspicion from the viceroy. Dufferin was concerned that Hume was planning 'a Political Convention of delegates on the lines adopted by O'Connell previous to the Catholic emancipation', or one that would adopt the methods of Parnell and his party.[56] In fact, many regional political associations of native Indians, who wanted Dufferin to pursue Riponesque reform, were established across the country. Some of these, Briton Martin Jr. claims, took some inspiration from the Irish Land League, although that is not to suggest that they were imitations.[57] In December 1885 delegates of many of these associations gathered in Bombay to form the first Indian National Congress. Womesh Chandra Bonnerjee was the first president.

O'Donnell has in fact claimed that the Indian National Congress sprang from his own organisation in London, the Constitutional Association of India. The evidence for this is thin. Anil Seal refers to the Constitutional Association in his classic *The Emergence of Indian Nationalism*, but uses O'Donnell as his source.[58] O'Donnell's description is of a meeting of 250 Indian gentlemen at the London home of the wealthy Indian expatriate Mohun Tagore. He proudly explains that he was the only non-Indian.[59] O'Donnell gives the impression of being reluctant to work with his Irish Party colleagues or, perhaps, to share the credit for a founding role in the Indian nationalist movement. He conflicted with his colleagues frequently, sometimes in the newspaper press.[60] He admits that he was 'careful' to invite some other MPs to meetings of his Constitutional Association of India, including one Irish MP, Edmund Leamy.[61] Those Irishmen who worked in a greater liberal tradition (or an O'Connellite tradition), alongside people like Bright and Fawcett, seem to have had more luck than the lone Frank Hugh O'Donnell. Irish aid to Indian reformers was partially contingent on the Irish Party's healthy relationship with the British Liberals.

In the face of opposition from Dufferin, Congress leaders worried that their efforts were not being recognised or understood in Britain, and several different schemes were used to correct that. The first was the short-lived Indian Telegraph Union, established in 1885 by Hume, who was concerned that the British public was not receiving accurate accounts of events in India, or positive accounts of Congress. The Union sent news to British newspapers, but its funding quickly ran out; Irish newspapers do not seem to have been recipients of the Indian Telegraph Union's news reports.[62] In 1887 Naoroji was appointed as an agent of the Congress in London, but lack of time and money prevented him from exercising much influence.[63] Money was found for a lecture series, though, with Bradlaugh and Bonnerjee giving public speeches in Northampton in 1888.[64] Ireland was not on the British–Indian lecture circuit.

Finally, over 1888 and 1889, a budget was set by Congress for an Indian Political Agency in London.[65] William Digby became its secretary and responsible for running its affairs. Much like the Irish home rulers' attempts to appeal to Conservatives in the 1870s, the Indian Political Agency began its life by trying to convince Conservatives that it was an apolitical organisation committed only to Indian reform.[66] After the failure of many Conservatives to join, it eventually aligned itself with the Liberal Party, conceding that this was the most practical strategy but still keenly asserting that its origins were independent.[67] The Indian Political Agency maintained a library of Indian source material, including all Parliamentary papers relating to India, and also served as a reference on Indian affairs: it hoped that MPs who needed facts about India would consult its offices.[68]

The Indian Political Agency was soon supplemented by a British Committee of the Indian National Congress (BCINC, or British Committee). Sir William Wedderburn chaired the British Committee in close consultation with Naoroji. Wedderburn was, like Hume, a Scottish retired Indian Civil Servant and he served as Congress president in 1889. This committee began producing a journal in February 1890, first titled *India: A Journal for the Discussion of Indian Affairs*, then later simply *India*. Wedderburn argued that a periodical was necessary, not only to publicise the cause of the British Committee but also to ensure that accurate news coverage of Indian affairs was available in Britain.[69] He argued that the reports that filtered into the British press were untrustworthy and biased. Webb agreed with him, and encouraged his fellow Quakers to read *India* for its 'treating of Indian questions from the standpoint of educated Indians and their British sympathisers'.[70]

India ran articles on all aspects of Indian politics and economics, reprinted all speeches and bills from the House of Commons that dealt with Indian affairs and publicised the work of Congress. Indian affairs also became personified in individuals who worked for the cause, including Naoroji, but particularly Wedderburn. Although Wedderburn's efforts for Indian reform were sustained, and his sincerity and humanitarian principles have not been called into doubt, reading *India* does give the impression that it was Wedderburn's personal propaganda machine. The fact that Wedderburn also wrote a biography of Hume, a founder of the Congress, has also solidified Wedderburn's position in this aspect of history.

Oddly, O'Donnell did not author articles for *India*, although Irish issues and people made occasional appearances in the writing in *India*. In the reprinted Parliamentary debates Swift MacNeill appears as one of the MPs who most frequently spoke on Indian issues in Parliament. His comparisons to Ireland were recurrent, but his speeches were based on in-depth knowledge of Indian affairs, and the frequency and quality of his Indian speeches leave no doubt that he cared about India for India's sake, not just for Ireland's. Still, he claimed that his appreciation of Indian grievances stemmed from his Irishness, and that Irish MPs would necessarily fill the void left by Bradlaugh:

> Unfortunately, since his death, the affairs of India have been sadly neglected; the Indian Government have taken advantage of his death to do this in every way; it has shown itself cruel and heartless in dealing with these suffering people. I am glad to tell the House that I have the sympathy of my colleagues from Ireland in this matter, and that as far as we are concerned we intend in season and out of season to bring forward the grievances of India, and insist on a remedy being applied.[71]

Swift MacNeill made great efforts to fill Bradlaugh's shoes, and frequently called the Under-Secretary for India, George Curzon, to account for events in India. McCarthy's contribution to Indian parliamentary questions is also in evidence through Bradlaugh's correspondence with Digby, where there are several references to McCarthy working on Indian bills and subjects.[72] Swift MacNeill's Irish intervention seemed appropriate to other politicians interested in Indian reform. The Scottish socialist and later leader of the Labour party James Keir Hardie contributed an 1893 article to *India* about Indian democracy, quoting Daniel O'Connell and crediting him with having argued against the character of British rule in India in the 1840s.[73] Irish intervention in Indian affairs required little explanation to many political observers.

Thus, by the early 1890s several developments in Irish–Indian relations had taken place. Wedderburn's correspondence with Naoroji frequently mentions Naoroji's connections with the Irish MPs, referring to them as his 'particular friends'.[74] The apparent plan to elect Naoroji to an Irish seat never came to fruition, though it seems probable that some individuals – including O'Donnell in 1878 and Davitt in 1883 – took the plan seriously. Several reasons have been suggested why these plans failed: lack of enthusiasm from the Irish leadership, concerns about alienating the electorate and reluctance on the part of Naoroji at a time when Irish home rule looked like a real possibility.

By 1892, Naoroji had perhaps changed his mind about the likelihood of home rule being quickly achieved, and after the death of Bradlaugh in 1891 there was serious pressure to find a new 'Indian' MP and to ensure that the hard work of the BCINC affected parliamentary opinion. Naoroji turned to Michael Davitt and asked, for the third time, if he could be chosen for an Irish constituency. Davitt replied that,

> Owing to the unhappy division in our Home Rule party I very much fear it will be impossible to obtain the assent of the Nationalist constituencies to a candidate of so complete an outsider as yourself. Unfortunately the feeling is a bitter [one] on both sides of the matter of fighting a dead issue that the country could not be educated up to the diplomatic level of returning you for an Irish seat. Personally I would be glad if it could be done, but I am convinced that it would be impossible.[75]

Not all Indians were convinced by Naoroji's candidacy. Motilal Ghose wrote to his friend Digby that he and Bonnerjee were sceptical about what an Indian could achieve in Parliament:

> We are after Professor MacNeill, and as Bonnerjee knows him also so I hope you will both do your best to induce him to take the place of Mr Bradlaugh. I don't talk of Mr Dadabhai because we want an Englishman or an Irishman in position who will be more useful to us than Dadabhai with all his ability and patriotism.[76]

Fortunately for Naoroji, he was selected as a Liberal candidate for the London seat of Central Finsbury. His platform in the 1892 election was a standard Liberal one, including a vigorous defence of the plan for home rule for Ireland. During the election he faced particularly xenophobic campaigning from Lord Salisbury, leader of the Conservatives, who argued that the British public could not elect a 'black man'.[77] In spite of, or perhaps because of, Salisbury's remarks, Naoroji was elected with a tiny margin.

The election of Naoroji to Parliament was a great boost to his cause of Indian reform. Wedderburn was also elected to Parliament, in an 1893 by-election, and decided to use his new position to resuscitate an Indian Parliamentary Committee. He did so by arranging a dinner party for 'a few leading independent members' whom he deemed interested in Indian reform. A committee was formed from these attendees, with Wedderburn as chair. The 17 members included two Irishmen, J. G. Swift MacNeill and Alfred Webb.[78] Both Webb and MacNeill were also part of the 11-member working committee. Wedderburn reports that the committee grew to 154 members by the end of the session, and that it was successful in lobbying the government to appoint the Welby Commission to enquire into Indian expenditure.[79] However, the absence of any bills or reports prepared by this committee, though, makes it difficult to be certain of its membership.[80] In the journal *India*, a list of membership taking into account new members was printed in May 1894. It lists 125 members, of whom 25 were Irish. In his 1893 presidential address to the Congress, Naoroji applauded the efforts of this 'Indian Parliamentary Committee', and claimed that India had the support of some 70 or 80 Irishmen;[81] this would have been virtually the entire Irish Party. Naoroji's statement is akin to saying that the Irish Party supported Indian reform, although we know that it did not have any pro-Indian platform. There is a slight suggestion that membership may underestimate Irish support. When Wedderburn and Naoroji were trying to get MPs to support a petition about the Indian Budget Wedderburn wrote to Naoroji that 'I can see that the Irish MPs may feel the difficulty you refer to about signing.' Without Naoroji's preceding letter to Wedderburn, though, it is unclear what that difficulty was.[82]

Those 25 that were on the membership list printed in *India* included prominent members of the party – J. F. X. O'Brien, Justin McCarthy and David Sheehy – and some less prominent members. Importantly, neither John Dillon nor John Redmond – now leading the Anti-Parnellite and Parnellite factions, respectively – was Committee members. During the general election in the summer of 1895, the Liberals lost nearly a hundred MPs to the Conservatives; the Irish Parliamentary Party gained one seat. The effect on the Indian Parliamentary Committee immediately after the election was that membership was reduced to 85, but there was an increase in the Irish membership from 25 to 28. The new Irish committee members were not, however, newly elected: they had all sat during the previous parliament. All of the Irish MPs on the Committee were members of the Irish Parliamentary Party; there were no Irish Unionist MPs belonging to the Committee. Davitt, who sat briefly in the House in 1893 and was re-elected in 1895, is not listed.

Several salient points about this committee are worth noting. First, it was largely symbolic: it seems to have done little in terms of creating reports or bills for Parliamentary use, but Committee membership was a public commitment on the part of MPs towards Indian reform and the Committee raised the profile of Indian issues within Parliament. Second, Irish MPs made up a substantial part of the committee. Working from the membership lists mentioned above, Irish MPs made up 20 per cent of the Committee in May 1894 when they held just 12 per cent of parliamentary seats. In August 1895 they made up nearly a third of the Committee although their Parliamentary representation remained at 12 per cent. When Naoroji served as Congress president in 1893, he emphasised the strong Irish participation on the Indian Parliamentary Committee in his presidential address, and expressed his 'special thanks to the Irish, Labour and Radical members' of the House. He also passed on an enthusiastic message from Davitt: 'Don't forget to tell your colleagues at the Congress that every one of Ireland's home rule members in Parliament is at your back in the cause of the Indian people.'[83] This might have been an exaggeration on Davitt's part, but it probably is a realistic representation of the momentum felt by those Irish who did take part in Indian affairs.

To see Webb's selection as president of the Congress as the culmination of exclusively positive, unimpeded Irish–Indian collaboration, though, would not be completely accurate. There were both detractors from, and obstacles to, a joint Irish–Indian political strategy. Indian nationalists in the 1880s and 1890s were more eager to present their loyalty to the Crown and the moderation of their proposed reforms; while it had become unacceptable to toast the Queen at Irish nationalist meetings, it was completely the norm to do so at Indian nationalist meetings in London.[84] Some Indian nationalists were wary of allying themselves with the Irish nationalists whose politics may have cast doubt on the moderation of Indian nationalist demands. Cumpston has argued that 'the association of Indian nationalism with Irish torment did not aid the Indian cause in parliament.'[85] Some Indians might have recognised that other members of the House were sceptical about the Irish Party and still associated it with obstructionism or even Fenianism; some Indians may have simply wanted to detach themselves from the complications of Irish politics and deal directly with the luminaries in the Liberal and Conservative parties. Although it is difficult to find explicit statements it is possible that the Irish were seen, for reasons either snobbish or strategic, as undesirable political allies.

Another bulwark to Irish–Indian collaboration was frustration from Indians who were competing with the Irish for the resources of Parliament. Frustration is expressed in the pages of *Fraternity*: that Irish issues were time-consuming, that the Irish representatives were effective at monopolising Commons time with Irish issues and that the status of home rule in the Liberal Party's platform meant that the leaders of that party were less concerned with Indian reform. *Fraternity*'s editor complained that the Indian Budget debate was put off until a day when 'the debating powers of the House were almost exhausted by the Irish

Question', and the leaders of the Liberal Party had already retired. Only a small number of individuals were left to debate the Indian budget, and it was perhaps with some bitterness that *Fraternity* wrote that 'India did not dare come in the way of Ireland – that great little country, championed by the greatest of British statesmen.'[86] This was an argument that Webb had himself made in 1883, when he argued that minor Irish issues were being discussed in Parliament and they would be better dealt with in an independent Irish parliament. In the meantime, he asked, 'And is it not deplorable that after weeks and months of Parliamentary business interspersed with such small considerations, questions like the Indian budget, upon which the welfare of millions may largely depend, are shuffled through in a few hours?'[87]

An Irish president for an Indian Congress

Indian frustrations, and rifts within Indian nationalism, become clear when the Congress committee began searching for a president for the 1894 Congress. By July 1894, Dinshaw Wacha (a young Indian nationalist and member of the Madras Organising Committee) wrote to Naoroji that they were interested in inviting an MP to preside. 'Our Madras friends say Mr Blake MP (formerly of Canada) is likely to accept the presidentship of the coming Congress if he is properly approached on the subject', and Wacha hoped that Naoroji and Wedderburn could be the ones to approach him with the invitation.[88] Wacha admitted that Naoroji and Wedderburn 'will best know whom to select', and that they would also consider a Muslim named Mr Syami, but that it would be most desirable to have an MP. He exclaimed in his letter, 'What a capital thing it would be!'[89]

Naoroji and Wedderburn were appointed to approach Blake on the matter.[90] Blake was an unusual Irish nationalist, since he was Canadian. Born to Galwegian parents in Canada, he had lived his entire life in Canada until he was elected to the South Longford seat in 1892. In Canada he was an accomplished lawyer and had led the Canadian Liberal Party. He had a firm intellectual commitment both to federalism in the British Empire and to Irish nationalism. His ideas and status were obviously attractive to Indian nationalists, although there is little record of his supporting Indian causes in Parliament: he was not, for example, a member of the Indian Parliamentary Committee.

Unfortunately, Naoroji struggled to get an answer. The minutes of the British Committee reveal the following chain of events:

Mr Naoroji said that he had approached Mr Sexton and several other Irish Members who viewed the matter favourably, but Mr Blake was in Canada and nothing could be settled until his return on the 7th Nov. It was resolved that the invitation to Mr Blake, received by telegram, should be forwarded to Mr Sexton asking him to communicate with Mr Blake. Mr Naoroji was asked to write to Mr Davitt asking him if, in the event of Mr Blake declining the invitation, he would accept the office of President of the Congress. Mr Dillon's name was also mentioned in case both Messrs. Blake and Davitt declined.[91]

Whether the Madras committee had specified so or not, by asking Naoroji to secure a president the search had been narrowed to his 'particular friends', the Irish MPs. This was reflected in the invitation that was forwarded to Blake, which asked him to support the Congress's moderate demands, 'recognising the gallantry of your own fight for an independence far greater than that we seek for ourselves'.[92]

In the meantime, Naoroji wrote to Davitt asking if he would accept the presidency if Blake were to decline. However, Davitt did not think that his acting as President would serve the cause of Indian nationalism and he urged Naoroji instead to 'redouble your efforts' to procure Blake as president. Blake 'would make an ideal chairman', Davitt argued, given his experience as a Crown minister in Canada and his personal friendships with Gladstone and Rosebery.[93] Like the Irish, Davitt recognised that Indians were also striving for respectability, and he thought that his own presence could bring the Congress into disrepute:

> my former political 'delinquencies' will be raked up – my conviction for Fenianism, Land Leaguism, the Parnell Commission etc; and though *my* countrymen and many Englishmen think no worse of me for my career; (and though it is to myself a matter of boast and not for apology or regrets) you and your friends in London are called upon to consider whether or not I would be the *wisest* selection in the event of Mr Blake declining to go.[94]

At Naoroji's request Davitt followed up by contacting Blake directly, and Blake responded that he had not yet received the invitation, although he had read about it in the press. He expected to decline the invitation because he could not spare the time, although he told Davitt that he thought 'the proposal highly honourable' and that he 'would be glad to do anything I can for the cause anywhere'.[95]

In early November Blake confirmed that he would not be able to attend because of his commitments to appear before the Privy Council. With only a few weeks until the president would have to sail for India, Naoroji hastily conducted 'several interviews' with MPs, including Thomas Sexton and John Dillon. After the Congress was finished, Wedderburn wrote of 'thanking the Irish leaders for their selection', implying that it was during one of these interviews that Webb was selected, possibly at the suggestion of the Irish Party leadership.[96] Webb accepted the invitation immediately, remarking in his autobiography that 'it must have been my attitude in Parliament towards Indian questions that led to this most flattering proposal being made.'[97] Hume was quickly dispatched to meet with Webb and brief him about the issues to be discussed at Congress.[98] Webb departed on 22 November 1894, with a small send-off celebration at Liverpool Street station in London organised by the London Indian Society.[99]

Thus, Webb was not the first choice of the Congress organisers, but the fourth or fifth. However, he was the ultimate choice for a high-profile position, and his selection was undoubtedly due to Naoroji's determination to honour an Irish MP with the presidency. Bizarrely, the Congress organisers in Madras had been convinced that Blake would accept their invitation, although it is unclear how they developed this belief. This was embarrassing for the Congress and, perhaps, for Webb, although he seems to have been so flattered by the invitation that he did not mind. *India* recognised the awkwardness of the situation and decided to confirm rather than deny reports:

> As readers of *India* are aware, the office of the President of the Indian National Congress this year was offered in the first instance to Mr E. Blake, MP Mr Blake would have gladly accepted the invitation had not certain Canadian cases in which he will shortly appear before the Judicial Committee of the Privy Council, and which it was found impossible to postpone, prevented him. In these circumstances Mr Alfred Webb, whose interest in Indian affairs is well known, graciously accepted the office. Mr Webb will bear with him to India a message of hope from the House of Commons, and especially from the Irish members who, by their votes in Parliament have rendered signal service to the Indian reform movement.[100]

In the first ten years of the Congress seven men had served as president. Five of them were Indian: Womesh Chandra Bonnerjee in 1885 and 1892, Naoroji himself in 1886 and 1893, Badruddin Tyabji in 1887,

Sir Pherozeshah Mehta in 1890 and Panambakkam Ananda Charlu in 1891. The other two were both Scottish but were long-term residents of India: George Yule was a merchant based in Calcutta and was president in 1888, and William Wedderburn was president in 1889. To date, Webb has been the only Congress president to never have lived in India – in fact, the only time he visited the country was during his presidential tour.[101] For some Congress politicians, this was not acceptable. In his lengthy account of his political life, including his own Congress presidency in 1895, Surendranath Banerjea makes only a brief mention of Webb:

> Mr Webb, an Irish Member of Parliament, presided over the Madras Congress of 1894. I believe that his election as President of the Congress did not meet with the approval of Mr W. C. Bonnerjea. The latter's view was, and it is held by many, that the President of the Indian National Congress should, save in exceptional cases, be an Indian.[102]

Yet inviting an Irishman was, the organisers hoped, another way to bring Indian issues to the attention of the British public. In his 1891 presidential address, Charlu argued that, to further educate the British people about the situation in India, an annual Congress meeting would have to be held in London.[103] This idea was also toyed with in the British Committee meetings, but there was substantial opposition because it would mean that many delegates would be unable to attend.

Perhaps Bonnerjea's idea of 'exceptional' circumstances would have meant the securing of a more high-profile non-Indian. In 1894, Webb was a member of the Indian Parliamentary Committee but not of the British Committee of the Indian National Congress. He spoke little in Parliament, although he had raised an Indian bill in the summer of 1894. That he was the fourth or fifth Irishman considered seems to show that Naoroji was personally determined to have an Irish president, in spite of opposition from some of his Congress colleagues. Whether his invitation prompted jealousy or resentment from other 'friends of India' – such as the dozen other Scottish and Englishmen on the British Committee, or the members of the Parliamentary Committee – is unknown. *India* acknowledged that there was much public speculation about the choice of Webb, and it quoted from the *Pioneer*, which 'abuses Mr Webb, and says that the leaders of the Congress movement in this country are to be pitied in that they have failed to secure a star company of actors this year'.[104] Even private circulars of the Congress organising committee dwelled more on the absence of Hume at the upcoming Congress than the presence of Webb.[105]

However, any fears that an Irish president would taint the Indian movement with radicalism were unfounded. Most commentators were struck by Webb's gentle demeanour. The *Times of India*, hardly a pro-Congress paper, applauded Webb's eloquence and moderation.[106] *India* reported that 'the Anglo-Indian journals with one accord betray painful signs of disappointment and disgust at Mr Webb's abstinence from the language of abuse'.[107] Webb provided no fodder for anti-Congress cannons.

Webb arrived in Bombay after 3 weeks at sea and he was met by Wacha, who served as his 'chaperone' over the duration of the trip and kept Naoroji updated through letters.[108] The main point of Webb's itinerary was to preside at the Congress meetings in Madras 26–29 December, attended by over 1100 delegates from across India, an unusually high number.[109] On his journey to and from Madras Webb also attended receptions, greeted delegations and received and made speeches.

Webb had quickly prepared a presidential speech before he left for India. The speech was one of the highlights of the Congress programme and was expected to last approximately one hour. Wacha was pleased with the address when he read it on Webb's arrival; he found it 'thoughtful and readable', noting with some relief in a letter to Naoroji, 'he has steered clear of Ireland – having deleted the abundant references there were when first drafted and read by you.'[110] Webb's speech did differ slightly from other Congress speeches of the era. Principally, he made the unusual decision to address the crowd directly as 'you' whereas others used 'we' or an impersonal style, perhaps because he was not an Indian himself, but also reflecting his less formal style. The speech was wide-ranging, making short comments on many of the subjects that would be discussed. Webb began by summarising the Congress's history and praising its past presidents. He then addressed his own suitability as president, acknowledging that 'my nationality is the principal ground for my having been selected.'[111] However, he believed that he was particularly qualified because of his upbringing as an abolitionist, and he quoted William Lloyd Garrison and Daniel O'Connell to demonstrate that he believed in universal liberties beyond national borders. He presented his political credentials to the Congress, in a passage that also reveals much about his thoughts on Irish politics and his own identity:

I hate tyranny and oppression wherever practised... I am a member of the Irish Parliamentary Party. I am one of the Indian Parliamentary Committee. I am a Dissenter, proud of the struggles of my Quaker forefathers for freedom of thought and action: a Protestant returned by a Catholic constituency – a Protestant living in a Catholic country, testifying against craven fears of a return to obsolete religious bitterness and intolerance – fears in your country and in mine worked upon to impede the progress of liberty.[112]

The rest of Webb's speech reflected many of his social preoccupations. He argued that the fate of India and 'the entire Empire is concerned in the speedy settlement of the Irish question', repeating his 1883 argument that Irish home rule would allow Parliament to concentrate on imperial affairs. He affirmed that there were benefits to imperial unity, but also that the recognition of Indian nationality was an essential part of imperial unity. He condemned the poverty of India and pointed to racial pay discrimination in the imperial military. He called for reform of the Indian legislative councils to make them more representative, and of the judicial system to make it more fair. Webb also broached three subjects that had a slightly moralistic element: he castigated the 'drink traffic' and called it one of the 'lowest products of Western civilization', he congratulated the Congress on fighting the Cantonment Acts and he urged the Congress to formulate a policy against opium trafficking.[113]

One diplomatic incident passed during the Congress that tested Webb's presence as chair. Webb ruled Miss Henrietta Muller, an English delegate, and Mr R. Venkata Ratnam out of order for trying to move a motion against the nomination of an individual to the Subject Committee, on account of that person having 'a stain on his character'. That person was Eardley Norton, a Madras lawyer and member of the BCINC. Ratnam wrote to Webb after the Congress to protest that he had been unfairly treated, and Webb replied that Ratnam had no right to disrupt the proceedings of the Congress for matters concerning character. Politics, Webb argued, was about compromise, especially in India, 'where a nation is to be built up by agreement for certain great ends amongst peoples of the most divergent forms of thought regarding religions and morals'.[114]

Wacha was pleased with Webb's 'firmness' in keeping the matter under control but Webb admitted in his autobiography that Miss Muller caused him some embarrassment back in London because they belonged to some of the same philanthropic circles: she was a prominent feminist and the sister of Eva Bright McLaren and she had followed Annie Besant in becoming a Theosophist.[115] This may be the reason that Webb's reply to Ratnam was published as a pamphlet: Webb felt the need to publicly state his version of events. These events also seem to have influenced the farewell address he made as he left Madras. Congratulating the Congress and the friends he had made, he remarked on the spirit of the delegation and the sense of unity it expressed. He encouraged them to continue to put aside class differences to work together, and then concluded, 'There is one other request... that I would desire to urge upon you, that you should put from you the demon of personality. Never let the question of personality enter into your proceedings.'[116] Webb knew from personal experience what negative effect personality might have on political progress, and also what intense feelings of friendship and unity politics promised.

After the Congress finished Wacha took Webb on a tour of India, taking in Delhi and the Taj Mahal at Agra and attending receptions at Bombay, Poona, Sholapore, Seconderabad, Adoni, Guntakal and Arkonam.[117] Webb was delighted but slightly overwhelmed by the music, fireworks, garlands and photographers that appeared wherever he went, explaining to one crowd that 'I am a quiet man, accustomed to lead a quiet life doing in a quiet way my duty to my fellow-citizens and to myself.'[118] Delegations met Webb along his route when his train stopped at stations, and sometimes he recalled 'we were roused up in the night and I in my pyjamas had to receive addresses and listen to bands of music.'[119] The delegations presented him with testimonials that showed the esteem with which they viewed Webb: many were on parchment with gold script and decoration, or enclosed in ornate silver cases. These thanked him for his visit, explained to him grievances in the locality and urged him to use his knowledge to lobby for Indian reform as an MP. 'We trust that the testimony of our condition thus obtained at first hand will enable you to speak with some degree of knowledge from your place in Parliament,' the residents of the Koloba district in Maharashtra wrote.[120] The testimonials came in flowery and eloquent language, and some revealed an English education that was technically correct but had other ironic connotations. Chiefly, one wrote to Webb that 'We are confident that your catholic and wide-reaching sympathies will be with us too.'[121]

Webb departed from Bombay in January. His final message to his audience was one of solidarity with Indians who were being mistreated in South Africa, and he declared the equality of all men and what he believed was the contractual nature of the Empire: 'If the Empire cannot for you enforce parity of treatment in any one of its Colonies, the sooner the better it turns that Colony off on its own account.'[122] Webb's speeches and overall demeanour as president were almost unanimously praised in the press. Wacha thought his speech had been 'universally approved' and admired for its 'native simplicity and deference'.[123] The speech was partially reprinted in the *Manchester Guardian* and the BCINC decided to print several hundred copies for distribution to MPs, the British press, and Liberal associations and clubs.[124] Webb's presidency had been an overall success: for him personally, for Naoroji, who had worked for two decades to forge Irish–Indian connections, for the Congress, which had a respectable patron, and for the Irish Party, which proved that it had more than domestic politics in its sights. Overall, Webb's presidency was the triumph of cosmopolitan nationalism in the imperial capital.

8
'Politics is a difficult and anxious game'[1]: An Assessment of Webb

Webb returned from India optimistic about what Irish and Indian nationalists could achieve together in Parliament, but his optimism was short-lived. His disputes with Healy led to a loss of confidence and his resignation from Parliament, and over the subsequent years his belief in the ability of Parliament to justly rule the Empire waned as a new theatre of conflict opened in South Africa. Webb remained in contact with his Indian friends, and he remained as vocal as ever in promoting a responsible position in international affairs, but he also sensed that Ireland was changing. The period 1895–1908 was one in which many different models were being argued for the future of Ireland; some of these groups professed to be apolitical but, as Webb pointed out, in disavowing politics they were making a political statement themselves.[2] F. S. L. Lyons has described W. B. Yeats at the turn of the twentieth century as 'desperately trying to hold a middle position between the anonymity of cosmopolitanism and the parochialism of Irish Ireland'.[3] Webb was in a different quandary: he was trying to remain an Irish cosmopolitan, not for the sake of compromise but because he embraced both Irishness and internationalism. New cultural movements presented new challenges to Webb in this era, as he continued to balance Indian lobbying, treasury duties for the Irish Party and his social and international conscience.

Webb in political life, 1895–1908

Webb returned from India in February 1895, suffering from malaria and barely able to attend the luncheon held in his honour at the National Liberal Club. This was attended by over 50 of his fellow MPs and members of the Indian Parliamentary Committee, including Naoroji, Wedderburn, Justin McCarthy, John Dillon, Swift MacNeill and some others who were not MPs, including Allan Octavian Hume.[4] Even J. F. X. O'Brien attended in support of his close friend, in spite of his deep aversion to the National Liberal Club and any event that was associated with English power.[5]

Webb also returned to an Irish Party that was deeply divided over the actions of T. M. Healy and some of his colleagues. Webb became convinced that if Healy was permitted to flout Party decisions and publicly criticise colleagues, then 'the Party Pledge has become a mockery'.[6] In August 1895, just a few weeks after he was re-elected unopposed for West Waterford, Webb resigned his seat. Reactions within the Irish Party were mixed. Some colleagues were probably unimpressed by Webb's threats of resignation, and even Healy himself was sceptical about Webb's determination to resign, and believed 'he will be got to continue' (though Healy was prepared for Webb's resignation and already scheming about the candidates he would like to see replace Webb).[7] Webb wrote to J. F. X. that 'I much regret that you and others I love and respect should not approve of the step I have taken,' but he was convinced that his decision was correct.[8] Webb was not the only one to resign over party discipline – John Morrogh had resigned in 1893 for the same reason.[9] However, Webb's decision to resign in protest at the party's failure to censure Healy was yet another resignation in his political career. Webb had become convinced that he was unsuited to Parliament, feeling the role of MP did not best employ his skills. As early as August 1894, he had drafted a letter to McCarthy explaining that he did not intend to stand for election again. Perhaps in one of his more negative moods, when he felt frustrated by the lack of progress towards home rule, he wrote:

> I do feel that in a permanent home of my own in Dublin, and with ample leisure, I would be more likely to be of service to the cause than here. At home I certainly exercise some influence, by letters and intercourse I then have much more to do with eminent people. Here I am measured and considered solely by parliamentary standards. I am, as you are aware, no speaker; thoughts and feelings seethe through and possess me, but I never can be sufficiently at my ease in the House to give them utterance. You may imagine how I suffer through this incapacity. ... To be socially pleasant all round in the House is beneficial, but I feel too hot and indignant to sustain that attitude. ... Somehow it feels to me easier in Ireland, to bear the process by which Ireland is being ruined, than here in Parliament to watch the machinery by which that ruin is being accomplished.[10]

Webb did stand for re-election, his confidence and optimism perhaps bolstered by his experience at Madras, but the Healy feud was the final straw that pushed him to resign. He complained that Healy's 'vile slanders' and bullying 'place me on my bed under the doctor's care at a time when I should be fighting the elections'.[11] If his colleagues would not vote to condemn Healy's actions and remove him from the Party, Webb concluded that he had no option but to resign.

After his resignation Webb and Lizzie departed on an extended holiday, returning to Australia where he had lived in the 1850s and visiting friends across the United States. Webb's letters to J. F. X. became more frequent and sentimental as he prepared to take his trip, the preparation for his departure on such a massive voyage perhaps enhancing the feelings of upheaval as he left Parliament behind. Webb even allowed himself to pen a bit of poetry, to mark the momentous occasion of his final duties as treasurer of the Parliamentary fund, in a letter to O'Brien:

> My boat is on the shore,
> And my barque is in the bay,
> But e'er I go, dear friend,
> I sign my last cheque here today.[12]

As disappointed as J. F. X. might have been, the individuals who were the most affected by Webb's resignation were not his Irish colleagues, but the Indian nationalists to whom he had pledged his leadership and support just 8 months previously.

Irish–Indian relations after 1894

The Congress had made a major investment in Webb and had hoped to reap benefits in Parliament. Webb wrote to Naoroji immediately after his resignation and explained that 'losing opportunities of helping or at least showing sympathy with India is the bitterest pill I have to swallow in leaving Parliament'.[13] The response to Webb's resignation in *India* expressed muted disappointment:

> Supporters of the Indian National Congress will have heard with profound regret of the intended resignation of Mr Alfred Webb MP... It may not yet, we hope, be too late for Mr Webb to reconsider his decision. Even if he should not, we may congratulate ourselves upon the fact that, while India will be deprived of his good office in the House

of Commons, he will still remain President of the Indian National Congress and a member of the British Committee.[14]

The paper also quoted an extract from Webb's letter of resignation, arguing that the Irish Party was failing to control 'baseless attacks upon the character and patriotism of Mr Blake and other members of the [Irish Party] Committee'.[15] Given Blake's good reputation with readers of *India*, this comment may have made Webb's actions more excusable.

The British Committee of the Indian National Congress (BCINC) had other reason to be concerned, because in the same election that Webb was returned unopposed for the third time, Naoroji lost his seat. Proving that Naoroji had been serious about the possibility of running for an Irish parliamentary in the 1870s and 1880s, he now wrote to Davitt, in 1896, to inquire whether it might be possible. On National Liberal Club stationery, he explained to Davitt that he had lost his seat, and 'unfortunately a reactionary Indian is in the House'.[16] He asked Davitt, 'on behalf of India', to 'help me obtain an Irish seat'. Davitt wrote his reaction, coming at a time when the Irish Party was in shambles, in the top margin of Naoroji's letter: 'No hope.'[17] Significantly, in spite of three previous failed attempts, Webb's resignation from Parliament and the splintering of the Liberal–Irish alliance, Naoroji was still interested in representing India from an Irish seat, and this demonstrates the sincerity of the previous negotiations regarding Irish seats (and also, possibly, the desperation Naoroji felt in 1896).

Naoroji's interest in Irish affairs remained deep and sincere after Webb's resignation from Parliament, and the two remained friends. That Naoroji was probably always the driving personality in relations between Irish and Indian nationalists in the 1880s and 1890s is credited by a lead article in the *Freeman's Journal* in May 1897.[18] Covering a speech made by Naoroji in Edinburgh, and referring with obvious irony and distaste to Salisbury's 'black man' comment, the newspaper detailed the troubles of Indians and the cruel famine afflicting the country. Explaining that 'what happened in Ireland in the forties is happening in India today', the paper condemned the government for failing to prevent the famine and paraphrased Naoroji's argument for drain theory (the idea that resources and wealth were being 'drained' out of India). Furthermore, it referred to Webb, 'whose devotion to the interests of the subject peoples of India was fittingly recognised by election to the presidency of the Indian National Congress'. It drew attention to Webb's condemnation of the leniency of the Indian magistrates' sentences for English men convicted of assaulting Indian women.[19] Two conclusions can be drawn from this article. First, Naoroji was interacting with Irish issues after it had ceased to be obviously politically expedient for him to do so. Second, neither he nor Webb was portrayed in the main Irish nationalist newspaper as in any way eccentric or unusual for their fusing of Indian and Irish nationalist politics.

Naoroji never returned to Parliament, although he tried again in London, standing as a radical candidate in North Lambeth in 1902. Naoroji consulted Webb as to whether he should make Irish issues part of his election platform.[20] Webb sent him a message of support, remarking that he personally had no desire to return to Parliament, although 'I think I may say that I might be back at Westminster any time I desired.' It seemed cruel to Webb that things should be so difficult for Naoroji: 'I long for you to be again in – and I wish it were as easy for you as it might be for me – and you have the powers and qualities for effective influence there, which I have not.'[21] Naoroji's qualities were also recognised by younger, radical Irish nationalists in the early 1900s. Eleven of them signed a message of support for the Congress (of which Naoroji was to be president) in 1906 in the socialist journal *New International Review*, arguing that 'when Indians have effective control of their own country, we believe that many of the serious economic and social problems of India will be solved.'[22]

Webb continued to receive letters of support and congratulations long after his own Congress presidency and he remained in communication with Congress leaders. He wrote letters of support to Congress committees and to *India*, expressing his views on political developments and referring to the Congress organisers as his 'brethren'.[23] He also wrote articles for British and Irish newspapers about Indian affairs and urged his readers to turn to *India* and the Congress as the most reliable sources of information on the situation in India. He sought information from Naoroji and Ripon to allow him to draft his speeches and articles on India.[24] His Indian colleagues were appreciative. An Indian newspaper reported in 1897 that Webb was addressing meetings in Dublin on Indian subjects, and 'that dear old Irishman, who presided at our latter Madras Congress, and who gained our love, has not forgotten us'.[25] An article of Webb's in the *British Friend* in May 1898 also was positively 'reviewed' in several Indian newspapers, and applauded as a sign that Webb was still actively lobbying for Indian reform.[26]

Webb also lobbied Irish Party MPs to lend their support to Indian causes and events. Writing to Timothy Harrington in 1897, he argued: 'As a matter of duty, and policy, it is most desirable to help our Indian friends. They are really very good fellows, and are much more helpless than ever we Irish were (since the Penal days) in the face of official tyranny.'[27] He invited colleagues to meet Indian nationalists Dinshaw Wacha and G. K. Gokhale when, visiting Britain to testify at the Welby Commission, they took the opportunity to do a lecture tour of the United Kingdom. Webb arranged the Irish talk, held at the Friends Institute in Dublin. His invitation to the event stated that the event would be 'entirely unconnected with any political or religious organization', and that it would be of considerable contemporary significance:

> Few men are better qualified to give information regarding Indian affairs [than Wacha and Gokhale]. ... In view of the acknowledged increasing importance of Indian questions, and of the famine at present prevailing, it is to be hoped that many thoughtful persons will avail themselves of this opportunity of at first hand enlightening themselves concerning a country with whose fortunes ours are interwoven.[28]

Webb also communicated privately with Dillon that Gokhale and Wacha were hoping to have the opportunity to meet him, and that 'both on account of our national movement, and of their movement for greater political consideration, I think it would be desirable you should meet'.[29] They were, Webb explained, keen followers of Irish affairs, and 'Professor Gokhale indeed has a more accurate knowledge of Irish history and Irish politics than, perhaps, some men in the [Irish] Party.'[30]

Webb's contact with Indian nationalists had a social and personal element. He referred to Gokhale and Wacha to be 'my best Indian friends',[31] and he signed letters to Naoroji with an unusually personal and informal closing, 'your old friend'.[32] Gokhale invited Webb and Lizzie to his daughter's wedding in India, although they were unable to attend.[33] Webb and Lizzie also socialised with Naoroji's daughter Manekbhai, one of the earliest Asian women to qualify as a doctor in the United Kingdom. She studied at Edinburgh and moved to Dublin around 1896. Little is known about her, but she was probably supported by the Lady Dufferin Fund. This was established by the Irish-born vicereine of India to train female doctors, in order to treat female patients in India who could not be examined by male doctors for religious and cultural reasons.[34] Webb and Lizzie invited Manekbhai to their home for Sunday lunches and offered to set up an introduction for her at the Women's Hospital in Dublin, where Webb's cousin worked.[35]

Losing faith in the Imperial Parliament

Webb's imperial optimism and his excitement about Congress's potential were somewhat short-lived. Although he did not lose confidence in his Indian friends, he did become disillusioned with the political process through which they hoped to make reforms. The outbreak of the Boer War (1899–1902) infuriated Webb and caused him to lose confidence in that institution which had promised so much opportunity for both Irish and Indian nationalists: Parliament. Webb's total disgust with the Boer War hardened his attitudes towards Britain, changed the conciliatory language he usually used and caused him to throw away some of the suggestions for imperial unity he had made in the previous decades. In 1866 Webb had argued in favour of special Irish regiments in the army, with distinctive uniforms;[36] in 1894 he had written that it was entirely possible to build 'a union of hearts' between Britain and Ireland.[37] Five years later, he had completely changed his mind and was now arguing that Ireland was sullied by such regiments in the Boer War:

> And let me protest against the disgrace being put upon our National Emblem, the Shamrock, in being about to be for the future (if only in the Army, where I cannot understand how any thoughtful Irishman can find himself) – associated in remembrance with one of the most iniquitous wars ever waged by a Pagan or reputably Christian nation.[38]

Michael Davitt was similarly disgusted. 'I am told that fully 3,000 Reservists have left Dublin during the past ten days for service in the British Army!,' he wrote to Webb.[39] He believed that this was a symptom of social problems and it boded badly for the home rulers: 'Drink, *dirty* homes, anti-National education, animal indulgences and other debasing agencies are to blame for this abominable humiliation. Above all there is a want of a *real* National spirit in Ireland at the present time which fills me with foreboding.'[40]

Davitt and Webb ploughed their shared anger about the Boer War into organising anti-war events in Dublin. They raised a subscription in the *Freeman's Journal* on behalf of the Boer War Ambulance Fund, based in Holland, and for the 'Transvaal Sick and Wounded'.[41] The usual suspects – Dublin Quakers like the Harveys and Deborah Webb – contributed. Webb and Davitt also wrote an address to Paul Kruger, president of the [Boer] South African Republic, assuring him that 81 out of the 102 Irish MPs had voted against the government in the decision to go to war. They wrote in the address that their 'hearts bleed' for the Boers 'under the oppressor's heel'.[42]

Webb's acceptance of the idea of benevolent imperialism – his belief that imperialism might bring something positive to colonised people – was completely lost when the Boer War broke out in 1899. He believed the war was entirely unprovoked, and merely an act of aggression, which he compared to Hasting's conquest of India.[43] He also complained of injustice within British South Africa, referring to testimonies given at the 1896 Indian National Congress of discrimination against Indians working in South Africa and repeating the sentiments he had expressed in his own 1894 presidential address. If Britain required its Indian subjects to carry identification cards in South Africa, Webb argued, it ultimately was a hypocritical government which was unable to protect its own subjects.[44] Webb also became convinced that Britain was not sincere in allowing Irish participation in democratic debate. He wrote a furious letter to the *Freeman's Journal*, asserting the right of Irish politicians to support the Boers publicly:

> Of all the ludicrously impudent, self-sufficient, pretentious, preposterous, priggish, conceited exhibitions of feeling we have ever had from the other side of the Channel... the horror being expressed at some of our members cheering the news of the late Boer victory exceeds... The other side have all the power in their hands; the Removable magistrates, the jury-packing, the expensive bribery, the concentration camps. ... The least they might do would be to leave us the free expression of our feelings. But no![45]

Neither Webb nor Davitt appears to have associated with the more radical Irish Transvaal Committee led by young nationalists like Maude Gonne and Willie Redmond. This group used a language that probably would have horrified Webb ('Remember Ninety-Eight. Remember the Penal Laws. Remember the Famine', one poster urged), and he is not listed as a subscriber to their funds.[46] Webb was furious at the turn he felt British politics had taken, but he was still a constitutional home ruler.

Looking around the world, Webb saw the dark side of imperialism manifested. Echoing his 1856 Statistical Society talk, he spoke of imperialism as a mask for economic aggression:

> There is something almost sickening in this "imperial" talk of assuming and bearing burdens for the good of others. ... Wherever empire

(I speak of the United Kingdom) is extended, and the climate suits the white man, the aborigines are, for the benefit of the white man, cleared off or held in degradation for his benefit.[47]

Furthermore, he believed these ideas were spreading beyond the United Kingdom. The Spanish–American War seemed to Webb to be a sad proof that 'the US has commenced to follow the example of European countries' in imperialistic wars.[48] He was angered by the American occupation of the Philippines,[49] although his take on the Spanish–American War was slightly silly:

> Protestant and lover of the US as I am, I cannot but feel for Spain, and cannot but remember her sympathy with us 300 years ago. (Although she would have burned me were I living then. But if living then I suppose I would have been a good Catholic, as George Fox was not born until later).[50]

Lover of the US that he was, his interest in the plight of African-Americans did not wane after the abolition of slavery. Despite R. D.'s dislike for Frederick Douglass, Webb and he remained in contact and Douglass visited Webb in Dublin 'to renew old memories of the '40s' sometime around 1890.[51] Reviewing Booker T. Washington's autobiography in 1901, he described the current state of affairs in the United States as 'terrorism' against former slaves.[52] In 1906 he wrote that 'slavery has been abolished... But we now have the lynchings, unhuman torturings, and colour prejudice.'[53] Webb's conviction that British democracy had become a sham was strengthened in 1904, when Tibet was invaded. Webb was appalled by what he saw as the 'wickedness' of the invasion, and the fact that 'the unfortunate Tibetans asked only to be let alone.'[54]

Over 10 years, Webb's idealistic internationalism had thus reached a dramatic high in London and Madras, and then come crashing down in South Africa.

Webb and the Irish Party post-1895

Just as Webb did not abandon his international causes, he never strayed far from the Irish Party. Although he and Lizzie had a long and eventful round-the-world trip, Webb could not put politics out of his mind. While in Australia he visited sites associated with John Mitchel's imprisonment in the 1840s (his anecdotes supplying lectures when he returned to Ireland).[55] His trip also overlapped with Davitt's Australian tour, and the two addressed some of the same audiences in Tasmania.[56]

It is not completely clear what Webb did on his return to Ireland. He admitted to Dillon that he was looking forward to being 'amongst my books again', since 'I feel too old and worn out to be good for much.'[57] However, by 1897 he was corresponding with J. F. X. O'Brien about financial matters again, and complaining that there was a need to 'place affairs on a business basis' in Dublin following the resignation of a poor office manager.[58] In 1898 he was not listed as one of the Parliamentary Fund treasurers on the stationery. However, he was one of nine honourary treasurers of the Evicted Tenants Fund, and apparently one of the more active ones.[59] The extent to which Webb moved around between different treasury roles in his career probably indicates that his skills were highly in demand, though his personality was not considered essential to give prestige to any one position.

The respect with which Webb was held as a treasurer, and probably his reputation as a neutral and inoffensive individual, was demonstrated in July 1900. Webb was approached by John Redmond, leader of the newly reunified Irish Party, to become joint Treasurer of the Central Directory (in other words, one of the most important financial positions in the Party). Webb responded that he was not suited to the job; that he had resigned twice from positions as treasurer and he considered himself likely to do it again. The reason was that he had been brought up 'with very severe ideas regarding money affairs, and cannot divest myself of these ideas in public affairs – ideas of the duty of not spending what one has not got. And in politics – especially election times – all such notions would often be thrown to the wind'. The loose management of funds had created 'anguish' for Webb in the past because he has felt 'morally responsible for all obligations incurred'.[60] He then offered his services in a more minor role: for example, as secretary of the Election Fund. Redmond consented.[61]

Webb ended up, by 1902, controlling the bank accounts for the Parliamentary Fund, the New Defence Fund and the United Irish League, and he sometimes relied on J. F. X. to help him when he confused the funds.[62] However, he relished his job, and reflected that 'the fact of having now again an opportunity of working for the cause makes me much healthier and happier than I was up to eighteen months ago.'[63] In 1902 Webb was 68 years old and showed no intention of retiring.

The late 1890s presented many challenges to which Webb had to react. His joy at being able to work for the national cause was, as always, tempered by his tendency towards pessimism and despair. In 1896 a

Irish Race Convention was held in Dublin to try to unify the warring factions in Irish nationalism; Webb drafted the ten resolutions which included the expected call for home rule, and also demands for land and taxation reform, the franchise for labourers, a Catholic university and the promotion of 'our ancient Irish tongue by the children of the Gael'.[64] The Convention was not successful in its aims; partly because the main offenders, Redmond and Healy, did not attend. Healy dismissed Webb's resolutions as 'not very startling'.[65]

The failure of attempts at unity, combined with his feeling that the country was apathetic, caused Webb moments of despair. He was convinced that 'The [Parnell] Split (necessary as it was on our consciences) has left deadly germs that will long rest in the soul of Irish thought.'[66] He was 'jealous' of the public attention that was given to non-political issues, such as the fate of the Giant's Causeway.[67] He was angry at the effort that had been put into the centennial celebrations of 1798 and explained to J. F. X. that he was not helping to organise the celebrations, because he believed that the time and money devoted to them was at the expense of helping evicted tenants. Using unusually militaristic language, he explained that 'we went to war for home rule', and 'we should not be letting the campaign starve and rushing home to hurrah for and erect memorials to those who fell in previous conflicts.'[68] Webb's deep frustration with what he perceived as the country's neglect for the nationalist cause made him pine for 'old Fenian days when the country was shook [sic] to its foundations with great hopes'.[69] In this vein, he wrote to the *Freeman's Journal* in 1899 that he no longer considered unity to be essential; rather, that the country needed to be lifted out of its 'political torpor' by the majority in the home rule movement (i.e. the non-Healyite anti-Parnellites) and that it should 'pull itself together and assert itself'.[70] Webb's tone is not the utopian or idealistic one he used decades earlier; it is the tone of a man who had grown impatient. He perhaps was responding to the energy surrounding William O'Brien's United Irish League, although there is a lack of sources to know if Webb agreed with O'Brien's land policies; Webb was probably more intent on securing a stable reconciliation within the Irish Party.

In his pessimism, Webb had even begun to doubt the motives of the Catholic clergy in Ireland, whom he had never criticised publicly (although he had referred to clerical influence in his 1886 letter to C. H. Oldham). He cynically suggested: 'Having reached an assured position largely through popular national support, they now appear satisfied and I believe in their heart of hearts do not want home rule. ... I greatly fear many are jealous of the money we are receiving.'[71] Webb's conclusion was perhaps made in anger; as a treasurer, he would have known that (at least from sources available from the late 1890s) Catholic clergy raised and contributed substantial funds for the Party.[72]

Another challenge for Webb, and the Party, came from the Gaelic revival movement. One of the hobbies which Webb took up after his retirement from Parliament was the study of the Irish language, under the auspices of the Gaelic League (Conradh na Gaeilge), which was formed in 1893 with the goal of promoting Irish as a living, spoken and written language. Webb joined the League, probably in 1895, and began taking classes for beginners. His attitude towards the language was summed up in an article he wrote to the *Freeman's Journal* in 1900:

> I have been a member of the [Gaelic] League for some years, and, although too old to be able ever to attain but a very elementary knowledge of the language, find in its study...one of the greatest pleasures of my leisure. As attaching young people to the land of their birth, as developing Irish genius, as a broadener and strengthener of the mind, as a preparation for the study of other languages, I would gladly see it find its place in every school in Ireland.[73]

However, Webb was extremely uncomfortable with the politicisation of the Gaelic League, as well as its condemnation of English literature and criticism of the Irish Parliamentary Party. These developments, he felt, showed a lack of respect for the 'old nationalism' – reaching back to O'Connell and including the home rule movement – that sought change through British institutions, namely parliament. He warned that Irish people must not lose sight of the goal of an independent Irish government, and that the example of Wales had demonstrated how too much focus on the language could hold back the home rule movement. Ultimately, he argued, 'if we all spoke Irish tomorrow we should not necessarily be nearer that goal [of home rule].'[74]

The growing friction came to a head in September 1901, when *An Claidheamh Soluis*, the journal of the Gaelic League, explicitly attacked the Irish Party. Webb vented his anger and frustration through his usual public outlet, the *Freeman's Journal*. In particular, he resented the suggestion, which he felt the League had offered, that parliamentary government was a distinctly 'English' idea. He was also genuinely hurt by the attack, since the Irish Party was the only political party to support the League,[75] and because he was an active supporter himself and personally acquainted with the League's leadership. Webb knew Eoin Mac Neill through taking classes at the Central Branch of the Gaelic League and Mac Neill had approached Webb for advice about setting up Cló Chumann, a printing business to print *An Claidheamh Soluis* and other Irish-language texts. Webb warned Mac Neill against proceeding, telling him the business would certainly lose money.[76]

Webb's sentiments were echoed by other members of the United Irish League. His colleague David Sheehy was particularly in favour of taking a hard line against the Gaelic League, believing that it was trying to destablilise the Irish Party. He also voiced frustration at what he saw as the hypocrisy of the Gaelic League: 'All I say to their demands for Irish speeches on platforms in Irish speaking districts, is that they ought to begin first themselves.'[77]

Webb's misgivings about the Gaelic League ran deep. Writing to J. F. X. to inquire about a rumour that he had been heckled at a Gaelic League meeting, Webb shared his suspicions: 'That League is I fear playing a double game – outwardly seeking our assistance, really against us. I mean to give up my membership in it.'[78] Webb also became convinced that his old nemesis was responsible, and that the League 'is being largely worked in Healyite interest'.[79] However, the situation was being diffused: 'Douglas Hyde has promised Redmond that if we privately do our best to encourage Irish speaking at meetings in Irish districts, he will see that there is no more abuse of us.'[80] In case of ongoing conflict, Webb was considered the right man to forge conciliation with Gaelic League. T. Sexton considered that the Party 'can rely upon Webb to do whatever is most conciliatory and kind'.[81]

The problems between the Party and the Gaelic League represent more than a brief episode in politics; they are symptomatic of larger debates about Irishness in the late-nineteenth and early-twentieth centuries, and the relationship between Englishness and Irishness. Through his interest in international affairs, and friendliness with individuals of different national allegiances, Webb represented one type of Irish nationalism. Although he supported Irish industries and learned Irish, Webb did not fit in with 'Irish Ireland'.[82] He was also bemused by new cultural events in Ireland. He attended an Irish Literary Theatre performance of two of Yeats's plays in 1904, but remarked to Dillon that he found them to be 'extraordinarily dreamy mythic affairs', one of which 'none of us could make any sense of'.[83] He was impressed by the wide turnout of people, 'the Yates [sic] and Gaelic League factions, Judge Madden and his family, Maude Gonne McBride [sic] a great figure, Mr and Mrs Coffy, Stephen Gwynn (that is an admirable Childrens Tales from Irish History his wife has just written), Mr Gill'.[84] Webb was aware of all these individuals, and may have known Yeats for a long time (if they had met in one of the Dublin societies they both frequented). However, he was in awe neither of them nor of their art. Webb was certainly concerned about public apathy towards Irish political questions, but he did not believe, as Yeats did, that Irish public life was losing energy and could be reinvigorated through a literary movement; on the contrary, he believed that certain cultural nationalists were deliberatively trying to divert energy from the political movement.[85] Webb also believed that apathy was not simply an Irish problem, and that other cultural innovations had a role: 'I am beginning to fear that the general political lethargy all over the world is due to people being so much engaged with the new power of cycling.'[86]

Webb engaged directly with the Gaelic League and articulated his philosophical differences from Irish Ireland in a piece titled 'The Gaelic League and politics' in *Dana: an Irish magazine of independent thought* in September 1904. *Dana* was edited by Frederick Ryan and John Eglinton and, for its short life from May 1904 until April 1905, published social, cultural and literary articles. The tone was respectful but controversial, and contributors included Æ, Stephen Gwynn, and Oliver Gogarty. *Dana* is best known for publishing James Joyce's first poem, 'Song'.

Webb's article was not a critique of the Gaelic League; it was the defence of political strategy, and a critique of a certain 'section' of the League. Webb explained that he had long been a member of the League, and was an enthusiast for the Irish language and 'everything Irish that is good, and true, and useful, and beautiful'. He also recognised that many people felt alienated from politics through the unfortunate divisions within the Irish Party (which, he argued, would have happened 'amongst leaders of other peoples similarly circumstanced').[87] However, Webb was adamant that politics is 'one of the first duties of man', and that 'in few countries is attention to politics more necessary than in Ireland'. This was for both domestic and international reasons: he made his familiar argument, that Irish people had a historical experience that made them particularly understanding of colonisation and better qualified to argue on behalf of colonised people.[88]

Webb was convinced that 'it is impossible that a language movement, an art movement, or a manufacture movement can ever take the place of a political movement.' He blamed certain 'sections' of the Gaelic League who 'sought to draw an amount of energy from politics, and to produce in the younger generation a feeling that politics do not matter – a fatal error, since it is just upon such apathy that the cause of reaction in every country flourishes'.[89] He reached two conclusions in his 1908 *Thoughts in retirement*, a collection of political maxims: first, that 'In states where vital questions are unsettled, "non-political" associations are dead weight against change,' and 'Those who "do not take any part in politics" are generally at heart ardent Conservatives.'[90]

Webb argued in *Dana* that political apathy was numbing Irish people's minds to the real grievances of 'British interference' in Ireland. Poor political rule was the cause of Irish distress, but he believed that people had become distracted by the ideological red herrings of Irish modernity, culture and language. Although some members of Irish Ireland were in favour of industrial modernisation, in their bid to de-Anglicise Ireland they also advocated ridding Ireland of 'British' cultural imports and resurrecting dying aspects of Irish culture to replace them, in particular the Irish language.[91] Webb worried that this was tantamount to arguing that Ireland would have to return to a pre-modern, pre-British state to rediscover its cultural identity. He rejected the idea that modernity was not Irish; he argued that Irish people had contributed much to the modern world, and that when Ireland had been fully Irish-speaking it was not a free democratic state. Webb believed that ignorance of political questions was thus a misguided form of escapism. He asked his readers: 'Is it not best to look hopefully forward, garnering the experiences of the ages and of all peoples, rather than seek to live in and by the far past of our own country alone?'[92] It is tempting to see the newer cultural movements of the late 1890s – both Yeats's and Moran's brands of cultural nationalism – as counterpoints to an Irish Party that was tired and stale. Except Webb was not a home ruler in 1905 because he had run out of ideas, or because he was clinging to the past; he was actually articulating an unusual vision of a modern Ireland that embraced multiculturalism, international responsibility, as well as Irish language.

Douglas Hyde tried to console Webb that the Gaelic League was doing steady work for Ireland, so that 'I think whether Ireland gets home rule or not, we are training up a good effective class of men in the Gaelic League, who will make the most of whatever happens.'[93] But Webb had not given up on home rule, neither in 1895 nor in 1908. He was certainly frustrated – he complained to Dillon that it was particularly difficult for him to see Protestant apathy towards nationalism, when 35 years earlier he had hoped that Disestablishment would turn Protestants into home rulers.[94] Depressive as he was, and in spite of his fears of public apathy, Webb was so passionate about home rule that he could not entirely give up:

> It must be comparatively easy for Catholics to keep up *springing* hope regarding the cause. I keep up hope, for without it I would not care to live, and in that hope whether it reaches its position or not in my

time, I shall die. ... It subsists in a few of us of the elder generation – I do not see the sign of the throb of it in the younger.[95]

Webb never truly retired but became decreasingly active in public life after 1905. In 1907 Lizzie died after a brief illness; many of Webb's political colleagues sent condolences. Webb was devastated, but as she had also been a committed nationalist, he believed 'the best tribute I can pay to my wife's memory is to try and continue the work in which so much of her heart lay'.[96]

On 31 July 1908, Webb died while on a holiday in Scotland.

An assessment of Webb

Webb's reputation as a gentle Quaker, both in some contemporary and most modern accounts, is challenged by his resilience. He retained his principles and passions in 50 years of public life. Close examination of his public speeches and writings has also demonstrated that Webb understood completely the political issues in which he was embroiled, and therefore his controversial statements were not peculiar utterances of a man who was out of touch, but courageous statements of deep personal conviction. A weak person simply would not have lasted through the turbulence of the home rule movement in this era. The greatest challenge Webb faced in his political career seems to have been his own tendency towards depression, which sometimes skewed his perspective on events and consumed his self-confidence.

Webb's tendency to resign from nearly every movement he ever joined may be a legacy of his Quaker upbringing, with its emphasis on avoiding conflict; but Webb also had faith in his abilities to ease tensions and reconcile warring factions within his own party. He also crossed barriers in life that some of his colleagues would have found insurmountable: barriers of class, nationality, race and religion. A twenty-first-century view might be that Webb was a stressed workaholic, prone to depression, who sought personal affirmation through his public life and became easily dejected when others failed to appreciate his hard work. Another explanation is simply that he was a sensitive person of elevated moral standards, who committed himself completely when he gave his support to any cause, and who resigned whenever he could not give his full moral backing.

Webb also seems to have been very sure of the role he was meant to occupy in politics. He often emphasised how hard he worked and, more specifically, how he worked harder than his colleagues, such as when he described himself as 'in truth one of the most earnest and active members' of the home rule movement.[97] Webb volunteered to do many tedious tasks that received little public acknowledgement, such as being treasurer, editing proceedings of conferences and running events behind the scenes. He does not seem to have sought public attention for himself but nor was he modest in explaining what his own role had been.

Webb raises questions for historians about authenticity and representativeness. Webb certainly was 'a minority several times over',[98] an unusual person whose life brought together many disparate groups, ideas and movements. This does not give cause to disregard his experience. Any individual who has risen to prominence in public or political life is, by definition, exceptional and therefore unrepresentative of 'ordinary' people and society. Webb's experience of international engagement certainly cannot be read as typical of nineteenth-century Ireland, but it was authentic and it reveals the diversity of thought and practice that nineteenth-century Ireland sustained. His local engagement also reveals diversity and progressive thought within Ireland. Without even considering the impact of nationalism, Webb is the window through which we can view a society that produced a wide range of original thinkers and activists. Webb's experiences reveal literary and reading groups, a wealth of charitable organisations, people who were debating openly about birth control and prostitution, large crowds gathering to listen to the experiences of an African-American former slave, famine relief funds, and intellectuals who believed that Ireland's problems could be solved through economic and 'statistical' enquiry.

Webb was an unusual home ruler. He was Protestant; he had an international outlook and a profound interest in foreign affairs; he publicly displayed great sensitivity and deep emotional attachment to other individuals in politics; and he was a liberal with no trace of Anglophobia. However, labelling Webb as unusual is taking a great assumption about the character of the Irish Party in this era. Indeed, it is an overstatement of the discipline that Charles Stewart Parnell imposed upon the Party. The Irish Party was not homogenous; no political party is. From the establishment of the Home Government Association in 1870, the idea of home rule was based on an attempt to unite all individuals who supported a domestic parliament for Ireland. It tried to unite both liberals and conservatives on a national platform, and although the disappearance of Conservatives from the infant Home Government Association has been emphasised,[99] this should not lead to the conclusion that the Home Rule League was a liberal organisation. The traditional Irish nationalist leaning towards the Liberal Party was based on a belief that

that party was friendliest towards the Irish cause. The home rule MP Jeremiah Jordan explained this in an 1889 newspaper interview, when he argued that if Ireland achieved its parliament in Dublin the Irish Party would naturally split along liberal–conservative lines: 'Mr Parnell might lead the more Conservative section of an Irish Parliament and Mr Davitt the more democratic. We should have some men more extreme than Mr Davitt.'[100]

Webb is representative of a subculture within Irish politics in this time: one that was cosmopolitan, outward-looking and liberal. However, to explain the existence of a subculture within the Party does not indicate that there was automatically friction or coldness between party members. A study of the correspondence of this era demonstrates that nationalism created a frame upon which deep personal friendships were constructed within the Irish Party, sometimes among those of differing views (the best example being that of Webb and J. F. X. O'Brien). Furthermore, an institutional perspective yields information about organisational hurdles, the dedication of both groups and individuals, who really did the work, and what kind of effort was put into the movement. In this case, through examining Webb's experience as treasurer of several institutions and organisations of Irish nationalism, it becomes clear that one of the major factors in determining the strategy of the movement was money. Virtually all nationalist organisations in the period 1860–1910 were strapped for cash. Funding affected staffing, publicity, which seats were contested, who became a member and the ability of MPs to work both in Parliament and in Ireland. As treasurer of the Home Rule League, the Irish Parliamentary Party, the National League and the Evicted Tenants Fund, Webb experienced these frustrations on a daily basis. There are countless letters between nationalists regretting that they are unable to do what they want to do, or what they felt the movement required, because of insufficient funds. Without this knowledge, it would be tempting to read ideological impulses into political events and decisions where they did not necessarily exist.

Webb's experiences represent just one facet of the Irish–Indian connection; it is not the only way in which Irish and Indian people interacted in the Victorian era, but it is an important and fascinating account that should not be ignored. Likewise, the history of the Irish Party is not the only history of late-Victorian Ireland, just as the history of the Indian National Congress is not the only history of colonial India. This study has used archival research in both Ireland and India, but further research could take into account a wider range of Indian sources to ensure that the fullest picture of Irish–Indian political interaction is described.

It also reveals the fabric of multicultural social relations in late-nineteenth-century Britain, in which individuals from the periphery of the British Empire met at the imperial core and found an international context to their nationalism. Webb's experiences, while fascinating in their own right, point to a broad and rich political culture in late-Victorian Dublin and London, one that extended beyond elected politics into the realm or voluntary and associational culture. It suggests the importance of associational culture in shaping political events, even in a country like Britain where parliamentary democracy was firmly established. Associations could provide political access to those who were, by nature of their nationality, ethnicity, gender or social class, not easily part of the elected political elite; the cooperation among Naoroji, O'Connor and Butler is one example of individuals optimising their contacts through associational culture to create their own political opportunities. Although enacting change through parliament remained the ultimate goal for Webb and Naoroji, much of their political network and reputation was established through their work for organisations supporting causes like temperance, suffragism and anti-slavery. Webb and Naoroji were passionate about the issues they supported, but they were also politically savvy and creative in using these organisations to shift political power to their ultimate goals, that of national political change in their respective countries.

Webb's interest in international affairs was genuine and consistent, though it stretched beyond the concerns of most of the Irish Party leaders, including Isaac Butt and Parnell. By studying Webb's politics, it is possible to identify a subculture within Irish nationalism that was cosmopolitan and open-minded; this diversity of thought would be obscured if sources were limited to the public pronouncements of the Irish Party's leaders. Webb's life sheds new light on Irish attitudes towards the British Empire and towards colonised people, contributing to the debate about Ireland's ambiguous position in the Empire as both peripheral and metropolitan. Webbs' experiences fit into a longer line of internationalist thought in Irish politics, one that remained a nearly constant, if normally subordinate, discourse in Irish nationalist thought throughout the twentieth century. The international angle of Irish political history is not surprising or new: as a small island, Ireland has been a site of migration for thousands of years, and Irish people have sought political cooperation from several major European powers in the past few centuries. What is peculiar to the internationalism espoused by

Webb, Davitt and McCarthy was its moral and ethical element: Webb keenly felt that the Irish had a responsibility to collaborate with and assist other 'suffering people', not simply to extract their assistance for immediate Irish political gain.

Webb's thought was appreciated by many other liberal-minded Londoners, and in the 1890s individuals such as Webb, Naoroji and Edwards joined together in an optimistic climate. Forty years ago, Anil Seal argued that 'the nationalist movements in India were not the creation of imperialism'.[101] Yet, obviously, the specific context for the nationalist movements of the 1880s and 1890s was an imperial one, in the widest sense: the specific goals of nationalists both Indian and Irish concerned changes with the relationship between their countries and Britain, through the mechanisms of the Parliament in Westminster. This was a parliament that, individuals like Webb and Naoroji believed, had responsibilities towards people throughout the Empire. For a few years during the 1890s, their hopes of responsible Parliamentary imperial governance began to be realised.

Notes

1 'How rich my life has been, not in itself but in its associations': An Introduction to Alfred Webb

1. DFHL, Webb autobiography, f. 1.
2. Alfred Webb, *A Compendium of Irish Biography: Comprising Sketches of Distinguished Irishmen, and of Eminent Persons Connected with Ireland by Office or by their Writings* (Dublin, 1878).
3. Tony Ballantyne, *Orientalism and Race: Aryanism in the British Empire* (Basingstoke, 2002), p. 3.
4. Leela Gandhi, *Affective Communities: Anti-Colonial Thought, fin-de-siècle Radicalism and the Politics of Friendship* (Durham and London, 2006).
5. Described as 'metaphoric kinship' by Thomas Hylland Eriksen, *Ethnicity and Nationalism: Anthropological Perspectives* (2nd edn, London, 2002), p. 106. On nationalism see also Anthony D. Smith, *Nationalism and Modernism: A Critical Survey of Recent Theories of Nations and Nationalism* (London, 1998); Benedict Anderson, *Imagined Communities: Reflections on the Origin and Spread of Nationalism* (London, 1991); Ernest Gellner and John Breuilly, *Nations and Nationalism* (London, 2005).
6. For a review of the debate see S. J. Connolly, 'Eighteenth-Century Ireland: Colony or *ancien régime*?' in D. George Boyce and Alan O'Day (eds), *The Making of Modern Irish History: Revisionism and the Revisionist Controversy* (London, 1996), pp. 15–33; for more recent discussion, see Terence McDonough (ed.), *Was Ireland a Colony? Economics, Politics and Culture in Nineteenth-Century Ireland* (Dublin, 2005).
7. See, for example, Roy F. Foster, *Paddy and Mr Punch* (London, 1993); L. P. Curtis, *Apes and Angels: The Irishman in Victorian Caricature* (Newton Abbot, 1971) and *Anglo-Saxons and Celts: A Study of Anti-Irish Prejudice in Victorian England* (Bridgeport, CT, 1968); Robert Young, *The Idea of English Ethnicity* (London, 2007); Jennifer M. Regan, '"We Could Be of Service to Other Suffering People": Representations of India in the Irish Nationalist Press, c. 1857–1887,' *Victorian Periodicals Review*, vol. 41, no.1 (Spring 2008), pp. 61–77; Scott Boltwood, '"The ineffaceable curse of Cain": Race, Miscegenation, and the Victorian Staging of Irishness,' *Victorian Literature and Culture*, vol. xxix, no. 2 (2001), pp. 383–396.
8. Thus unsurprisingly, in the nineteenth-century volume of the Oxford history of the British Empire, the chapter on Ireland in the Empire was written by a specialist in Irish emigration. David Fitzpatrick, 'Ireland and the Empire' in Andrew Porter (ed.), *The Oxford History of the British Empire*, vol. III: *The Nineteenth Century* (Oxford, 1999), pp. 495–521.
9. Edward M. Spiers, 'Army Organisation and Society in the Nineteenth Century' in Thomas Bartlett and Keith Jeffery (eds), *A Military History of Ireland* (Cambridge, 1996), pp. 335–357; Michael Silvestri, 'The "Sinn Féin

of India": Irish Nationalism and the Policing of Revolutionary Terrorism in Bengal, 1905–1939,' *Journal of British Studies* (October, 2000) and ' "An Irishman is Specially Suited to be a Policeman": Sir Charles Tegart and Revolutionary Terrorism in Bengal,' *History-Ireland* (Winter 2000).
10. Studies of the experience of Empire in domestic Britain include John MacDonald MacKenzie (ed.), *Imperialism and Popular Culture* (Manchester, 1986); Catherine Hall, *Civilising Subjects: Metropole and Colony in the English Imagination, 1830–1867* (Oxford, 2002). One example of work that has probed the Irish experience of Empire is Keith Jeffery (ed.), *An Irish Empire?: Aspects of Ireland and the British Empire* (Manchester, 1996).
11. Tadhg Foley and Maureen O'Connor (eds), *Ireland and India: Colonies, Culture and Empire* (Dublin, 2006); Stephen Howe, *Ireland and Empire: Colonial Legacies in Irish History and Culture* (Oxford, 2000); Kevin Kenny (ed.), *Ireland and the British Empire* (Oxford, 2004); Jeffery, *An Irish Empire*.
12. G. K. Peatling, 'Interactions from the Periphery: Some Irish Religious Minorities and India, c. 1850–1923' in Foley and O'Connor, *Ireland and India*, p. 103.
13. Kate O'Malley, *Ireland, India and Empire: Indo-Irish Radical Connections 1919–1964* (Manchester, 2008).
14. Scott B. Cook, *Imperial Affinities: Nineteenth Century Analogies and Exchanges between India and Ireland* (London and New Delhi, 1993), p. 25.
15. Howard V. Brasted, 'Indian Nationalist Development and the Influence of Irish Home Rule, 1870–1886,' *Modern Asian Studies*, vol. xiv (1980), pp. 37–63.
16. Jonathan Schneer, *London 1900: The Imperial Metropolis* (New Haven, 1999).
17. Antoinette Burton, *At the Heart of Empire: Indians and the Colonial Encounter in Late-Victorian Britain* (Berkeley, 1998), p. 1.
18. See also Rozina Visram, *Asians in Britain: 400 years of History* (London, 2002); Michael Fisher, *Counterflows to Colonialism: Indian Travellers and Settlers in Britain, 1600–1857* (New Delhi, 2004).
19. Alfred Webb, *Alfred Webb: The Autobiography of a Quaker Nationalist*, ed. Marie-Louise Legg (Cork, 1999). To assist the reader, when citing from Webb's autobiography I will in the first instance cite from the published work (Webb, *Autobiography*) because it is more accessible. Unpublished extracts will be cited from the original manuscript (DFHL, Webb autobiography).
20. Webb, *Autobiography*, p. 1.
21. The Press Cutting Agency wrote to one of Webb's political colleagues offering to 'send you all entries from the press relating to yourself personally and to any special subjects in which you are interested' for a fee. It claimed that its clients included many MPs, the Chinese Legation and the Home Rule Union. See Press Cutting Agency, London, to Jeremiah Jordan, 1 August 1885 (PRONI, Jordan papers, MS D/2073/4/2).
22. Webb, 'The Propriety of Conceding the Elective Franchise to Women' in *Journal of the Statistical and Social Inquiry Society of Ireland*, vol. iv, no. 8 (1868), pp. 455–461; Alfred Webb (ed.), *The Opinions of Some Protestants regarding Their Irish Catholic Fellow-Countrymen*, 3rd edn, enlarged, with resolutions of the Irish Protestant Home Rule Association (Dublin, 1886).
23. Alfred Webb, *Thoughts in Retirement* (Dublin, 1908).

24. Linda Colley, *The Ordeal of Elizabeth Marsh: A Woman in World History* (London, 2007), p. 300.
25. For example, Maria Luddy, *Women and Philanthropy in Nineteenth-Century Ireland* (Cambridge, 1995); Margaret H. Preston, *Charitable Words: Women, Philanthropy, and the Language of Charity in Nineteenth-Century Dublin* (Westport, CT, 2004).

2 'Interested in people of all countries, especially of America': A Quaker Family in the Atlantic World

1. DFHL, Webb autobiography, f. 15; Webb, *Autobiography*, p. 19.
2. William Lloyd Garrison to Wendell Garrison, 27 July 1872, BPL, MS A.1.1. v.8. p. 20.
3. Correspondence between R. D. Webb and George Combe from 1848 to 1849 is in TCD, Webb papers, MS 4787. Combe and Hodgson were both radicals, inspired by Massachusetts' educational models, and joined with Jacob Bright and James Lucas in advocating for Manchester educational reform. See D. K. Jones, 'Lancashire, the American Common School, and the Religious Problem in British Education in the Nineteenth Century', *British Journal of Educational Studies*, vol. xv, no. 3 (October, 1967), pp. 292–306.
4. DFHL, Webb autobiography, f. 28.
5. Maurice J. Wigham, *The Irish Quakers: A Short History of the Religious Society of Friends in Ireland* (Dublin, 1992), p. 18.
6. Richard S. Harrison, *Richard Davis Webb: Dublin Quaker Printer (1805–72)* (Skibbereen, 1993), p. 2.
7. Webb, *Autobiography*, pp. 30–31.
8. The term 'Quaker', though originally more of a nickname, can be used interchangeably with the word 'Friend' to describe a member of the Society of Friends.
9. Webb, *Autobiography*, p. 23.
10. Society of Friends, *Rules of Discipline of the Yearly Meeting of Friends in Ireland with Advices Issued and Adopted Thereby* (2nd edn, Dublin, 1841), p. 33.
11. Webb, *Autobiography*, p. 27.
12. Society of Friends, *Rules*, p. 96.
13. Ibid., p. 16.
14. Webb, *Autobiography*, p. 29.
15. Wigham, *Irish Quakers*, p. 32.
16. Legg, 'Introduction', in Webb, *Autobiography*, p. 6.
17. Society of Friends, *Rules*, p. 169.
18. Ibid., p. 166.
19. Ibid., p. 20.
20. Olive C. Goodbody and P. Beryl Eustace, *Quaker Records Dublin: Abstracts of Wills* (Dublin, 1957).
21. Mary E. Daly, *Dublin: The Deposed Capital, a Social and Economic History, 1860–1914* (Cork, 1984), p. 33.
22. Society of Friends, *Rules*, p. 22.
23. DFHL, Webb autobiography, f. 250.
24. Webb, *Autobiography*, p. 29.
25. DFHL, Webb autobiography, f. 250.

26. Webb, *Autobiography*, p. 18.
27. Richard Robert Madden (1798–1886) is known for *Literary Remains of the United Irishmen of 1798* (Dublin, 1887). He also had been a doctor in Jamaica where he supported freeing slaves. For more on Madden see Nini Rodgers, *Ireland, Slavery and Anti-Slavery: 1612–1865* (Basingstoke, 2007), passim; Cian McMahon, 'Struggling against Oppression's Detestable Forms: R. R. Madden and Irish Anti-Slavery, 1833–1846', *History Ireland*, vol. xv, no. 3 (May/June 2007), pp. 24–29.
28. DFHL, Webb autobiography, f. 250.
29. Webb, *Autobiography*, p. 26.
30. Ibid., p. 20.
31. Ibid., p. 32.
32. Ibid., p. 29.
33. Ibid., p. 18.
34. DFHL, Webb autobiography, f. 250.
35. Harrison, *Webb*, p. 64.
36. Webb, *Autobiography*, p. 57.
37. Anne Vernon, *A Quaker Businessman: The Life of Joseph Rowntree, 1836–1925* (London, 1958), p. 29.
38. William Bennett, *Narrative of a Recent Journey of Six Weeks in Ireland, in Connexion with the Subject of Supplying Small Seed to Some of the Remoter Districts* (London and Dublin, 1847), p. 3.
39. DFHL, Webb autobiography, f. 400.
40. R. D. Webb to Anne Weston, 26 September 1857 (BPL, Anti-Slavery papers, MS A.9.2. 29. 25).
41. Abby Kimmer to R. D. Webb, cited in Douglas C. Riach, 'Ireland and the Campaign against American slavery, 1830–1860' (PhD thesis, University of Edinburgh, 1975), p. 389.
42. Harrison, *Webb*, p. 67.
43. Ibid., p. 66.
44. As described in 'Mr Alfred Webb, of Dublin', clipping from unidentified American newspaper, 30 May 1874 (NLI, Webb papers, MS 1746).
45. DFHL, Webb autobiography, f. 400.
46. See Roy Foster, 'Protestant Magic', in his *Paddy and Mr Punch* (London, 1993), p. 220. For a wider study of Gothicism, see Luke Gibbons, *Gaelic Gothic: Race, Colonization and Irish Culture* (Galway, 2004).
47. Thad Logan, *The Victorian Parlour: A Cultural Study* (Cambridge, 2001), p. 106.
48. Ibid., quotes in p. 147, pp. 172–173.
49. Marianne Elliott, *Robert Emmet: The Making of a Legend* (London, 2003), p. 97.
50. Thomas C. Kennedy, *British Quakerism 1860–1920: The Transformation of a Religious Community* (Oxford, 2001), p. 244.
51. Ibid., p. 247.
52. Alfred Webb, 'To the editor of the *New York Nation*', 18 June 1875, newspaper clipping (NLI, Webb papers, MS 1745).
53. Society of Friends, *Rules*, p. 242.
54. Webb, *Autobiography*, p. 34.

55. Alfred Webb, 'The position and prospects of the temperance cause in Ireland', letter to editor of the *Irish Times*, 12 May 1885 (NLI, Webb papers, MS 1745).
56. Alfred Webb, draft of letter to editor of *Freeman's Journal*, 1904 (NLI, Webb papers, MS 1747).
57. Kennedy, *Quakerism*, p. 273.
58. Webb, *Autobiography*, p. 26.
59. For extremely detailed coverage of Irish anti-slavery and in particular R. D. Webb's role, see Riach, 'Ireland and the Campaign' and Rodgers, *Ireland, Slavery and Anti-Slavery*.
60. Entry for Francis Davis. Harrison, *A Biographical Dictionary of Irish Quakers* (Dublin, 1997), p. 38.
61. Letter from William Lloyd Garrison to Samuel Haughton, 24 March 1873, in Samuel Haughton, *Memoir of James Haughton: With Extracts from His Private and Public Letters* (London and Dublin, 1877), p. 289.
62. Haughton, *Memoir*, p. 44.
63. Ibid., p. 22.
64. Ibid., pp. 62, 75. It is not known whether this peace society was affiliated with the Peace Society run by William Allen (1770–1843), mentioned in Kennedy, *Quakerism*, p. 242.
65. William Lloyd Garrison, preface to Frederick Douglass, *Narrative of the Life of Frederick Douglass, An American Slave* (Boston, 1845).
66. Harrison, *Webb*, pp. 50–51.
67. Riach, 'Ireland and the campaign', pp. 285, 389.
68. Ibid., pp. 287–288.
69. Harrison, *Webb*, p. 2.
70. For France, see any of the work of Robert Darnton, for example Robert Darnton and Daniel Roche (eds), *Revolution in Print: The Press in France, 1775–1800* (London and Berkeley, 1989). For the press and nationalism, see Benedict Anderson, *Imagined Communities: Reflections on the Origin and Spread of Nationalism* (London, 1983).
71. Records of a Dublin letterpress, NLI, MS 139.
72. Legg, 'Introduction', in Webb, *Autobiography*, p. 1.
73. DFHL, Webb autobiography, f. 18.
74. Ibid., f. 245.
75. Daly, *Dublin*, pp. 45, 50.
76. Records of a Dublin letterpress (NLI, MSS 139–140); Men's bill book of a Dublin printing office (NLI, MS 141).
77. DFHL, Webb autobiography, f. 18.
78. 26 April 1846, ibid.
79. 28 March 1846, ibid.
80. November 1846, ibid.
81. 28 March 1846, ibid.
82. November 1846 (NLI, MS 141).
83. May 1847, ibid.
84. Carmel Quinlan, *Genteel Revolutionaries: Anna and Thomas Haslam and the Irish Women's Movement* (Cork, 2002), p. 110.
85. Ibid., p. 25.
86. Ibid., p. 53.

87. Invitation to a private event for the Dublin Branch of the National Association for the Repeal of the Contagious Diseases Acts (NLI, Webb papers, MS 1745).
88. Anna Parnell to Webb, 8 March 1881 (NLI, Rosamond Jacob papers, 22,143/22–25).
89. D. J. O'Donoghue, 'Webb, Alfred John (1834–1908)', rev. Alan O'Day, *DNB*.
90. Harrison, *Webb*, p. 44.
91. Quinlan, *Genteel Revolutionaries*, p. 125.
92. DFHL, Webb autobiography, f. 271.
93. Ibid., f. 299.
94. Webb to J. F. X O'Brien, 29 November 1891 (NLI, J. F. X. O'Brien papers, MS 13,431/2).
95. Mona Hearn, *Thomas Edmondson and the Dublin Laundry: A Quaker Businessman 1837–1908* (Dublin, 2004); Charles Delheim, 'The Creation of a Company Culture: Cadburys, 1861–1931', in *The American Historical Review*, vol. xcii, no. 1 (February 1987), pp. 13–44; Allen Warren, 'Forster, William Edward (1818–1886)', *DNB*.
96. Webb, *Autobiography*, p. 22.
97. NLI, MSS 139–140; compare to Fergus A. D'Arcy, 'Wages of Labourers in the Dublin Building Industry, 1667–1918', in *Saothar*, vol. xiv (1989), pp. 17–32.
98. Alfred Webb's letter of resignation to Dublin Monthly Meeting, 1 October 1857 (DFHL, Dublin Monthly Meeting minutes, Port. 64, Folder 1.6p), emphasis in original.
99. Minute on the case of Alfred Webb, February 1858 (DFHL, Dublin Monthly Meeting minutes, Port. 64, Folder 1.2h).
100. DFHL, Webb autobiography, f. 285.
101. In this case, prostitution. Alfred Webb, *Eternal Punishment* (Dublin, 1876) [3-page open letter, published as a pamphlet].
102. DFHL, Webb autobiography, f. 299.
103. Webb, *Autobiography*, p. 47.
104. DFHL, Webb autobiography, f. 286.
105. Webb, *Autobiography*, p. 36.
106. Letter from Webb to unknown newspaper, 'The Society of Friends and Resistance to Law', 31 October 188[6?] (NLI, Webb papers, MS 1745).
107. DFHL, Webb autobiography, f. 367.
108. Cited in Anonymous, *The Society of Friends in Ireland and Home Rule: A Letter from a Member of the Society of Friends in Ireland to a Fellow-Member* (Dublin, 1893), p. 22.
109. Anonymous, *Home Rule*, p. 22.

3 'The labours and responsibilities nearly killed me': Webb and Social Activism in Victorian Dublin

1. Webb, *Autobiography*, p. 48.
2. Theories of social capital belong more to political scientists than to historians, but it is a useful concept, as articulated here by Putnam: 'Social capital here refers to features of social organization, such as trust, norms,

and networks, that can improve the efficiency of society by facilitating coordinated actions.' See Robert D. Putnam, *Making Democracy Work: Civic Traditions in Modern Italy* (Princeton, 1993), p. 167.
3. Mary E. Daly, *The Spirit of Earnest Inquiry: The Statistical and Social Inquiry Society of Ireland 1847–1997* (Dublin, 1997), p. 2.
4. Maria Luddy, *Women and Philanthropy in Nineteenth-Century Ireland* (Cambridge, 1995), p. 5. Luddy is using 'reform' and 'benevolent' as proposed by Anne M. Boylan, 'Women in Groups: An Analysis of Women's Benevolent Organisations in New York and Boston, 1797–1840,' in *Journal of American History*, vol. lxxi (1984), pp. 497–523.
5. Luddy, *Philanthropy*, p. 5.
6. Ibid., p. 147.
7. For examples of studies of women philanthropists and reformers, see Luddy, *Philanthropy*; Judith Walkowitz, *Prostitution and Victorian Society: Women, Class and the State* (Cambridge, 1980); Margaret H. Preston, *Charitable Words*; and F. K. Prochaska, *Women and Philanthropy in Nineteenth-Century England* (Oxford, 1980).
8. NLI, Webb papers, MSS 1745–1747.
9. Some of these articles have sometimes been incorrectly attributed to A. V. Dicey, a mistake rectified in Christopher Harvie, 'Ideology and Home Rule: James Bryce, A. V. Dicey and Ireland, 1880–1887,' in *The English Historical Review*, vol. xci, no. 359 (1976), p. 301.
10. DFHL, Webb autobiography, f. 367.
11. The Cork St. Hospital had ties with the Society of Friends. Wigham cited in Hearn, *Edmondson*, p. 23.
12. DFHL, Webb autobiography, f. 349.
13. For full discussion of the nineteenth-century use of the term 'statistical' see Daly, *Spirit*, pp. 9–10, 13.
14. R. D. Collison Black, 'History of the Society' in *Statistical and Social Inquiry Society of Ireland, Centenary Volume 1847–1947* (Dublin, 1947), p. 11.
15. M. J. Cullen, *The Statistical Movement in Early Victorian Britain: The Foundations of Empirical Social Research* (Hassocks, Sussex, 1975), p. 148.
16. Black, 'History,' p. 66; Daly, *Spirit*, p. 13. The niece was the daughter of James Haughton's brother William Haughton. James Haughton had a son named Samuel Haughton who published his correspondence in S. Haughton, *Memoir of James Haugton: With Extracts from His Private and Public Letters* (Dublin and London, 1877). As in many Irish Quaker families, the Haughtons married within the extended family and recycled names. This Samuel Haughton should not be confused with Samuel Haughton, the Trinity College Dublin scientist, who was a cousin and who married his own half-cousin Louisa Haughton. The scientist Samuel Haughton's mother was also from the Hancock family.
17. Daly, *Spirit*, p. 30.
18. For example, the Webbs printed: *The Statistical and Social Inquiry Society of Ireland: List of Members of the Society* (Dublin, 1864).
19. Black, 'History,' p. 62.
20. Ibid., p. 25.
21. Ibid.
22. Alfred Webb, 'The Progress of the Colony of Victoria,' in *Journal of the Statistical and Social Inquiry Society of Ireland*, vol. i, Part 11 (1856), p. 361.

23. Webb, 'Victoria,' p. 362.
24. Ibid., p. 361.
25. Ibid., p. 367.
26. Ibid., p. 372.
27. Ibid., pp. 362–363.
28. The speech was delivered on 20 December 1867. Alfred Webb, 'The Propriety of Conceding the Elective Franchise to Women,' in *Journal of the Statistical and Social Inquiry Society of Ireland*, vol. iv, Part 8 (1868), pp. 455–461.
29. See Deirdre Raftery, 'Frances Power Cobbe' in Mary Cullen and Maria Luddy (eds), *Women, Power and Consciousness in 19th-Century Ireland: Eight Biographical Studies* (Dublin, 1995) pp. 89–124.
30. Webb, 'Propriety,' p. 458.
31. Ibid., pp. 457–458.
32. Copy of Webb's speech to Statistical and Social Inquiry Society, 21 December 1880 (NLI, Webb papers, MS 1745); Alfred Webb, 'Impediments to Savings from Cost and Trouble to the Poor of Proving Wills,' in *Journal of the Statistical and Social Inquiry Society of Ireland*, vol. viii, Part 57 (1880–1881), pp. 182–187.
33. Copy of Webb's speech to Statistical and Social Inquiry Society, 15 June 1896, also undated clipping of article in the *New Age* (NLI, Webb papers, MS 1745). Alfred Webb, 'Symposium on Crime: The Sherborn Massachusetts Reformatory Prison for Women,' in *Journal of the Statistical and Social Inquiry Society of Ireland*, vol. x, Part 77 (1896–1897), pp. 326–333.
34. See p. 59. 15 January 1876 (NLI, Records of a Dublin letterpress, MS 140).
35. Quinlan, *Genteel Revolutionaries*, p. 144.
36. R. F. Foster, *W. B. Yeats: A Life. Vol. 1: The Apprentice Mage, 1865–1914* (Oxford, 1997), pp. 41–42.
37. Marie O'Neill, 'The Dublin Women's Suffrage Association and Its Successors,' in *Dublin Historical Record*, vol. xxxviii, no. 4 (September 1985), p. 126.
38. J. S. Mill to J. E. Cairnes, 1 September 1867, in Francis E. Mineka and Dwight N. Lindley (eds), *Collected Works of John Stuart Mill*, vols xiv–xvii, *The Later Letters of John Stuart Mill 1849–1873* (32 vols, Toronto and London, 1972 and 1991), vol. xvi, letter 1145, p. 1315.
39. Quinlan, *Genteel Revolutionaries*, p. 113.
40. J. S. Mill to R. D. Webb, 24 February 1868, in Marion Filipiuk, Michael Laine and John M. Robson (eds), *Collected Works of John Stuart Mill*, vol. xxxii, *Additional letters of John Stuart Mill* (32 vols, Toronto and London, 1991), vol. xxxii, letter 1194A, p. 189.
41. For information about Tod see Maria Luddy, 'Isabella M. S. Tod (1836–1896),' in Luddy and Cullen, *Women, Power & Consciousness*, pp. 197–230.
42. O'Neill, 'Dublin Women's Suffrage Association,' p. 127.
43. 'Lecture by Mrs Fawcett,' *Freeman's Journal*, 19 April 1870.
44. O'Neill, 'Dublin Women's Suffrage Association', p. 128.
45. O'Neill cites 12 miscellaneous letters in NLI, Eva Gore-Booth papers, Ms 1651, but these refer to the suffrage movement in Great Britain, particularly Manchester. Lydia Becker is one of the main correspondents. Quinlan refers to DWSA annual reports but I have been unable to locate them.

46. 'National Society for Women's Suffrage,' *Freeman's Journal*, 21 January 1876.
47. K. D. Reynolds, 'Sturge, Eliza Mary (1842–1905)', *DNB*.
48. *Freeman's Journal*, 21 January 1876.
49. Berkeley Hill, 'Statistical Results of the Contagious Diseases Acts,' in *Journal of the Statistical Society of London*, vol. xxii, no. 4 (December 1870), pp. 463–485.
50. Walkowitz, *Prostitution*, p. 74.
51. Alfred Webb, printed letter addressed to MPs urging them to repeal CDAs, 27 May 1880 (NLI, Webb papers, MS 1745).
52. Walkowitz, *Prostitution*, p. 93.
53. For information on Newman see Quinlan, *Genteel Revolutionaries*, pp. 37–43 and J. G. Sieveking, *Memoir and Letters of F. W. Newman* (London, 1909).
54. Luddy, *Philanthropy*, p. 139.
55. C. S. Parnell to Webb, 14 June 1881 (NLI, Rosamond Jacob papers, MS 33,143/4).
56. Anonymous [Alfred Webb?], 'Private advice to boys and young men,' n.d. [marked '1870' in pencil], R. D. Webb and Sons, Printers, Dublin. This is a very short printed article.
57. Webb, Private advice.
58. Alfred Webb, printed letter addressed to MPs urging them to repeal CDAs, 27 May 1880 (NLI, Webb papers, MS 1745).
59. Alfred Webb, *Eternal Punishment*.
60. Alfred Webb, printed letter addressed to MPs urging them to repeal CDAs, 27 May 1880 (NLI, Webb papers, MS 1745).
61. See Elizabeth B. Van Heyningen, 'The Social Evil in the Cape Colony 1868–1902: Prostitution and the Contagious Diseases Acts,' in *Journal of Southern African Studies*, vol. x, no. 2 (April 1984), pp. 170–197.
62. Antoinette Burton, *Burdens of History: British Feminists, Indian Women, and Imperial Culture 1865–1915* (Chapel Hill and London, 1994), discussion of attitudes towards Indian CDAs, pp. 130–140.
63. Alfred Webb, Congress address (1894), in A. M. Zaidi (ed.), *Congress Presidential Addresses, Vol. 1 1885–1900* (5 vols, New Delhi, 1985), pp. 206–207.
64. Webb, *Autobiography*, p. 34.
65. Harrison, *Webb*, p. 59; Edward H. Milligan, 'Knight, Anne (1786–1862)', *DNB*.
66. R. D. Webb to 'My dear Friend', 16 July 1862 (BPL, Anti-slavery papers, MS A.9.2. 30. P. 70).
67. DFHL, Webb autobiography, ff. 280–281.
68. Ibid., p. 279.
69. Ibid., p. 340.
70. Webb to J.F.X. O'Brien, 16 June 1897 (NLI, J. F. X. O'Brien papers, MS 13,431/4).
71. Webb to J. F. X. O'Brien, 7 April 1897 (ibid.).
72. Webb to Dillon, 9 January 1895 (TCD, Dillon papers, MS 6760/1685).
73. Webb to J. F. X. O'Brien, 5 March 1891 (NLI, J. F. X. O'Brien papers, MS 13,431/2).
74. Webb to Dillon, 19 February 1907 (TCD, Dillon papers, MS 6760/1752).
75. Sophie O'Brien (Mrs William O'Brien), *My Irish Friends* (London and Dublin, 1937), pp. 62–66.

76. For some of Deborah's published poems see 'Miss Deborah Webb', in Evelyn Noble Armitage, *The Quaker Poets of Great Britain and Ireland* (London, 1896), pp. 289–293. Deborah's poems are unusual in this anthology: whereas most of the poetry is religious in theme, one of her contributions was 'John Brown's March,' glorifying the militant American abolitionist who led a revolt at Harper's Ferry in 1859.
77. For example, see receipt for donation from Miss Deborah Webb, 18 November 1898, Irish Parliamentary Fund cash book (NLI, J. F.X. O'Brien papers, MS 9234); Record of donation from Miss D. Webb, 29 October 1896, Irish National Fund account book (ibid., MS 9236).
78. Anne Colman, 'Far from Silent: Nineteenth-Century Irish Women Writers', in Margaret Kelleher and James H. Murphy (eds), *Gender Perspectives in Nineteenth-Century Ireland: Public and Private Spheres* (Dublin, 1997), p. 209.
79. Armitage, *Quaker Poets*, p. 290.
80. Deborah Webb in Armitage, *Quaker Poets*, p. 290.
81. DFHL, Webb autobiography, f. 364.
82. For discussion of these terms see Chris White, 'General introduction' in Chris White (ed.), *Nineteenth-Century Writings on Homosexuality: A Sourcebook* (London, 1999), pp. 1–8. For a twentieth-century Irish view, see Anne Owens Weekes, 'A Trackless Road: Irish Nationalisms and Lesbian Writing', in Kathryn Kirkpatrick (ed.), *Border Crossings: Irish Women Writers and National Identity* (Tuscaloosa and London, 2000).
83. Entry for Anne Webb (DFHL, Pamela Bradley, 'Index of Persons named in Alfred Webb's autobiographical manuscript', 1996).
84. DFHL, Webb autobiography, f. 305.
85. Armitage, *Quaker Poets*, p. 290.
86. DFHL, Webb autobiography, f. 359.
87. Haslam in Quinlan, *Genteel Revolutionaries*, p. 62.
88. Quinlan, *Genteel Revolutionaries*, pp. 32–33, 68–99.
89. Minutes, 7 May 1883 (Dublin City Archives, Dublin City Council minutes).
90. Letter of resignation from Alfred Webb, dated 16 June 1884, Minutes, 1 August 1884 (Dublin City Archives, Dublin City Council minutes).
91. Minutes, 11 August 1884 (Dublin City Archives, Dublin City Council minutes).
92. *Irish International Exhibition, 1907* (Dublin, 1907), p. 22.
93. Robert Kane, *The Industrial Resources of Ireland* (Dublin, 1845).
94. Webb, *Autobiography*, pp. 46–47.
95. Davitt to Webb, n.d. [marked 'Richmond Prison, Sunday', 1882?] (TCD, Davitt papers, MS 9490/4956).
96. *Freeman's Journal*, 10 September 1881.
97. Ibid., 14 September 1881.
98. *Irish Builder*, 15 January 1882.
99. *Freeman's Journal*, 31 August 1881.
100. Advertisement in *Freeman's Journal*, 29 September 1881, capitalisation in original.
101. *Irish Builder*, 15 June 1882.
102. Ibid., 15 July 1882.
103. Ibid., 1 January 1882; Daly, *Dublin*, p. 60.
104. *Irish Builder*, 1 September 1882.

184 Notes

105. Webb, *Autobiography*, p. 48.
106. *Irish Builder*, 15 July 1882.
107. Lord Mayor quoted in 'Opening the Exhibition', *Freeman's Journal*, 16 August 1882.
108. 'The National Exhibition', *Freeman's Journal*, 16 August 1882.
109. For other exhibition catalogues see *Irish International Exhibition, 1907*; Department of Agriculture and Technical Instruction for Ireland, *Ireland: Industrial and Agricultural* (Dublin, 1902).
110. Webb, *Autobiography*, p. 48.
111. Clipping of letter to editor from Alfred Webb, *Freeman's Journal*, 14 December 1904 (NLI, Webb papers, MS 1747).
112. Alfred Webb, 'Free education in Ireland (from a correspondent)', clippings from *Manchester Guardian*, 29 December 1891 and 13 January 1892 (NLI, Webb papers, MS 1746).
113. DFHL, Webb autobiography, f. 353.
114. Draft letter, May 1876, Webb to Dr William Reeves (NLI, Webb papers, MS 1745).
115. DFHL, Webb autobiography, f. 355.
116. *Nation*, undated (NLI, Webb papers, MS 1745).
117. *Irish Times*, 16 July 1878 (ibid.).
118. *Melbourne Advocate*, 4 October 1879 (ibid.).
119. *Express*, 25 July 1878 (ibid.).
120. Henry Boylan, *A Dictionary of Irish Biography* (New York, 1978).
121. Roy F. Foster, *Charles Stewart Parnell: The Man and His Family* (Hassocks, Sussex, 1976), p. 117.
122. T. W. Moody, *Davitt and Irish Revolution 1846–82* (Oxford, 1981), p. 479.
123. *Freeman's Journal*, 20 March 1886 (NLI, Webb papers, MS 1745).
124. For example, 'If you would damn the Castle / As you have dammed the Nile / Our lands like those of Egypt, /Would then begin to smile.' The final 'i' in 'smile' is punctuated with a 'smiley face' drawing. Webb to J. F. X. O'Brien, 30 December 1902 (NLI, J. F. X. O'Brien papers, MS 13,431/6).
125. DFHL, Webb autobiography, f. 390.
126. Quinlan, *Genteel Revolutionaries*, p. 23.
127. DFHL, Webb autobiography, f. 341.
128. Webb, *Autobiography*, p. 54.
129. Untitled draft, dated '88' (NLI, Webb papers, MS 1745).
130. Webb to Sir Charles Gavan Duffy, 5 August 1892 (NLI, Gavan Duffy papers, MS 8005/36).
131. Thanks to Dr Michael McAteer, Queen's University Belfast, for advising me on the Irish Literary Society. See Foster, *Yeats*, pp. 118–122.
132. Webb to Sir Charles Gavan Duffy, 5 August 1892 (NLI, Gavan Duffy papers, MS 8005/36).

4 'Some curious characters floated on the surface': Webb's Entry into Nationalist Politics

1. Alfred Webb, describing the home rule movement, in Webb, *Autobiography*, p. 40.
2. Terence de Vere White, *The Road of Excess* (Dublin, 1946); David Thornley, *Isaac Butt and Home Rule* (London, 1962).

3. Roy Foster has used Webb's autobiography, but mainly as a source for politics in the 1880s. Roy Foster, *Charles Stewart Parnell*, pp. 372n, 389n.
4. PRONI, Home Rule Association papers, MS D/213. Obviously, outgoing correspondence from these organisations is to be found in the papers of individuals, and there is correspondence between administrators of these organisations, but I am not aware of any other source material produced in its entirety by these organisations.
5. Richard J. Hayes (ed.), *Manuscript Sources for the History of Irish Civilization* (Boston, 1965).
6. Alvin Jackson uses this source (PRONI, Home Rule Association papers, MS D/213) in his *Home Rule: An Irish History, 1800–2000* (London, 2003), but, as he is mainly concerned with the high politics of the organisation, does not make use of much of the more quotidian correspondence. D/213 is not mentioned in any of the following: Thornley, *Butt*; White, *Excess*; Alan O'Day, *Irish Home Rule 1867–1921* (Manchester, 1998).
7. See J. H. Whyte, *The Independent Irish Party, 1850–9* (Oxford, 1958).
8. 'Revised Rules of the Irish National League,' J. B. Dillon, 15 April 1864, attached to John Martin to Daunt, 28 April 1864 (NLI, Daunt papers, MS 8047/1).
9. Note the tendency of organisations to refer to themselves by different names, even in official documents such as constitutions.
10. 'Revised Rules of the Irish National League,' J. B. Dillon, 15 April 1864, attachment to Martin to Daunt, 28 April 1864 (NLI, Daunt papers, MS 8047/1).
11. John Martin to Daunt, 22 February 1866 (NLI, Daunt papers, MS 8047/1).
12. John Martin to Daunt, 13 August 1866 (ibid.).
13. Webb, *Autobiography*, p. 37.
14. 'Ulster Custom' refers to the broad concept that tenants would be able to sell their interest in the holdings for a fair price, taking into account improvements they had made on property.
15. This is not widely cited, but an 1870 letter refers to Butt as a 'brother' and states 'because I know, that you are a Freemason, for yourself told me so'. It is, of course, possible that the writer was mistaken or had been misled by Butt: Jacque [sic] Spyre to Butt, 13 April 1870 (NLI, Butt papers, MS 8692/5).
16. Webb, *Autobiography*, p. 37.
17. DFHL, Webb autobiography, f. 294.
18. John Brown, a militant abolitionist, captured American army arsenals in Harper's Ferry, West Virginia, 1859, with the intention of freeing slaves. He was captured, tried and executed by the government.
19. Webb, *Autobiography*, p. 38.
20. Ibid.
21. Ibid.
22. R. V. Comerford, *The Fenians in Context* (2nd edn, Dublin, 1998), p. 36.
23. Webb, *Autobiography*, p. 39.
24. Alfred Webb, 'Why are So Many Irishmen Disloyal?' *Manchester Examiner and Times*, 20 February 1866 (NLI, Webb papers, MS 1745).
25. John Martin to Daunt, 16 October 1865 (NLI, Daunt papers, MS 8047/1).
26. Webb, 'Why are So Many Irishmen Disloyal?'
27. Ibid.

28. Alfred Webb, letter to the editor of the *Daily News*, 30 July 1868 (NLI, Webb papers, MS 1745).
29. Webb, *Autobiography*, p. 39.
30. A. M. Sullivan, *New Ireland* (London, 1877), pp. 301–303.
31. Ibid.
32. Alfred Webb, letter to editor of *New Ireland*, 24 May 1870 (NLI, Webb papers, MS 1745).
33. Webb, *Autobiography*, p. 42.
34. 'Constitution and Rules of the Home Government Association of Ireland,' Marked 'proof', 18 July 1870 (NLI, Webb papers, MS 1745).
35. Rule 5, 'Constitution and Rules of the Home Government Association of Ireland,' Marked 'proof', 18 July 1870 (NLI, Webb papers, MS 1745).
36. Isaac Butt, *Irish Federalism: Its Meaning, Its Objects, and Its Hopes* (Dublin, 1870).
37. Legally, 'Repeal' of the Act of Union would not have technically restored a parliament. However, the Repeal campaign overlooked certain practicalities and legalities, and based its argument on precedent: that Ireland could and should have a parliament because it had had one before the Union.
38. For example, see John Martin to Daunt, 26 July 1870 (NLI, Daunt papers, MS 8047/2).
39. Rule 34, 'Constitution and Rules of the Home Government Association of Ireland,' Marked 'proof', 18 July 1870 (NLI, Webb papers, MS 1745).
40. Webb to A. M. Sullivan, 13 May 1871 (ibid.).
41. Webb to A. M. Sullivan, 19 September 1870 (ibid.).
42. Webb, *Autobiography*, p. 43.
43. Webb to Daunt, 2 March 1871 (NLI, Daunt papers, MS 8048/6).
44. Webb to Daunt, 21 June 1871 (NLI, Daunt papers, MS 8048/6).
45. Webb, *Autobiography*, p. 43.
46. Webb to A. M. Sullivan, 19 September 1870 (NLI, Webb papers, MS 1745).
47. Possibly the 'Moonlighters', a society led by Anna Dunville Webb, of which Webb had been a member (see Chapter 2). Webb to John Martin, 25 March 1871 (ibid.).
48. Ibid.
49. Webb to A. M. Sulllivan, 13 May 1871 (NLI, Webb papers, MS 1745).
50. Alfred Webb, 'To the Members of Council of the Home Government Association Who Usually Attend Council Meetings,' 13 May 1871 (NLI, Webb papers, MS 1745).
51. Webb to Butt, 14 June 1871 (NLI, Butt papers, MS 8693/5).
52. For a more detailed discussion see R. V. Comerford, 'The Home Rule Party 1870–77,' in W. E. Vaughan (ed.), *A New History of Ireland, vol. vi: Ireland under the Union II – 1870–1921* (Oxford, 1996), pp. 5–9.
53. Sullivan does not indicate that he and his colleagues used mob intimidation or threatened violence, as Michael Hurst has argued that they did. Hurst, however, is almost completely reliant on the Devonshire papers in his examination of the Kerry election and seems to take for granted that the Fenians were trying to exert violent influence on the home rule campaign. Michael Hurst, 'Ireland and the Ballot Act of 1872,' in *The Historical Journal*, vol. viii, no. 3 (1965), pp. 343–348.
54. Comerford, 'The Home Rule Party,' p. 8.

55. Webb to Daunt, 15 March 1871 (NLI, Daunt papers, MS 8048/6).
56. Blennerhassett to Butt, 7 February 1872 (NLI, Butt papers, MS 8694/1).
57. Galbraith to Butt, 28 September 1871 (ibid., MS 8693/5).
58. Daunt to unknown recipient, late September 1873 (PRONI, Home Rule Association papers, MS D/213).
59. Daunt to unknown recipient, late September 1873 (ibid.).
60. Daunt to unknown recipient, 26 July 1873 (ibid.).
61. Daunt to unknown recipient, 26 July 1873 (ibid.).
62. Daunt to H. K. Martin, 23 July 1873 (ibid.).
63. Daunt to M. Clarke (Scotland), 11 July 1873 (ibid.).
64. For example, the following are to correspondents in England: McAllister to John Laverty, 4 December 1873; McAllister to James Madden, 21 March 1874; McAllister to J. Taylor, 2 April 1874; McAllister to M. Brennan, 7 May 1874 (ibid.).
65. Daunt to J. J. Egan, 30 July 1873 (ibid.).
66. For example, on receiving £46 from New Zealand home rulers, the Council resolved:

> we hail this remittance, coming as it does in succession to others received from Quebec, Buenos Ayres, Massachusetts, Cape Colony and other places where the Irish People are settled, as a convincing proof that the home rule movement has obtained the support of the Irish race all over the world.

McAllister to Mr Dennihy (Christchurch, New Zealand), 27 August 1875 (PRONI, Home Rule Association papers, MS D/213).
67. Jackson, *Home Rule*, p. 5.
68. John Martin to Butt, 20 May [1870?] (NLI, Butt papers, MS 8692/7).
69. Jason Ingoldsby to Butt, n.d. [1870?] (ibid., MS 8692/11).
70. Daunt, Rev. Galbraith, and John Martin. Webb to Daunt, 6 July 1871 (NLI, Daunt papers, MS 8048/6).
71. Webb to Daunt, 14 August 1871 (ibid.).
72. Webb to Daunt, 21 February 1871 (ibid.).
73. Letter marked 'Not Sent – by Advice of Mr Blunden,' Daunt to J. Barry, 25 July 1873 (PRONI, Home Rule Association papers, MS D/213).
74. Lawrence J. McCaffrey, 'Home Rule and the General Election of 1874 in Ireland,' in *Irish Historical Studies*, vol. ix, no. 34 (September 1954), pp. 190–212.
75. O'Day, *Irish Home Rule*, p. 32.
76. Mayor of Cork, 18 November 1873, *Proceedings of the Home Rule Conference Held at the Rotunda, Dublin, on the 18th, 19th, 20th and 21st November, 1873* (Dublin, 1874), p. 56.
77. A. M. Sullivan, 18 November 1873, *Proceedings*, p. 67.
78. Chairman William Shaw, 19 November 1873, *Proceedings*, p. 106.
79. Fergus A. D'Arcy, 'Religion, Radicalism and Rebellion in Nineteenth-Century Ireland: The Case of Thaddeus O'Malley,' in Judith Devlin and Ronan Fanning (eds), *Religion and Rebellion* (Dublin, 1997).
80. E. R. King-Harman, 18 November 1873, *Proceedings*, pp. 60–61.
81. Cahill, 20 November 1873, *Proceedings*, p. 149.

82. John Martin, 18 November 1873, *Proceedings*, p. 42. Simple repeal was understood as the repeal of the Act of Union and the implied restoration of the 1782 parliament.
83. Speech of Isaac Butt, *Proceedings*, 18 November 1873, p. 27; also cited in White, *Road of Excess*, p. 278.
84. For example, Thornley has described Butt's 'curious imperial nationalism which was so often to prove unexplicable to the young men around him in the home rule movement'. Thornley, *Butt*, p. 20.
85. Regan, 'Perceptions of India,' passim and especially pp. 37, 46–47.
86. Galbraith, 19 November 1873, *Proceedings*, p. 70.
87. Sir Joseph Neale McKenna, 20 November 1873, *Proceedings*, pp. 108–112.
88. McCarthy Downing, 21 November 1873, *Proceedings*, p. 197.
89. Alfred Webb, 21 November 1873, *Proceedings*, p. 198.
90. John Martin to unknown recipient, 11 January 1875 (PRONI, Home Rule Association papers, MS D/213).
91. John Martin to unknown recipient, 11 January 1875 (PRONI, Home Rule Association papers, MS D/213).
92. Sullivan, *New Ireland*, p. 264.
93. Thornley, *Butt*, pp. 177–178.
94. White, *Road of Excess*, p. 291.
95. My emphasis. Webb to Captain Dunne, 23 May 1874 (PRONI, Home Rule Association papers, MS D/213).
96. For example, J. McAllister to C. Martin, 23 July 1873, J. McAllister to John Laverty, 4 December 1873 (ibid.).
97. Webb to Mitchell Henry, 19 December 1873, in Thornley, *Butt*, pp. 174–175.
98. Webb to Daunt, 13 June 1874 (NLI, Daunt papers, MS 8048/6).
99. Comerford, 'The Home Rule Party,' p. 23.
100. Webb to Daunt, 23 July 1874 (NLI, Daunt papers, MS 8048/6).
101. Alfred Webb, *Why I Desire Home Rule* (Dublin 1874), pp. 2–6.
102. Webb, *Why I Desire Home Rule*, pp. 15–16.
103. Ibid., p. 17.
104. Ibid., p. 18.
105. Ibid., p. 22.
106. Ibid., p. 25.
107. Ibid., p. 17.
108. Ibid., pp. 19, 30.
109. For a detailed discussion of 1874 obstructionism, see Thornley, *Butt*, pp. 227–240.
110. Alfred Webb, 'To the Members of Council of the Home Government Association Who Usually Attend Council Meetings,' 13 May 1871 (NLI, Webb papers, MS 1745).
111. O'Day, *Irish Home Rule*, p. 44.
112. M. Kirwan to Butt, 5 July 1876 (NLI, Butt papers, MS 13,257). The outcome of this plea is unknown.
113. Motion of Mr Meldon MP, Home Rule League invitation to meeting and notice of motion, 18 July 1876 (NLI, Home Rule scrapbook, MS 3272).
114. J. McAllister to Rev. Peter Butte, C. C., 22 March 1876 (PRONI, Home Rule Association papers, MS D/213).
115. O'Day, *Irish Home Rule*, p. 48.

116. J. McAllister to unknown recipient (illegible), 2 November 1877 (PRONI, Home Rule Association papers, MS D/213).
117. Butt to Delaney, 29 September 1877 (NLI, Delaney papers, MS 10,512/2).
118. Butt to Delaney, 29 December 1877 (ibid.).
119. Mitchell Henry, to the editor of the *Freeman's Journal*, 6 June 1877 (NLI, Home Rule scrapbook, MS 3272).
120. Jackson, *Home Rule*, p. 24; White, *Road of Excess*, p. 284.
121. 'Mr A. M. Sullivan's Bid for the Leadership of the Home Rule Party,' in *The Irishman*, 27 July 1876 (NLI, Home Rule scrapbook, MS 3272).
122. J. McAllister to Webb, 6 December 1876 (PRONI, Home Rule Association papers, MS D/213).
123. J. McAllister to Webb, 6 March 1876 (ibid.).
124. Galbraith was urged to reconsider; the outcome is unknown. J. McAllister to Galbraith, 29 December 1877 (ibid.).
125. J. McAllister to A. M. Sullivan, 25 February 1878 (ibid.).
126. J. McAllister to F. H. O'Donnell, 11 March 1878 (ibid.).
127. 'Irish Home Rule League. List of person proposed [for Council membership]...,' January 1877 (NLI, Home Rule scrapbook, MS 3272).
128. J. McAllister to John Denvir, 31 October 1876 (PRONI, Home Rule Association papers, MS D/213).
129. Confidential, printed letter sent by League to 200 gentlemen, 20 November 1876 (NLI, Home Rule scrapbook, MS 3272).
130. J. McAllister to James Collins, 20 July 1878 (PRONI, Home Rule Association papers, MS D/213).
131. J. McAllister to Council of Home Rule League, 2 August 1878 (ibid.).
132. J. McAllister to J. F. Hogan, 19 November 1878 (PRONI, Home Rule Association papers, MS D/213).
133. White, *Road of Excess*, p. 179.
134. Webb to the editor of the *Nation*, 20 December 1876 (NLI, Webb papers, MS 1745).
135. 11 October 1878, 19 October 1878, 6 November 1878, *Freeman's Journal*.
136. Alfred Webb, 'The Home Rule Movement,' *Freeman's Journal*, 11 October 1878.
137. Alfred Webb, 'Public Opinion in Ireland,' *Freeman's Journal*, 6 November 1878.
138. Webb, *Autobiography*, p. 45.
139. Ibid., p. 46. Parnell was elected to Parliament in 1875.
140. Ibid., p. 46.
141. Several letters between from Webb to Parnell from this era are in NLI, Rosamund Jacob papers, MS 33,143/3.

5 'I am willing to take any dangerous part': Webb in the World of Parnell and Gladstone

1. Webb to Harrington, 21 September 1887 (NLI, Harrington papers, MS 8576/50).
2. For general histories of the Land League, see Richard Vincent Comerford, 'The Land War and the Politics of Distress, 1877–82,' in Vaughan, *A New*

History of Ireland, pp. 26–52; Paul Bew, *Land and the National Question in Ireland, 1858–82* (Dublin, 1978).
3. Webb, *Autobiography*, p. 46.
4. Parnell to Webb, 31 December 1880 (NLI, Rosamund Jacob papers, MS 33,143/3).
5. 'To some friends in prison, Christmas 1881,' clipping of printed poem signed 'A. W.' (NLI, Webb papers, MS 1745).
6. Clipping from *Freeman's Journal*, 14 April 1882 (NLI, Webb papers, MS 1745).
7. Alfred Webb, 'For use of Members of Parliament: How English outrages are dealt with: A memorandum suitable for consideration at the present time,' a 2-page pamphlet, 24 May 1882 (NLI, Webb papers, MS 1745).
8. Anna Parnell to Webb, 3 November 1881 (NLI, Rosamund Jacob papers, MS 33,143/22-25).
9. Webb, *Autobiography*, p. 48.
10. Anna Parnell to Webb, 8 March 1881(NLI, Rosamund Jacob papers, MS 22,143/22-25).
11. Webb, *Autobiography*, p. 49.
12. Anna Parnell to Webb, 8 March 1881 (NLI, Rosamund Jacob papers, MS 33,143/22-25).
13. Webb, *Autobiography*, p. 47.
14. Ibid., pp. 49–50.
15. Constitution of Irish National League, n.d. [1882] (NLI, Harrington papers, MS 8581/3, 8582/4).
16. Devoy telegram to James O'Connor, cited in Comerford, 'The Politics of Distress, 1877–82,' in Vaughan, *A New History*, p. 31.
17. C. S. Parnell to Webb, 10 March 1883 (NLI, Rosamund Jacob papers, MS 33,143/12).
18. Michael Davitt to Webb, n.d. [sent from Richmond Prison, probably 1882] (TCD, Davitt papers, MS 9490/4956); Michael Davitt to Webb, n.d. (ibid., MS 9490/4979).
19. Letters to chairman, Organising Committee, Irish National League, 18–19 October 1882 (NLI, Harrington papers, MS 8582/3).
20. Handwritten note outlining executive, unsigned, n.d. (NLI, Harrington papers, MS 8582/4).
21. Parnell to Webb, 11 November 1883 (NLI, Harrington papers, MS 8581/1).
22. Webb, *Autobiography*, p. 51.
23. Ibid., p. 45.
24. 'North City Ward Meeting,' clipping from unidentified newspaper, 6 March 1885 (NLI, Webb papers, MS 1745).
25. 'The Field Testimonial,' open letter soliciting donations, n.d. (NLI, Webb papers, MS 1745).
26. Webb, *Autobiography*, p. 51.
27. Alfred Webb, 'To editor of the *Freeman*,' 27 September 1883 (NLI, Webb papers, MS 1745).
28. Letter of resignation from Alfred Webb, dated 16 June 1884, minutes, 1 August 1884 (Dublin City Archives, Dublin City Council minutes).
29. Margaret O'Callaghan, *British High Politics and a Nationalist Ireland: Criminality, Land and the Law Under Forster and Balfour* (Cork, 1994), pp. 117–118.

30. Webb, *Autobiography*, p. 51.
31. Alfred Webb, 'To some of my nationalist friends,' printed letter, 27 January 1886 (NLI, Webb papers, MS 1745).
32. Webb, *Autobiography*, p. 49.
33. C. S. Parnell to Webb, 12 February 1883 (NLI, Rosamund Jacob papers, MS 33,143/8).
34. C. S. Parnell to Webb, 11 June 1884 (ibid., MS 33,144/19).
35. Davitt to Webb, 17 June 1884 (TCD, Davitt papers, MS 9490/6957).
36. Sophie O'Brien (Mrs William O'Brien), *My Irish Friends* (London and Dublin, 1937), p. 62.
37. Webb, *Autobiography*, p. 49.
38. Biggar to Harrington, 18 March 1888 (NLI, Harrington papers, MS 8576/4).
39. Webb, *Autobiography*, p. 45.
40. D. B. [Alfred Webb], 'The Irish Question,' *New York Nation*, 27 September 1883, reprinted as a pamphlet.
41. D. B. [Alfred Webb], 'The Government of Ireland,' *New York Nation*, 20 December 1883, reprinted as a pamphlet.
42. Webb describing fear of Catholicism: Alfred Webb, *Why I Desire Home Rule*, p. 22.
43. A. V. O'Connor, 'Oldham, Alice (1850–1907),' in *DNB*.
44. F. S. L. Lyons, *Culture and Anarchy in Ireland 1890–1939* (Oxford, 1979), p. 35.
45. Webb to C. H. Oldham, 22 June 1886 (NLI, Oldham autograph letter).
46. Alfred Webb (ed.), *The Opinions of Some Protestants*.
47. Thomas Henry Webb in Webb, *Opinions of Some Protestants*, p. 28.
48. Webb, *The Opinions of Some Protestants*.
49. Minutes of Dublin meeting, 24 November 1886 (NLI, IPHRA papers, MS 3657).
50. T. M. Healy, *A Word for Ireland* (Dublin, 1886).
51. Minutes of Dublin meeting, 29 May 1886 (ibid.).
52. Minutes of Dublin meeting, 8 October 1886 (ibid.).
53. James Loughlin, 'The Irish Protestant Home Rule Association and Nationalist Politics, 1886–93,' in *Irish Historical Studies*, vol. xxiv, no. 95 (May 1985), p. 351.
54. Minutes of Dublin meeting, 3 June 1886 (NLI, IPHRA papers, MS 3657).
55. Minutes of Dublin meeting, 20 October 1886 (ibid.).
56. Minutes of Dublin meeting, 20 February 1888 (ibid.).
57. Minutes of Dublin meeting, 28 June 1886 (ibid.).
58. Loughlin, 'Irish Protestant Home Rule,' p. 344.
59. David Hamer, 'Morley, John, Viscount Morley of Blackburn (1838–1923),' in *DNB*.
60. Anthony F. Denholm, 'Robinson, George Frederick Samuel, First Marquess of Ripon (1827–1909),' in *DNB*.
61. Webb, *Autobiography*, p. 52.
62. *Proceedings in Connection With the Visit to Dublin of the Marquis of Ripon, K. G. and the Right Hon. John Morley, M.P., 1st to 3rd February, 1888* (hereafter *Visit to Dublin*) (Dublin, 1888), p. 23.
63. *Visit to Dublin*, p. 29.
64. Ibid., p. 32.

65. 'List of Recipients of Honorary Freedom of City of Dublin, Dublin City Council' (http://www.dublincity.ie/your_council/history/0050_freedom_of_the_city.asp) (28 April 2007).
66. Webb to Harrington, 21 September 1887 (NLI, Harrington papers, MS 8576/50).
67. J. J. Clancy to Harrington, 21 February 1890 (NLI, Harrington papers, MS 8576/8).
68. Webb to J. F. X. O'Brien, 16 March 1891, 20 March 1891, and 26 March 1891 (NLI, J. F. X. O'Brien papers, MS 13,431/2).
69. Webb complains of his lack of public speaking ability: Webb to J. F. X. O'Brien, 5 November 1891 (ibid.).
70. Alfred Webb, 'New Museum Library – to the Editor of the *Freeman*,' 12 February 1890 (NLI, Webb papers, MS 1745).
71. 'Mr Pinkerton, M. P. Interviewed [by M. P. Squirrel],' clipping of [Eastern?] *Daily*, 16 July 1889 (PRONI, Pinkerton papers, MS D/1078/P/2).
72. 'Home rule demonstration. Speech by Mr Pinkerton. An Irish concert'. Unidentified newspaper clipping, 21 March 1893 (ibid.).
73. Committtee Meeting Minutes, 18 June 1895 (NLI, Irish Parliamentary Party papers, MS 9223).
74. Elizabeth Isichei, *Victorian Quakers* (London, 1970), pp. 205–207.
75. Dublin Quakers were known for their opposition to home rule and wrote to the London Yearly Meeting in 1886 expressing their opposition. Philip Ashton, 'Divided Ideals: The Religious Society of Friends and the Irish Home Rule Controversy 1885 to 1886,' in *The Woodbrooke Journal*, no. 6 (summer 2000), pp. 15–17.
76. Alfred Webb M. P., 'Supply – Civil Service Estimates,' *Hansard*, 3, cccxlvi, 11 July 1893, pp. 1511–1516.
77. Alfred Webb M. P., 'Indian Opium Revenue. Resolution,' *Hansard*, 4, xiv, 30 June 1893, pp. 591–602.
78. Webb, *Autobiography*, pp. 56, 60.
79. Ibid., p. 56.
80. Webb's description of the Parnell Split: ibid., p. 76.
81. Joseph Biggar to T. M. Healy, 11 February 1886 (UCD, Healy papers, MS P6/B/10).
82. For sources on the Split see: Frank Callanan, *The Parnell Split, 1890–1* (Cork, 1992); F. S. L. Lyons, *Charles Stewart Parnell* (London, 1977); Paul Bew, *Charles Stewart Parnell* (Dublin, 1980); R. Barry O'Brien, *The Life of Charles Stewart Parnell* (London and New York, 1910).
83. Webb to J. F. X. O'Brien, 26 December 1891 (NLI, J. F. X. O'Brien, papers, MS 13,431/2).
84. Webb to J. F. X. O'Brien, 26 October 1891 (ibid.).
85. Webb, *Autobiography*, p. 59.
86. Webb to J. F. X. O'Brien, 2 January 1891 (NLI, J. F. X. O'Brien, papers, MS 13,431/2).
87. T. M. Healy to Maurice Healy, 12 March 1891 (UCD, Healy papers, MS P6/A/17).
88. Webb to J. F. X. O'Brien, 10 December 1890 (NLI, J. F. X. O'Brien, papers, MS 13,431/1). F. S. L. Lyons has dealt with the financial situation of the movement in the 1890s in his *Irish Parliamentary Party, 1890–1910* (2nd edn,

Westport, CT, 1975), passim and pp. 201–217, and therefore no attempt has been made here to cover the financial situation in detail.
89. Webb to J. F. X. O'Brien, 10 December 1890 (NLI, J. F. X. O'Brien, papers, MS 13,431/1).
90. Webb, *Autobiography*, p. 45.
91. Webb to J. F. X. O'Brien, 10 December 1890 (NLI, J. F. X. O'Brien, papers, MS 13,431/2).
92. Webb to J. F. X. O'Brien, 10 December 1890 (NLI, J. F. X. O'Brien, papers, MS 13,431/1).
93. Webb to J. F. X. O'Brien, 25 February 1891(ibid., MS 13,431/2).
94. Constitution of Irish National Federation, 10 March 1891 (TCD, Davitt papers, MS 9470/4181).
95. Proof of constitution of Irish National Federation, 10 March 1891 (NLI, J. F. X. O'Brien, papers, MS 13,431/2).
96. Constitution of Irish National Federation, 18 November 1892 (TCD, Davitt papers, MS 9470/4182).
97. Webb to J. F. X. O'Brien, 5 January 1891 (NLI, J. F. X. O'Brien, papers, MS 13,431/2).
98. Lyons explains that the initial amount was around £50,000, but that after taxes and fees it was closer to £39,000: Lyons, *Irish Parliamentary Party*, p. 23.
99. Dillon to Charles Stewart Parnell, 15 September 1891 (NLI, Harrington papers, MS 8577/1).
100. Archbishop Croke of Cashel to Davitt, 6 November 1892 (TCD, Davitt papers, MS 9472/4211); Davitt to Harrington, 23 October 1894 (NLI, Harrington papers, MS 8576/11).
101. Davitt to Harrington, 15 January 1896 (ibid.).
102. Davitt to Henry Campbell, 8 November 1894 (TCD, Davitt papers, MS 9472/4217).
103. Webb to [J. F. X. O'Brien?], n.d., probable postscript to 25 February 1891 (NLI, J. F. X. O'Brien papers, MS 13,431/2).
104. Webb to J. F. X. O'Brien, 25 February 1891 (ibid.).
105. Webb to J. F. X. O'Brien, 12 March 1891 (ibid.).
106. Lyons, *John Dillon: A Biography* (London, 1968), p. 178.
107. Committee minutebook 1893–1895 (NLI, Irish Parliamentary Party papers, MS 9223).
108. Resolution from Michael Davitt Branch of Irish National League of America, Holyoke, MA, 29 July 1883 (NLI, Webb papers, MS 1745); Archbishop William Walsh to Harrington, 10 December 1885 (NLI, Harrington papers, MS 85756/51).
109. Webb to Dillon, 20 August 1893 (TCD, Dillon papers, MS 6760/1670).
110. Resolution of Committee (Blake, Dillon, William O'Brien, T. P. O'Connor, Sexton, T. D. Sullivan), 17 April 1894 (NLI, Irish Parliamentary Party papers, committee minutebook 1893–1895, MS 9223).
111. Webb to Justin McCarthy, 21 January 1895 (NLI, J. F. X. O'Brien papers, MS 13,431).
112. Webb to Dillon, 28 June 1895 (TCD, Dillon papers, MS 6760/1670).
113. Callanan, *T. M. Healy* (Cork, 1996), p. 420.

194 Notes

114. For examples of Healy's treatment of Parnell at the beginning of the Split, see T. P. O'Connor, *Memoirs of an Old Parliamentarian* (2 vols, London, 1929), vol. ii, pp. 226–234.
115. Committee minutes, 1893–1895 (NLI, Irish Parliamentary Party papers, MS 9223).
116. Proof of Constitution of the Irish National Federation, March 1891 (NLI, J. F. X. O'Brien papers, MS 13,431/2).
117. Callanan, *Healy*, pp. 243, 448.
118. Webb, *Autobiography*, pp. 72, 77.
119. Callanan, *Healy*, p. 423.
120. *Irish Weekly Independent*, 24 August 1895.

6 'A union of hearts firmly based on love of Ireland': Cosmopolitan Friendship in the Imperial Metropolis

1. Alfred Webb MP, 'Liberals and Home Rule,' clipping from *Manchester Guardian*, 10 March 1894 (NLI, Webb papers, MS 1746).
2. Webb, *Autobiography*, p. 56.
3. Comte Crémont to Harrington, 29 April 1897 (NLI, Harrington papers, MS 8576/9); J. H. McCarthy to Harrington, 23 October 1886 (ibid., MS 8576/27).
4. Webb, *Autobiography*, pp. 60–65.
5. Webb to Dillon, 1 February 1894 (TCD, Dillon papers, MS 6760/1670).
6. Many of Webb's letters to Dillon in 1894 and 1895 express such depressed and unconfident views (TCD, Dillon papers, MS 6760).
7. Charles S. Parnell to Webb, 10 July 1882 (NLI, Rosamund Jacob papers, MS 33,143/6); Anna Parnell to Webb, n.d. (NLI, Jacob papers, MS 33,143/22-25).
8. Webb, *Autobiography*, p. 53.
9. Ibid.
10. Rules, Regulations, Bye-Laws, List of Members, July 1894 (NLC, records).
11. Rules, Regulations, Bye-Laws, List of Members, 1884, 1885, 1886, 1887, 1890 [missing 1888 and 1889] (NLC, records).
12. Alan O'Day, *The English Face of Irish Nationalism* (Dublin and Toronto, 1977), p. 30.
13. Elections Sub-Committee Minutes, 1889–1891 (NLC, records).
14. Elections Sub-Committee Minutes, 25 February 1891 (NLC, records).
15. Elections Sub-Committee Minutes, 27 March 1889 (NLC, records).
16. Lectures and Discussions Minutes, 5 September 1889 (NLC, records).
17. General Committee Minutes, 17 June 1897; Political Sub-Committee Minutes, 10 December 1897 (NLC, records).
18. Alfred Webb, 'Irish members and the Voluntary Schools Bill,' clipping of letter to the *Freeman's Journal*, [?] April 1897 (NLI, Webb papers, MS 1746).
19. Webb, *Autobiography*, p. 60.
20. Sophie O'Brien, *My Irish Friends*, pp. 62–66.
21. Webb, *Autobiography*, p. 60.
22. Ibid.
23. Draft of unpublished autobiography, edited by Webb (NLI, J. F. X. O'Brien papers, MS 16,695).

24. Webb, *Autobiography*, p. 56.
25. Draft of unpublished autobiography, edited by Webb (NLI, J. F. X. O'Brien papers, MS 16,695).
26. 'The Indian National Congress – the President's Views,' clipping from *Manchester Guardian*, 19 February 1895 (NLI, Webb papers, MS 1746).
27. Entry for 'cosmopolitan,' *Oxford English Dictionary* (2nd edn, Oxford, 1989).
28. Georgios Varouxakis, ' "Patriotism", "cosmopolitanism", and "humanity" in Victorian Political Thought,' in *European Journal of Political Theory*, vol. v, no. 1 (2006), p. 104.
29. Lyons, *Irish Parliamentary Party*, p. 37.
30. Senia Paseta, *Before the Revolution: Nationalism, Social Change and Ireland's Catholic Elite, 1879–1922* (Cork, 1999), p. 98.
31. Griffith in Paseta, *Before the Revolution*, p. 152.
32. Comerford, 'Ireland, 1870–1892,' in Vaughan, *New History*, p. xliv.
33. O'Day, *English Face*, pp. 25–30.
34. Ibid., p. 30.
35. Donal Sullivan to Webb, 8 October 1894 (TCD, Dillon papers, MS 6760/1670).
36. Invitations to Mr and Mrs Pinkerton 'Lady Tweedmouth at home,' 29 May, and 'Mrs James Bryce at home,' 19 July, 'Invitation to Mrs John Pinkerton to meet the Executive and members of the Women's National Liberal Association, Lady Brassey at home, 8 May,' n.d., [all 1886?] (PRONI, Pinkerton papers, MS D/1078/P/67).
37. Webb to Dillon, 1 February 1894 (TCD, Dillon papers, MS 6760/1672).
38. TCD, 'The Flight of the Webbs', clipping from unidentified Parnellite newspaper, n.d. (marked 1893) (NLI, Webb papers, MS 1746).
39. See, for example, Andrew G. Newby, 'Landlordism is Soon Going Skye-High: Michael Davitt and Scotland 1882–1887,' in *History Scotland*, vol. iii, no.4 (2003), pp. 45–52.
40. For further discussion of multicultural London, see Jonathan Schneer, *London 1900: The Imperial Metropolis* (New Haven, 1999 and 2001), especially chapters 7 and 8, 'London's radical and Celtic fringe' and 'Dadabhai Naoroji and the search for respect'.
41. For information on the Indian community in Britain, see Michael Fisher, *Counterflows to Colonialism*; Burton, *At the Heart of the Empire*; Visram, *Asians in Britain*.
42. There are many studies of the Irish in nineteenth-century Britain. See, for example: Roger Swift and Sheridan Gilley (eds), *The Irish in the Victorian City* (London, 1985); or Fintan Cullen and Roy Foster, *'Conquering England': Ireland in Victorian London* (London, 2005).
43. R. P. Masani, *Dadabhai Naoroji: The Grand Old Man of India* (London, 1939); David Lewis Jones, 'Naoroji, Dadabhai (1825–1917),' in *DNB*.
44. Josephine Butler to Dadabhai Naoroji, 12 January 1888 (NMML, Naoroji papers, MS 4A).
45. Correspondence from this organisation is in NAI, Naoroji papers, MS Acc. 406, reel 4, B-216.
46. Presidential speech of Alfred Webb, reprinted in A. M. Zaidi and Shaheda Zaidi (eds), *The Encyclopedia of Indian National Congress, vol. II: 1891–1895, the Age of Reforms* (Delhi, 1977), p. 481.

47. Omar Ralph, *Naoroji: The First Asian MP* (Antigua, 1997), p. 117.
48. Correspondence from this organisation is in NAI, Naoroji papers, MS Acc. 438, reel 36, N-77.
49. Clipping from *Madras Standard*, n.d. (NLI, Webb papers, MS 1746).
50. Presidential speech of Alfred Webb, reprinted in Zaidi and Zaidi, *Encyclopedia*, p. 480.
51. For a description of these societies and Empey and Edwards, see Schneer, *London 1900*, pp. 204–213.
52. Varouxakis, 'Victorian Political Thought,' pp. 100–118.
53. Editorial, *Fraternity*, July 1893.
54. *Fraternity*, January 1896.
55. Schneer writes that both Webb and Naoroji were on the executive committee of the SRUBM, although I have not seen Webb listed in the issues of *Fraternity*. Schneer, *London 1900*, p. 201.
56. 'Ireland / Fifty years of blameless life / Fifty years of war and strife / Fifty year's thy army's been an oppressing force / Fifty years employed thy subjects to coerce', Miss St Clair Knox, 'Jubilee Events in the Reign of Queen Victoria,' *Fraternity*, February 1896.
57. James O'Connor, St Patrick's Day Celebration Committee, London, to Naoroji, 16 March 1892 [NAI, Naoroji papers, MS Acc. 420, reel 18, I-42(2)]; John Ball, Clerkenwell Branch INLGB, to Naoroji, 20 June 1895 [ibid., I-42(7)].
58. John Dillon O'Flinn, Dulwich Branch INLGB to Naoroji, 17 February 1892 [ibid., I-42(4)].
59. C. E. Wilson, Sec., St Pancras branch INLGB, to Naoroji, 6 March 1894 [ibid., I-43(3)].
60. John Ball to Naoroji, 13 July 1892 [ibid., I-42(3)]; Thomas Daniel O'Connor to Naoroji, 14 July 1892 (ibid., I-43).
61. Robert J. Sheehey to Naoroji, 8 May 1894 [ibid., I-43(8)].
62. J. F. X. O'Brien to Naoroji, 11 August 1894 [ibid., I-43(10)].
63. M. Keating to Naoroji, 2 October 1901 (NAI, Naoroji papers, MS Acc 445, Reel 43, U-21(1)); M. Keating to Naoroji, 29 April 1904 [ibid., U-21(2)].
64. C. J. O'Donnell to Naoroji, 3 January 1902 (NAI, Naoroji papers, MS Acc 438, Reel 36, O-10).
65. C. J. O'Donnell to Naoroji, 20 June 1903 [ibid., O-10(2a)].
66. John Bunting, Holborn branch UILGB to Naoroji, 31 January 1906 (NAI, Naoroji papers, MS Acc 445, Reel 43, U-20); John Bunting to Naoroji, 8 February 1906 [ibid., U-20(1)].
67. Samuel Geddes to Naoroji, 19 October 1906 [NAI, Naoroji papers, MS Acc 420, Reel 18, I-40(3)].
68. Samuel Geddes to Naoroji, 10 October 1906 [ibid., I-40(2)].
69. Jackson, *Ireland 1798–1998* (Oxford and Malden, MA, 1999), p. 119.
70. James McConnel, 'Fenians at Westminster: The Edwardian Irish Parliamentary Party and the Legacy of the New Departure,' in *Irish Historical Studies*, vol. xxxiv, no. 133 (May 2004), pp. 41–64.
71. Davitt to Webb, 5 March 1885 (TCD, Davitt papers, MS 9490/4959).
72. Webb to J. F. X. O'Brien, 10 October 1898 (NLI, J. F. X. O'Brien papers, MS 16,696).

73. J. F. X. O'Brien autobiography, with notes by Webb (NLI, J. F. X. O'Brien papers, MS 16,695).
74. IRB stands for either Irish Revolutionary Brotherhood or Irish Republican Brotherhood, the secret society whose members were called Fenians.
75. Riach, 'Ireland and the Campaign against Anti-Slavery,' p. 342.
76. Webb to J. F. X. O'Brien, 14 August 1896 (NLI, J. F. X. O'Brien papers, MS 13,431/4).
77. Davitt to Webb, 9 March 1898 (TCD, Davitt papers, MS 9490/4961).
78. Sophie O'Brien, *My Irish Friends*, pp. 31–32.
79. Webb to J. F. X. O'Brien, 14 August 1896 (NLI, J. F. X. O'Brien papers, MS 13,431/4).
80. Webb to Mitchell Henry, 19 December 1873, in Thornley, *Butt*, pp. 174–175.
81. Davitt to Webb, 30 March 1906 (TCD, Davitt papers, MS 9490/4975).
82. John Martin to Daunt, 5 August 1870 (NLI, Daunt papers, MS 8047/2).
83. Webb, *Autobiography*, p. 43.
84. John Tosh, 'Masculinities in an Industrializing Society: Britain, 1800–1914,' in *Journal of British Studies*, vol. xliv, no. 2 (2005), pp. 330–342.
85. Rev. Charles O'Reilly, Treas. INL America, to Kenny, 9 August 1890 (NLI, Harrington papers, MS 8582/2).
86. William O'Brien to Joe Quinn, n.d. [1882?] (NLI, Quinn papers, MS 5930).
87. Ibid.
88. 'I heard that the cause of your delay in writing was – that you were gone mad about some girl': Andrew Kettle to Joe Quinn, 16 February 1885 (NLI, Quinn papers, MS 5930).
89. Webb to J. F. X. O'Brien, 13 July 1896 (NLI, J. F. X. O'Brien papers, MS 13,431/4).
90. Jordan to Pinkerton, 1 March 1902 (PRONI, Pinkerton papers, MS D/1078/P/71).
91. Jordan to Pinkerton, 1 March 1902 (ibid.). Some of these comments also give credit to the argument that the new, young recruits to the Party after 1890 did not integrate well with the old guard, as argued in Lyons, *Irish Parliamentary Party*, p. 161.
92. Jordan to Pinkerton, 23 April 1901 (ibid., MS D/1078/P/70).
93. T. M. Healy to Maurice Healy [his father], 28 February 1890 (UCD, Healy papers, MS P6/A/13).
94. Webb, *Autobiography*, pp. 74–75, 77.
95. See David Alderson, *Mansex Fine: Religion, Manliness and Imperialism in Nineteenth-Century British Culture* (Manchester, 1998).
96. There is a vast literature on this subject. For a few examples, see Christine Bolt, *Victorian Attitudes to Race* (London, 1971); Paul B. Rich, *Race and Empire in British Politics* (2nd edn, Cambridge, 1990); Ann McClintock, *Imperial Leather: Race, Gender and Sexuality in the Colonial Context* (New York, 1995).
97. For example, 'The Saxon is Practical, the Celt is Imaginative': 'Mr J. Cowen MP on Egypt and Ireland,' *United Ireland*, 21 February 1885.
98. Motilal Ghose to William Digby, 9 August 1892 (BLOIOC, Digby papers, MS Eur/D767/9). This in spite of the fact that one biography of Ghose presents him as a social conservative who was very afraid that India was being contaminated by loose British morals. Note that Ghose's first name can be spelt as two words or one; I have spelled it as one to avoid giving the impression

that 'Lal' is part of his surname. Paramananda Dutt, *Memoirs of Moti Lal Ghose* (Calcutta, 1935), passim and p. 75.
99. William Wedderburn, *Allan Octavian Hume, C. B., 'father of the Indian National Congress', 1829 to 1912* (London, 1913), p. 48.
100. George L. Mosse, 'Nationalism and Respectability: Normal and Abnormal Sexuality in the Nineteenth Century,' in *Journal of Contemporary History*, vol. xvii, no. 2 (1982), p. 223.
101. Sandra Swart, ' "A Boer and his gun and his wife are three things always together": Republican Masculinity and the 1914 Rebellion,' in *Journal of Southern African Studies*, vol. xxiv, no. 4 (1998), pp. 737–751.
102. George L. Mosse, 'Friendship and Nationhood: About the Promise and Failure of German Nationalism,' in *Journal of Contemporary History*, vol. xvii, no. 2 (1982), p. 351.
103. Lynn Hunt and Margaret Jacob, 'The Affective Revolution in 1790s Britain,' in *Eighteenth-Century Studies*, vol. xxxiv, no. 4 (2001), p. 496.
104. Webb, *Autobiography*, p. 57.
105. For some recent scholarly work on affect, see Gandhi, *Affective Communities*; Sara Ahmed, 'Affective Economies,' *Social Text*, 79, vol. xxii, no. 2 (Summer 2004), pp. 117–139; Jane Haggis and Margaret Allen, 'Imperial Emotions: Affective Communities of Mission in British Protestant Women's Missionary Publications c. 1880–1920,' *Journal of Social History*, vol. xli, no. 3 (Spring 2008), pp. 691–716.

7 'I stand beside you as a comrade': Irish and Indian Political Collaboration

1. Alfred Webb, 'Mr Webb's Valedictory Address at Bombay, 17 January 1894,' in *Indian Affairs: Speeches of Alfred Webb, Esq., MP, President, Tenth Indian National Congress* (Bombay, 1895), p. 39.
2. Obituary of R. D. Webb, *Old and New* (Boston, 1872) (NLI, Webb papers, MS 1745).
3. Entry for Richard Davis Webb. Harrrison, *Biographical Dictionary*, p. 102.
4. See quote, p. 89.
5. Webb, *Autobiography*, p. 34.
6. Covered in detail in *India*, June 1893. See also: Alfred Webb MP, 'Indian Opium Revenue. Resolution,' *Hansard*, 4, *xiv*, 30 June 1893, pp. 591–602.
7. Jason Alexander Mowatt, letter to *Evening Post* [New York?], 'Home Rule for Ireland: Mr Alfred Webb's Views Supported,' 12 December 1872 (NLI, Webb papers, MS 1745).
8. Alfred Webb, 'Home Rule on the Colonial Model: To the Editor of the *Freeman's Journal*,' 26 December 1885 (ibid.).
9. Ibid.
10. Alfred Webb, 'Indian Affairs,' *British Friend*, May 1890 (NLI, Webb papers, MS 1747).
11. Alfred Webb MP, 'Indian Opium Revenue,' *Hansard*, 4, *xiv*, 30 June 1893, pp. 591–602.
12. Alfred Webb, 'What Is Going on in Russia – To the Editor of the *Freeman*,' 11 November 1889 (NLI, Webb papers, MS 1745).

13. Alfred Webb MP, 'Supply – Civil Service Estimates,' *Hansard*, 3, cccxlvi, 11 July 1893, pp. 1511–1516.
14. Davitt to Webb, 29 November 1889 (TCD, Davitt papers, MS 9490/6860).
15. Sophie O'Brien, *My Irish Friends*, p. 65.
16. Speech by Alfred Webb to Belfast Young Ireland Society, clipping from unknown newspaper, autumn 1896 (NLI, Webb papers, MS 1747).
17. Galbraith, 19 November 1873, *Proceedings*, p. 70.
18. S. B. Cook, 'The Irish Raj: Social Origins and Careers of Irishmen in the Indian Civil Service, 1855–1914,' in *Journal of Social History*, vol. xx (1986), p. 510.
19. Kevin Kenny (ed.), 'The Irish in the Empire,' *Ireland and the British Empire*, pp. 105–106.
20. Sir Antony MacDonnell quoted in Cook, 'The Irish Raj,' p. 520.
21. 'Ireland and the "Empire",' *Nation*, 5 December 1857.
22. See Jennifer M. Regan, 'Perceptions of India in the Irish Nationalist Press, c. 1857–1887,' M.A. thesis, Queen's University Belfast, 2004.
23. Galbraith, 19 November 1873, *Proceedings*, p. 70.
24. Sir Joseph Neale McKenna and Mr McCarthy Downing MP, 20 November 1873, *Proceedings*, pp. 108–112.
25. There are dozens of such pamphlets and speeches, many held at the Special Collections of Queen's University Belfast. A few examples: Frederic Harrison, *Mr Gladstone – or Anarchy!* (London, 188[6?]); Rev. Malcolm MacColl, *Reasons for Home Rule* (London, 1886); George Coffey, *Home Rule: Answers to Objections* (London, 1888); W. E. Gladstone, *Speech on the Government of Ireland Bill* (London, 1886); Irish Loyal and Patriotic Union, *The Parnell Catechism: Questions and Answers on the Government of Ireland Bill* (Dublin, 188[6?]); Thomas E. Webb, *The Irish Question: A Reply to Mr. Gladstone* (Dublin, 1886).
26. 'Land League Meeting in Ballycastle,' clipping from unknown newspaper, 2 December 1880 (PRONI, Pinkerton papers, MS D/1078/P/1).
27. See letter declining to comment on the Party's views on the Eastern Question: J. McAllister to Patrick Loftus, Secretary of St Michael's Catholic Young Men's Society, Birmingham, 15 January 1878 (PRONI, Home Rule Association papers, MS D/213). See also discussion of lack of Party policy on Eastern Question, *Freeman's Journal*, 13–14 August 1878.
28. Cecil Rhodes to C. S. Parnell, 19 June 1888 (NLI, Parnell/Rhodes papers, MS 697).
29. Cecil Rhodes to C.S. Parnell, 19 June 1888 (ibid.).
30. C. S. Parnell to Cecil Rhodes, 23 June 1888 (ibid.).
31. Cecil Rhodes to C. S. Parnell, 24 June 1888 (ibid.).
32. Brasted, 'Irish Home Rule Politics and India 1873–1886: Frank Hugh O'Donnell and Other Irish "Friends of India",' PhD Thesis, University of Edinburgh, 1974, passim and pp. 85–95.
33. F. H. O'Donnell, *A History of the Irish Parliamentary Party* (2 vols, London, 1910).
34. Cumpston particularly relies on O'Donnell's *History*: Cumpston, Mary, 'Some Early Indian Nationalists and Their Allies in the British Parliament, 1851–1906,' *English Historical Review*, vol. lxxvi, no. 299 (April 1961), pp. 279–297.

35. O'Donnell, *History*, vol. ii, p. 431.
36. My emphasis. Frank Hugh O'Donnell, 'Mr O'Donnell MP and the Eastern Debate: To the Editor of the *Freeman*,' *Freeman's Journal*, 13 August 1878.
37. Phrase used by Brasted, 'Irish Home Rule Politics,' p. 5.
38. Eugene J. Doyle, *Justin McCarthy* (Dundalk, 1996), p. 8.
39. Cumpston, 'Early Indian Nationalists,' pp. 279–297.
40. Brasted, 'Irish Home Rule Politics,' p. 86.
41. Brasted, 'Irish Nationalism and the British Empire in the Late Nineteenth Century,' in Oliver MacDonagh, W. F. Mandle and Pauric Travers (eds) *Irish Culture and Nationalism, 1750–1950* (Dublin, 1983); Brasted, 'Indian Nationalist'.
42. Harrison, *Webb*, passim.
43. Ralph, *Naoroji*, pp. 48–49.
44. Edward Royle, 'Bradlaugh, Charles (1833–1891),' in *DNB*.
45. Callanan, *Healy*, pp. 116–117.
46. O'Donnell, *History*, vol. ii, p. 438.
47. Ibid., p. 428.
48. Ibid., pp. 428–429; Ralph, *Naoroji*, p. 88.
49. Michael Davitt, *The Fall of Feudalism in Ireland: or, The Story of the Land League Revolution* (London and New York, 1904), p. 447.
50. Naoroji cited in Masani, *Naoroji*, p. 234.
51. Naoroji, journal entry for 17 May 1886, cited in ibid., p. 238.
52. Naoroji's printed address to the Holborn Division of Finsbury electors, 30 June 1886 (NMML, Naoroji papers, MS 4A).
53. 'Mr Davitt Is in London,' *Freeman's Journal*, 26 June 1886; Masani, *Naoroji*, p. 244.
54. Ripon in Briton Martin Jr., *New India 1885: British Official Policy and the Emergence of the Indian National Congress* (Berkeley, 1969), p. 1.
55. Briton Martin, jr., 'Lord Dufferin and the Indian National Congress, 1885–1888,' in *Journal of British Studies*, vol. vii, no. 1 (November 1967), p. 74.
56. Dufferin quoted in Martin, 'Lord Dufferin,' pp. 77, 85.
57. Ibid., p. 84.
58. Anil Seal, *The Emergence of Indian Nationalism: Competition and Collaboration in the Later Nineteenth Century* (Cambridge, 1968), p. 258.
59. O'Donnell, *History*, vol. ii, pp. 439–441.
60. For example, his version of events at a meeting of the Home Rule executive, as described in his letter of 13 August 1878, was contested by the General Secretary: W. J. Oliver, 'Mr O'Donnell MP and the Home Rule Executive: To the Editor of the *Freeman*,' *Freeman's Journal*, 14 August 1878.
61. O'Donnell, *History*, vol. ii, p. 439. I have not found evidence of Leamy taking part in other Indian lobbying or political groups.
62. Wedderburn, *Hume*, p. 55.
63. Ibid., p. 87.
64. Roger T. Stearn, 'Bonnerjee, Woomes Chunder (1844–1906),' in *DNB*.
65. Wedderburn, *Hume*, pp. 87–88.
66. 'There is, happily, at the present time an entire freedom from party bias in the discussion of Indian questions, and in the administration of Indian affairs... It should be remembered that Indians are thoroughly Conservative in all their ideas; and hence form the natural allies of the Conservative

party': Frederic Pincott, 'Why Conservatives Should Support the Indian Congress,' *India: A Journal for the Discussion of Indian Affairs*, February 1890.
67. *India: A Journal for the Discussion of Indian Affairs*, 5 December 1890.
68. 'The Gazette of India and the Gazettes of subordinate Governments, all Blue Books relating to India, and all the principal Indian and Anglo-Indian newspapers are filed: everything is made freely available for enquiry': *India: A Journal for the Discussion of Indian Affairs*, February 1890.
69. Wedderburn, *Hume*, p. 97.
70. 'Indian Affairs,' letter from Alfred Webb to *British Friend*, May 1890 (NLI, Webb papers, MS 1747).
71. Swift MacNeill, speech in House of Commons on Appointments in the Indian Civil Service bill, 12 February 1892, in *India: A Journal for the Discussion of Indian Affairs*, 11 March 1892.
72. Charles Bradlaugh to William Digby, 21 February 1890 (BLOIOC, Digby papers, MS Eur/D767/7/145); Charles Bradlaugh to William Digby, 3 November 1890 (ibid., MS Eur/D767/7/47).
73. James Keir Hardie MP, 'The Democracy and India,' *India*, May 1893.
74. Wedderburn to Naoroji, 16 February 1894 [NAI, Naoroji papers, MS Acc. 450, reel 48, W-48(83)]. For references to Naoroji communicating with Irish MPs see also Wedderburn to Naoroji, 27 May 1893, 30 May 1893, 29 February 1894, 29 October 1894 [NAI, Naoroji papers, MS Acc. 450, reel 48, W-48(74, 75, 83 and 89)].
75. Davitt to Naoroji, 18 February 1892 [NAI, Naoroji papers, MS Acc. 409, reel 7, D-59(2)].
76. Motilal Ghose to William Digby, 9 August 1892 (BLOIOC, Digby papers, MS Eur/D767/9).
77. For more information on this incident see Antoinette M. Burton, 'Tongues Untied: Lord Salisbury's "Black Man" and the Boundaries of Imperial Democracy,' in *Comparative Studies in Society and History*, vol. xlii, no. 3 (2000), pp. 632–661.
78. Wedderburn, *Hume*, pp. 93–94.
79. Ibid., pp. 94–96.
80. The Indian Parliamentary Committee did not constitute the Royal Commission to inquire into the administration of Indian Expenditure (commonly known as the Welby Commission after Baron Welby, its head commissioner). Fifteen commissioners were appointed of whom three were members of the Parliamentary Committee: Wedderburn, Naoroji and Caine. See *Royal Commission on Administration of Expenditure of India. First Report Volume I. Minutes of Evidence*, vi, 1 [C.8258], H. C. 1896, xvi, 6.
81. Speech of Dadabhai Naoroji in A. M. Zaidi (ed.), *Congress Presidential Addresses, vol. I: 1885–1900* (5 vols, New Delhi, 1985), p. 157.
82. Wedderburn to Naoroji, 30 May 1893 [NAI, Naoroji papers, MS Acc. 450, reel 48, W-48(75)].
83. Davitt, quoted by Naoroji in his Presidential Address of 1893, in Zaidi, *Congress Presidential Addresses*, pp. 156–157.
84. At a dinner to honour Webb, the first toast was to 'The Queen Empress,' *India*, June 1895.
85. Cumpston, 'Early Indian Nationalists,' p. 286.

86. 'British Parliament and the Greatest British Dependency,' *Fraternity*, 15 November 1893.
87. D. B. [Alfred Webb], 'The Government of Ireland,' from *New York Nation*, 20 December 1883. Reprinted as a pamphlet, n.d.
88. Wacha to Naoroji, 27 July 1894 [NAI, Naoroji papers, MS Acc 448, Reel 46, W-1(250)].
89. Wacha to Naoroji, 21 August 1894 [ibid., W-1(254)]. See also letter from Wacha, reprinted in minutes of 21 August 1894 (NAI, Minutes of meetings of the BCINC, MS Acc. 1941, reel 2, vol. iii, p. 53).
90. Letter from Wacha, reprinted in minutes of 21 August 1894 (ibid.).
91. Minutes of 2 October 1894 (NAI, Minutes of meetings of the BCINC, MS Acc. 1941, reel 2, vol. iii, p. 57).
92. Copy of invitation from C. Sankaran Nair and secretaries of the Madras Congress to unknown (probably Blake), 19 September 1894 [NAI, Naoroji papers, MS Acc. 409, reel 7, C-230(1)].
93. Davitt to Naoroji, 5 October 1894, 29 August 1894 [ibid., D-59(4)].
94. Davitt to Naoroji, 5 October 1894 [ibid., D-59(4)], emphasis in original.
95. Edward Blake to Michael Davitt, 15 October 1894 (TCD, Davitt papers, MS 9347/516). For Naoroji's efforts to get an answer from Blake see minutes of 2 October 1894 and 13 November 1894 (NAI, Minutes of the meetings of the BCINC, MS Acc. 1941, reel 2).
96. Wedderburn to Naoroji, 25 January 1895 [NAI, Naoroji papers, MS Acc. 450, reel 48, W-48(91)].
97. For Webb's account of his Indian experience see Webb, *Autobiography*, pp. 67–72, quote p. 67.
98. Naoroji to Hume, 11 November 1894 [NAI, Naoroji papers, MS Acc. 434, reel 32, N-1(2541)].
99. Invitation from T. Nand, Hon. Sec. London Indian Society, n.d. (NMML, Naoroji papers, MS 4A).
100. *India*, December 1894.
101. The three non-Indians who were presidents after Webb – Henry Cotton, Annie Besant and Nellie San Gupta – all lived a significant part of their lives in India.
102. Surendranath Banerjea, *A Nation in Making: Being the Reminiscences of Fifty Years of Public Life* (London, 1925), p. 136.
103. P. Ananda Charlu, Indian National Congress presidential address, 1891, in Zaidi, *Congress Presidential Addresses*, pp. 117–119.
104. *India*, February 1895.
105. Congress Reception Committee circular, marked 'private,' 25 September 1894 [NAI, Naoroji papers, MS Acc. 409, reel 7, C-230(2)].
106. Quoted in *India*, February 1895.
107. Ibid.
108. Wacha to Naoroji, 17 December 1894 [NAI, Naoroji papers, MS Acc. 448, reel 46, W-1(269)].
109. See Judith Brown, *Modern India: The Making of an Asian Democracy* (2nd edn, Oxford, 1994), p. 181.
110. Wacha to Naoroji, 17 December 1894 [NAI, Naoroji papers, MS Acc. 448, reel 46, W-1(269)].

111. Alfred Webb, Presidential Address at 1894 Indian National Congress, reprinted in Zaidi and Zaidi, *Encyclopedia*, p. 469.
112. Alfred Webb, Presidential Address at 1894 Indian National Congress, in Zaidi and Zaidi, *Encyclopedia*, p. 470.
113. Ibid., pp. 480–482.
114. Alfred Webb, 'Mr Webb's vindication of his ruling on the Norton incident at the Congress,' letter to Mr R. Venkata Ratnam, 5 January 1895, reprinted in *Indian Affairs*.
115. Wacha to Naoroji, 5 January 1895 [NAI, Naoroji papers, Acc. 448, reel 46, W-1(270)]; Webb, *Autobiography*, pp. 68–69; Rosemary Auchmuty, 'Müller, (Frances) Henrietta (1845/6–1906),' in *DNB*.
116. Alfred Webb, 'Mr Webb's Goodbye at Madras,' in *Indian Affairs*.
117. Alfred Webb, 'Address to the Students of Madras,' in *Indian Affairs*.
118. Ibid.
119. Webb, *Autobiography*, p. 68.
120. Address to Alfred Webb from the Koloba district, 18 January 1895, copy (DFHL, Webb papers, MS Port. 43, folder 28). See also open letter to Alfred Webb from the 'fellow-subjects of Pen Taluka,' 18 January 1895 (ibid.).
121. Open letter to Alfred Webb from Mirasidars of Peralore and Sembian, December 1894 (ibid.).
122. Alfred Webb, 'Mr Webb's Valedictory Address at Bombay, 17 January 1894,' in *Indian Affairs*.
123. Wacha to Naoroji, 5 January 1895 [NAI, Naoroji papers, MS Acc. 448, reel 46, W-1(270)].
124. 'The Indian National Congress – the President's Views,' clipping from *Manchester Guardian*, 19 February 1895 (NLI, Webb papers, MS 1746).

8 'Politics is a difficult and anxious game': An Assessment of Webb

1. Webb to O'Neill Daunt, 16 December 1873 (NLI, Daunt papers, MS 8048/6).
2. Alfred Webb, 'The Gaelic League and Politics,' in *Dana: An Irish Magazine of Independent Thought*, September 1904, pp. 141–144.
3. Lyons, *Culture and Anarchy*, p. 71.
4. 'The Indian National Congress – the President's Views,' *Manchester Guardian*, 19 February 1895 (NLI, Webb papers, MS 1746).
5. Draft of J. F. X.'s unpublished autobiography, edited by Webb (NLI, J. F. X. O'Brien papers, MS 16,695).
6. Webb to J. F. X. O'Brien, 24 August 1895 (ibid., MS 13,431/4).
7. T. M. Healy to Maurice Healy, 6 July 1895 (UCD, Healy papers, MS P6/A/27).
8. Webb to J. F. X. O'Brien, 24 August 1895 (NLI, J. F. X. O'Brien papers, MS 13,431/4).
9. Lyons, *Irish Parliamentary Party*, p. 45.
10. Webb to Justin McCarthy (draft), 10 August 1894 (NLI, Webb papers, MS 1746).
11. Webb to Dillon, 17 August 1895 (TCD, Dillon papers, MS 6760/1681).
12. Webb to J. F. X. O'Brien, 29 August 1895 (NLI, J. F. X. O'Brien papers, MS 13,431/4).

13. Webb to Naoroji, 27 August 1895 [NAI, Naoroji papers, MS Acc. 450, reel 48, W-41(1)].
14. *India*, September 1895.
15. Ibid.
16. Sir Mancherjee Merwanjee Bhownaggree, Conservative MP for Bethnal Green, London 1895–1906.
17. Dadabhai Naoroji to Michael Davitt, 15 January 1896 (TCD, Davitt papers, MS 9348/529).
18. 'The Government of India,' *Freeman's Journal*, 31 May 1897.
19. Ibid.
20. Webb to Naoroji, 22 October 1902 [NAI, Naoroji papers, MS Acc. 450, reel 48, W-41(8)].
21. Ibid.
22. Fred Cutliffe, editor, to Naoroji, in *New International Review*, 4 December 1906 (NAI, Naoroji papers, MS Acc. 438, reel 36, N-91). The Irish nationalists were D. J. Cogan (W. Wicklow), William Duffy (S. Galway), James C. Flynn (N. Cork), John Hayden (S. Roscommon), Jeremiah Jordan (S. Fermanagh), Michael Joyce (Limerick City), Vincent Kennedy (W. Cavan), Hugh Law (W. Donegal), Thomas O'Donnell (W. Kerry), Patrick O'Hara (N. Monaghan) and J. J. O'Shea (W. Waterford).
23. Alfred Webb, draft of letter to Thirteenth Indian National Congress, 4 November 1897 (NLI, Webb papers, MS 1747); Alfred Webb, letter to the editor of *India*, 12 September [1899?] (ibid.).
24. Ripon to Webb, 23 August 1899 (TCD, Webb papers, MS 4787/61).
25. Clipping from unidentified Indian newspaper, 16 May 1897 (NLI, Webb papers, MS 1747).
26. Reviews clipped from several unidentified Indian newspapers, 1898 (ibid.).
27. Webb to Harrington, 17 August 1897 (NLI, Harrington papers, MS 8576/50).
28. Alfred Webb, 'The Wants and Wishes of India from the Indian Standpoint,' invitation to a talk by Gokhale and Wacha, 25 May 1897 (TCD, Dillon papers, MS 6852/11).
29. Webb to Dillon, 11 June 1897 (ibid., MS 6760/1698).
30. Webb to Dillon, 5 June 1897 (ibid., MS 6760/1700).
31. Ibid.
32. Webb to Naoroji, 22 September 1907 [NAI, Naoroji papers, MS Acc. 450, reel 48, W-41(7)].
33. Webb, *Autobiography*, pp. 67–68.
34. Daniel Sanjiv Roberts, ' "Merely birds of passage": Lady Hariot Dufferin's Travel Writings and Medical Work in India, 1884–1888,' in *Women's History Review*, vol. xv, no. 3 (July 2006), pp. 443–457; Antoinette Burton, 'Contesting the Zenana: The Mission to Make "Lady Doctors" for India, 1874–1885,' in *Journal of British Studies*, vol. xv (July 1996), pp. 368–397.
35. Webb to Naoroji, 20 October 1896 [NAI, Naoroji papers, MS Acc. 450, reel 48, W-41(2)]; Webb to Naoroji, 26 October 1896 [ibid., W-41(3)].
36. See p. 130.
37. Alfred Webb MP, 'Liberals and Home Rule,' clipping from *Manchester Guardian*, 10 March 1894 (NLI, Webb papers, MS 1746).
38. Alfred Webb, clipping of letter to the editor of *Freeman's Journal*, 8 March 1900 (NLI, Webb papers, MS 1747).

39. Davitt to Webb, 7 December 1899 (TCD, Davitt papers, 9490/6965), original emphasis.
40. Ibid., original emphasis.
41. See *Freeman's Journal*, October and November 1899.
42. 'An address from Ireland to his excellency Paul Kruger', written by Webb and signed by Webb, Davitt, and J. J. O'Kelly, n.d. (NLI, Webb papers, 1747).
43. Alfred Webb, 'Transvaal Sick and Wounded,' *Freeman's Journal*, 14 November 1899 (ibid.).
44. Alfred Webb, letter to the editor of *Freeman's Journal*, 16 November 1899 (ibid.).
45. Alfred Webb, 'The Irish Members and the Boers,' letter to the editor of *Freeman's Journal*, 16 March 1902 (ibid.).
46. Original in block capital letters. Address in minute book of Irish Transvaal Committee, 12 October 1899 (NLI, William Redmond papers, MS 19,933).
47. Alfred Webb, article on Rudyard Kipling, *Hindu*, 30 March 1899, reprint from the *New York Evening Post* (NLI, Webb papers, MS 1747). Webb seems to have used 'aborigine' as a general term, and not solely in reference to the native inhabitants of Australia.
48. Webb to J. F. X. O'Brien, 21 July 1898 (NLI, J. F. X. O'Brien papers, MS 13,431/5).
49. DFHL, Webb autobiography, f. 25.
50. Webb to Dillon, 5 June 1898 (TCD, Dillon papers, MS 6760/1713).
51. Webb, *Autobiography*, pp. 66–67.
52. Alfred Webb, review of Booker T. Washington's *Up from Slavery: An Autobiography*, clipping from *British Friend*, August 1901 (NLI, Webb papers, MS 1747).
53. DFHL, Webb autobiography, f. 25.
54. Alfred Webb, 'The invasion of Tibet,' clipping of letter to the editor of *Freeman's Journal*, 3 April 1904 (NLI, Webb papers, MS 1747).
55. Alfred Webb, 'On the footsteps of some of the men of '48', speech to Belfast Young Ireland Society, n.d. (NLI, Webb papers, MS 1747); Alfred Webb, 'A Pilgrimage to Tasmania,' letter to the editor of *Freeman's Journal*, 28 November 1895 (NLI, Webb papers, MS 1746).
56. 'Home Rule,' *Tasmanian News*, 29 November 1895 (ibid.).
57. Webb to Dillon, 9 January 1896 (TCD, Dillon papers, MS 6760/1685).
58. Webb to J. F. X. O'Brien, 9 November 1897 (NLI, J. F. X. O'Brien papers, MS 13,431/4).
59. Webb to J. F. X. O'Brien, 14 April 1897 (ibid.); Draft of Evicted Tenants Fund Report and Appeal, July 1898 (NLI, J. F. X. O'Brien papers, MS 13,431/5); Evicted Tenants Fund Report and Appeal and Statement of Accounts, July 1898 (NLI, Webb papers, MS 1747).
60. Webb to John Redmond, 6 July 1900 (NLI, Harrington papers, MS 8577/1).
61. Correspondence from Webb to J. F. X. O'Brien on United Irish League and General Election Fund letterhead, October 1900 (NLI, J. F. X. O'Brien papers, MS 13,431/5).
62. Webb to J. F. X. O'Brien, 24 September 1902 (NLI, J. F. X. O'Brien papers, MS 13,431/6).
63. Webb to J. F. X. O'Brien, 25 February 1902 (ibid.).

64. Alfred Webb, first ten motions, Irish Race Convention Agenda, 1–3 September 1896 (PRONI, Jordan papers, MS D/2073/4/1).
65. T. M. Healy to Maurice Healy, 1 September 1896 (UCD, Healy papers, MS P6/A/31).
66. Webb to O'Brien, 1 November 1898 (NLI, J. F. X. O'Brien papers, MS 16,696).
67. Webb to J. F. X. O'Brien, 14 August 1896 (ibid., MS 13,431/4).
68. Webb to J. F. X. O'Brien, 21 July 1898 (ibid., MS 13,431/5).
69. Webb to J. F. X. O'Brien, 14 August 1896 (ibid., MS 13,431/4).
70. Letter to Alfred Webb to the editor of *Freeman's Journal*, 15 April 1899 (NLI, Webb papers, MS 1747).
71. Webb to J. F. X. O'Brien, 5 December 1902 (NLI, J. F. X. O'Brien papers, MS 13,431/6).
72. See, for example, Irish National Fund Subscriptions 1897–1899 (NLI, J. F. X. O'Brien papers, MS 9232); Irish Parliamentary Party Receipts 1897–1898 (ibid., MS 9233); Irish Parliamentary Party receipt book, 1898–1899 (ibid., MS 9234); Parliamentary Fund account book 1896–1899 (ibid., MS 9236).
73. Alfred Webb, 'The Gaelic League and Nationality,' *Freeman's Journal*, 20 May 1900.
74. Alfred Webb, 'The Study of Irish', *Freeman's Journal*, 7 September 1899.
75. Alfred Webb, letter to the editor, *Freeman's Journal*, 28 September 1901.
76. Webb to Mac Neill, 13 June and 16 June 1899 (NLI, Eoin Mac Neill papers, MS 10,877). Mac Neill went ahead, lost a great deal of money, but had few regrets because ultimately it had 'the effect of making Irish printing an ordinary business matter in Dublin, and no longer a high-priced luxury'. Short typed paragraph quote, attributed to 'Tráchtas Mhic Neill,' n.d. (ibid.).
77. David Sheehy to J. F. X. O'Brien, 17 October 1901 (NLI, J. F. X. O'Brien papers, MS 13,431/6).
78. Webb to J. F. X. O'Brien, 12 October 1901 (ibid.).
79. Webb to J. F. X. O'Brien, 13 October 1901 (ibid.).
80. Webb to J. F. X. O'Brien, 23 October 1901 (ibid.).
81. T. Sexton to J. F. X. O'Brien, 2 November 1901 (ibid., MS 13,429).
82. For information on Irish Ireland see Patrick Maume, *The Rise and Fall of Irish Ireland: D. P. Moran and Daniel Corkery* (Coleraine, 1996); Patrick Maume, *The Long Gestation: Irish national life, 1891–1918* (Dublin, 1999), esp. Ch. 2.
83. Webb to Dillon, 27 April 1904 (TCD, Dillon papers, MS 6760/1730).
84. Ibid.
85. Webb, 'The Gaelic League and Politics,' p. 142.
86. Webb to Dillon, 19 May 1897 (TCD, Dillon papers, MS 6760/1696).
87. Webb, 'The Gaelic League and Politics,' p. 142.
88. Ibid., p. 142.
89. Ibid., p. 143.
90. Alfred Webb, *Thoughts in Retirement*, p. 1.
91. For a discussion of Douglas Hyde and Patrick Pearse's differing views on modernisation, see J. J. Lee, *The Modernisation of Irish Society, 1848–1918* (Dublin, 1989), pp. 137–148.
92. Ibid., p. 144.
93. An Craobhín [Douglas Hyde] to Webb, 2 October 1905 (TCD, Webb papers, MS 4787/28).

94. Webb to Dillon, 29 October 1903 (TCD, Dillon papers, MS 6760/1729).
95. Webb to Dillon, 22 June 1897 (ibid., MS 6760/1707).
96. Webb to Dillon, 22 February 1907 (ibid., MS 6760/1753).
97. Webb, *Autobiography*, p. 42.
98. G. K. Peatling, 'Interactions from the Periphery,' p. 103.
99. See, for example, David Thornley, 'The Irish Conservatives and Home Rule, 1869–73,' in *Irish Historical Studies*, vol. xi (1958–1959), pp. 200–222.
100. 'Mr Pinkerton, MP Interview [by MP Squirrel],' [Eastern?] *Daily*, 16 July 1889 (PRONI, Pinkerton papers, MS D/1078/P/2).
101. Seal, *Emergence*, p. 22.

Bibliography

Primary Sources

I. Archival Sources

Republic of Ireland:
Dublin City Archives

Dublin City Council Minutes, 1882–1884.
Dublin City Council Reports, 1882–1884.

Friends Historical Library Dublin

Autobiography of Alfred Webb, 1906.
Miscellaneous papers relating Alfred Webb and India, Portfolio 43, folders 28–29.
Miscellaneous Webb family photos, 229a, p. 67.

National Archives of Ireland

Port and Docks Board Records, 1880–1885.
Will of Alfred Webb, 1908.

National Library of Ireland

Isaac Butt papers, 8506, 8692–8694, 8705–8706, 13,257.
Daniel Crilly papers, 5937.
William O'Neill Daunt papers, 8047–8048.
George Delaney papers, 10,512.
Charles Gavan Duffy papers, 8005.
Eva Gore-Booth papers, 1651.
T. C. Harrington papers, 8576–8582, 9454.
Home Rule League Scrapbook, 3272.
Irish Protestant Home Rule Association papers, 3657.
Rosamond Jacob papers, 33,143.
Eoin Mac Neill papers, 10,877.
Men's Bill Book of a Dublin printing office, 141.
J. F. X. O'Brien papers, 5835, 9222–9225, 9232–9236, 13,432, 16,695–16, 696.
Mrs William O'Brien papers, 8507.
Charles Stewart Parnell and Cecil Rhodes correspondence, 697.
Joseph Quinn papers, 5930.
Records of a Dublin letterpress, 139–140.
William Redmond papers, 19,933.

Alfred Webb papers, 1745–1747.
Alfred Webb to C. H. Oldham, autograph letter, 1886.

University College Dublin

T. M. Healy papers, P6/A, P6/B.

Trinity College Dublin

Michael Davitt papers, 9470–9472, 9490, 9346–9349, 9590, 9596.
John Dillon papers, 6760, 6727, 6852.
R. D. and Alfred Webb papers, 4787.

Northern Ireland:
Public Record Office of Northern Ireland

Rev. J. B. Armour papers, D/1792.
Joseph Biggar papers, T/1160.
Home Rule Association Letterbook, D/213.
Jeremiah Jordan papers, D/2073.
John Pinkerton papers, D/1078.

England:
British Library Office of India and Oriental Collections

William Digby papers, Eur D767.

National Liberal Club

Elections Sub-Committee Minutes, 1889–1900.
General Committee Minutes, 1883–1900.
Lectures and Discussions Minutes, 1889.
Political Sub-Committee Minutes, 1895–1897.
Rules, Regulations, Bye-Laws, List of Members, 1884–1887, 1890–1891, 1893–1895.

Reform Club

Membership records, 1870–1900.

United States:
Boston Public Library

Anti-Slavery Papers, A.1.1, A.2.1, A.9.2.

India:
National Archives of India

Dadabhai Naoroji papers, account nos 407–450.

210 Bibliography

Minutes of the British Committee of the Indian National Congress, Account no. 1941.

Nehru Memorial Museum and Library

Dadabhai Naoroji papers, 4A.

II. Periodicals
Anti-Caste
Dana: An Irish Magazine of Independent Thought
Fraternity
Freeman's Journal
India: A Journal for the Discussion of Indian Affairs
Irish Builder
Thom's Irish Almanac and Official Directory
Journal of the Statistical and Social Inquiry Society of Ireland [Published on microfilm as *Economic and Social Investigations in Ireland: The Transactions of the Dublin Social Inquiry and Statistical Society, 1847–1919* (Reading, 1990).]

III. Official Publications
Alfred Webb MP, 'Indian Opium Revenue. Resolution', *Hansard*, 4, *xiv*, 30 June 1893, pp. 591–602.
Alfred Webb MP, 'Supply – Civil Service Estimates', *Hansard*, 3, cccxlvi, 11 July 1893, pp. 1511–1516.
Final Report of the Royal Commission on the Administration of the Expenditure of India, iv [Cd. 131], H.C. 1900, xxix, 553–748.
Minutes of Evidence Taken Before the Royal Commission on the Administration of the Expenditure of India, iii [Cd. 130], H.C. 1900, xxix, 1–502.
Royal Commission on Administration of Expenditure of India: First Report Volume I. Minutes of Evidence, vi, 1 [C.8258], H.C. 1896, xvi, 6.
Royal Commission on Condition of Poorer Classes in Ireland, Appendix C, Part 2: Report on City of Dublin, Appendix C, Part ii [36], H.C. 1836, xxx.

IV. Contemporary Published Works
Anonymous. *The Society of Friends in Ireland and Home Rule: A Letter from a Member of the Society of Friends in Ireland to a Fellow-Member*. Dublin, 1893.
Armitage, Evelyn Noble. *The Quaker Poets of Great Britain and Ireland*. London, 1896.
Banerjea, Surendranath. *A Nation in Making: Being the Reminiscences of Fifty Years of Public Life*. London, 1925.
Bennett, William. *Narrative of a Recent Journey of Six Weeks in Ireland, in Connexion with the Subject of Supplying Small Seed to Some of the Remoter Districts*. London and Dublin, 1847.
Brown, William W. *Narrative of William W. Brown, an American Slave*. London, 1849.
Butt, Isaac. *Irish Federalism: Its Meaning, Its Objects, and Its Hopes*. Dublin, 1870.
Coffey, George. *Home Rule: Answers to Objections*. London, 1888.

Daunt, W. J. O'Neill. *A Life Spent for Ireland: Being Selections from the Journals of the Late W. J. O'Neill Daunt*, edited by his daughter. London, 1896.
———. *Eighty-Five Years of Irish History, 1800–1885. 2nd edn with supplementary chapter bringing down the narrative to 1887*. London, 1888.
Davitt, Michael. *The Fall of Feudalism in Ireland: or, The Story of the Land League Revolution*. London and New York, 1904.
Department of Agriculture and Technical Instruction for Ireland. *Ireland: Industrial and Agricultural*. Dublin, 1902.
Douglass, Frederick. *Narrative of the Life of Frederick Douglass, an American Slave*. Boston, 1845. A digitalised version is available at http://www.history.rochester.edu/class/douglass/DUGLAS11.TXT (Consulted March 2005).
EML. *A Few Words on Women's Suffrage*. Dublin, 1873.
Gladstone, W. E. *Speech on the Government of Ireland Bill*. London, 1886.
Harrison, Frederic. *Mr Gladstone – or Anarchy!* London, 188[6?].
Haughton, Samuel. *Memoir of James Haugton: With Extracts From His Private and Public Letters*. Dublin and London, 1877.
Healy, T. M. *A Word for Ireland*. Dublin, 1886.
Hill, Berkeley. 'Statistical Results of the Contagious Diseases Acts'. In *Journal of the Statistical Society of London*, vol. xxii, no. 4 (December 1870), pp. 463–485.
Home Rule League. *Proceedings of the Home Rule Conference Held at the Rotunda, Dublin, on the 18th, 19th, 20th and 21st November, 1873*. Dublin, 1874.
———. *Proceedings in Connection with the Visit to Dublin of the Marquis of Ripon, K. G. and the Right Hon. John Morley, M. P., 1st to 3rd February, 1888*. Dublin, 1888.
Howitt, Mary. *An Autobiography, edited by her daughter*. 2 vols, London, 1889.
Irish International Exhibition, 1907. Dublin, 1907.
Irish Loyal and Patriotic Union. *The Parnell Catechism: Questions and Answers on the Government of Ireland Bill*. Dublin, 188[6?].
Johnson, William Forbes. *A Letter on Protection, to the Right Hon. Lord Stanley, in Which is Discussed the Probable Duration of the British Empire Under the Present Laws*. Dublin, 1850.
Kane, Robert. *The Industrial Resources of Ireland*. Dublin, 1845.
MacColl, Rev. Malcolm. *Reasons for Home Rule*. London, 1886.
McEvoy, John. *Suggestions for Dublin Municipal Reform*. Dublin, 1878.
Collected Works of John Stuart Mill, vols xiv–xvii, *The Later Letters of John Stuart Mill 1849–1873*. eds. Mineka, Francis E. and Lindley, Dwight N., and vol. xxxii *Additional Letters of John Stuart Mill*, eds. Filipiuk, Marion, Laine, Michael and Robson, John M. 32 vols, Toronto and London, 1972 and 1991.
O'Brien, R. Barry. *The Life of Charles Stewart Parnell*. London and New York, 1910.
O'Brien, Sophie (Mrs William O'Brien). *My Irish Friends*. London and Dublin, 1937.
O'Connor, T. P. *Memoirs of An Old Parliamentarian*. 2 vols, London, 1929.
O'Donnell, F. H. *A History of the Irish Parliamentary Party*. 2 vols, London, 1910.
O'Malley, Thaddeus. *Home Rule on the Basis of Federalism*. Dublin, 1873.
Sieveking, J. G. *Memoir and Letters of F. W. Newman*. London, 1909.
Smith, Joseph. *Supplement to a Descriptive Catalogue of Friends' books*. London, 1892. Reprinted. New York, 1970.
Society of Friends. *Rules of Discipline of the Yearly Meeting of Friends in Ireland with Advices Issued and Adopted Thereby*. 2nd edn, Dublin, 1841.

The Statistical and Social Inquiry Society of Ireland. *List of Members of the Society*. Dublin, 1864.
Sullivan, A. M. *New Ireland*. 2 vols, London, 1877.
Webb, Alfred. *Alfred Webb: The Autobiography of a Quaker Nationalist*. Ed. Marie-Louise Legg. Cork, 1999.
———. *Why I Desire Home Rule*. Dublin, 1874.
———. *Eternal Punishment*. Dublin, 1876.
———. *A Compendium of Irish Biography: Comprising Sketches of Distinguished Irishmen, and of Eminent Persons Connected with Ireland by Office or by Their Writings*. Dublin, 1878.
———, ed. *The Opinions of Some Protestants Regarding Their Irish Catholic Fellow-Countrymen*. 3rd edn, enlarged, with resolutions of the Irish Protestant Home Rule Association. Dublin, 1886.
———. *Indian Affairs: Speeches of Alfred Webb, Esq., M. P., President, Tenth Indian National Congress*. Bombay, 1895.
———. *Thoughts in Retirement*. Dublin, 1908.
Webb, Thomas E. *The Irish Question: A Reply to Mr. Gladstone*. Dublin, 1886.
Wedderburn, William. *Allan Octavian Hume, C.B., 'father of the Indian National Congress', 1829–1912*. London, 1913.
Zaidi, A. M., ed. *Congress Presidential Addresses, vol. I: 1885–1900*. 5 vols, New Delhi, 1985.

Secondary Sources

I. Books and Articles

Ahmed, Sara. 'Affective Economies.' In *Social Text*, 79, vol. xxii, no. 2 (Summer 2004), pp. 117–139.
Alderson, David. *Mansex Fine: Religion, Manliness and Imperialism in Nineteenth-Century British Culture*. Manchester, 1998.
Anderson, Nancy Fix. 'Bridging Cross-Cultural Feminisms: Annie Besant and Women's Rights in England and India, 1874–1933.' In *Women's History Review*, vol. iii, no. 4 (1994), pp. 563–580.
Anderson, Benedict. *Imagined Communities: Reflections on the Origin and Spread of Nationalism*. London, 1983.
Ashton, Philip. 'Divided Ideals: The Religious Society of Friends and the Irish Home Rule Controversy 1885 to 1886.' In *The Woodbrooke Journal*, no. 6 (summer 2000).
Balkin, Jordanna. 'The Place of Liberalism.' In *Victorian Studies*, vol. xlviii, no. 1 (2005), pp. 83–91.
Bayly, Christopher A. 'Ireland, India and the Empire, 1780–1914.' In *Transactions of the Royal Historical Society*, 6th series, vol. x, no. 10 (2000), pp. 377–397.
———. *The Birth of the Modern World, 1780–1914: Global Connections and Comparisons*. Oxford, 2004.
Bew, Paul. *Land and the National Question in Ireland, 1858–82*. Dublin, 1978.
———. *Charles Stewart Parnell*. Dublin, 1980.
Black, R. D. Collison. 'History of the Society.' In *Statistical and Social Inquiry Society of Ireland Centenary Volume 1847–1947*. Dublin, 1947, pp. 1–47.
Bolt, Christine. *Victorian Attitudes to Race*. London, 1971.

Boltwood, Scott. ' "The ineffaceable curse of Cain": Race, Miscegenation, and the Victorian Staging of Irishness.' In *Victorian Literature and Culture*, vol. xxix, no. 2, 2001, pp. 383–396.

Boyce, D. George and O'Day, Alan, eds. *Defenders of the Union: A Survey of British and Irish Unionism Since 1801*. London and New York, 2001.

Boylan, Anne M. 'Women in Groups: An Analysis of Women's Benevolent Organisations in New York and Boston, 1797–1840.' In *Journal of American History*, vol. lxxi (1984), pp. 497–523.

Boyle, John W. *The Irish Labor Movement in the Nineteenth Century*. Washington, 1988.

Brasted, Howard. 'Indian Nationalist Development and the Influence of Irish Home Rule, 1870–1886.' In *Modern Asian studies*, vol. xiv, no. 1 (1980), pp. 37–63.

———. 'Irish Nationalism and the British Empire in the Late Nineteenth Century.' In MacDonagh, Oliver, Mandle, W. F. and Travers, Pauric, eds. *Irish Culture and Nationalism, 1750–1950*. Dublin, 1983.

Brown, Judith M. *Modern India: The Origins of an Asian Democracy*. 2nd edn, Oxford, 1994.

Burton, Antoinette. *Burdens of History: British Feminists, Indian Women, and Imperial Culture, 1865–1915*. Chapel Hill and London, 1994.

———. 'Contesting the Zenana: The Mission to Make "Lady Doctors" for India, 1874–1885.' In *Journal of British Studies*, vol. xxxv (July 1996), pp. 368–397.

———. *At the Heart of the Empire: Indians and the Colonial Encounter in Late-Victorian Britain*. Berkeley, 1998.

———. 'Tongues Untied: Lord Salisbury's "Black Man" and the Boundaries of Imperial Democracy.' In *Comparative Studies in Society and History*, vol. xlii, no. 3 (July 2000), pp. 632–661.

Callanan, Frank. *The Parnell Split, 1890–1*. Cork, 1992.

———. *T. M. Healy*. Cork, 1996.

Candy, Catherine. 'Relating Feminisms, Nationalisms, and Imperialisms: Ireland, India and Margaret Cousins's Sexual Politics.' In *Women's History Review*, vol. iii, no. 4 (1994), pp. 581–594.

Chandra, Bipan et al. *India's Struggle for Independence*. New Delhi, 1989.

Clyde, Tom. *Irish Literary Magazines: An Outline History and Descriptive Bibliography*. Dublin, 2002.

Colley, Linda. *The Ordeal of Elizabeth Marsh: A Woman in World History*. London, 2007.

Colman, Anne. 'Far From Silent: Nineteenth-Century Irish Women Writers.' In Kelleher, Margaret and Murphy, James H., eds. *Gender Perspectives in Nineteenth-Century Ireland: Public and Private Spheres*. Dublin, 1997, pp. 203–211.

Comerford, R. V. 'Ireland, 1870–1921.' In Vaughan, W. E., ed. *A New History of Ireland, vol. vi: Ireland under the Union II – 1870–1921*. 8 vols, Oxford, 1996, pp. xliii–lvii.

———. 'The Home Rule Party 1870–77.' In Vaughan, W. E., ed. *A New History of Ireland, vol. vi: Ireland under the Union II – 1870–1921*. 8 vols, Oxford, 1996, pp. 1–25.

———. 'The Land War and the Politics of Distress, 1877–82.' In Vaughan, W. E., ed. *A New History of Ireland, vol. vi: Ireland under the Union II – 1870–1921*. 8 vols, Oxford, 1996, pp. 26–52.

——. *The Fenians in Context: Irish Politics and Society 1848–1882*. 2nd edn, Dublin, 1998.
Connolly, S. J. 'Eighteenth-Century Ireland: Colony or *ancien régime*?' In Boyce, D. George and O'Day, Alan, eds. *The Making of Modern Irish History: Revisionism and the Revisionist Controversy*. London, 1996, pp. 15–33.
——. 'Religion, Work-Discipline and Economic Attitudes: The Case of Ireland.' In Devine, Thomas Martin and Dickson, David, eds. *Ireland and Scotland 1600–1850: Parallels and Contrast in Economic and Social Development*. Edinburgh, 1983, pp. 235–245.
Cook, Scott B. *Imperial Affinities: Nineteenth Century Analogies and Exchanges Between India and Ireland*. London and New Delhi, 1993.
——. 'The Irish Raj: Social Origins and Careers of Irishmen in the Indian Civil Service, 1855–1914.' In *Journal of Social History*, vol. xx (1987), pp. 507–529.
Crangle, John V. 'Irish Nationalist Criticism of the Imperial Administration of India (1880–1884).' In *Quarterly Review of Historical Studies*, vol. xi, no. 4 (1972), pp. 189–194.
Cullen, Fintan and Foster, Roy. *'Conquering England': Ireland in Victorian London*. London, 2005.
Cullen, M. J. *The Statistical Movement in Early Victorian Britain: The Foundations of Empirical Social Research*. Hassocks, Sussex, 1975.
Cumpston, Mary. 'Some Early Indian Nationalists and Their Allies in the British Parliament, 1851–1906.' In *English Historical Review*, vol. lxxvi, no. 299 (April 1961), pp. 279–297.
Curtis, L. P. *Anglo-Saxons and Celts: A Study of Anti-Irish Prejudice in Victorian England*. Bridgeport, CT, 1968.
——. *Apes and Angels: The Irishman in Victorian Caricature*. Newton Abbot, 1971.
Dalmia, Vasudha. *Orienting India: European Knowledge Formation in the Eighteenth and Nineteenth Centuries*. New Delhi, 2003.
Daly, Mary and Dickson, David, eds. *The Origins of Popular Literacy in Ireland: Language Change and Educational Development 1700–1920*. Dublin, 1990.
Daly, Mary E. *Dublin: The Deposed Capital, a Social and Economic History, 1860–1914*. Cork, 1984.
——. *The Spirit of Earnest Inquiry: The Statistical and Social Inquiry Society of Ireland 1847–1997*. Dublin, 1997.
D'Arcy, Fergus A. 'Wages of Labourers in the Dublin Building Industry, 1667–1918.' *Saothar*, vol. xiv (1989), pp. 17–32.
——. 'Religion, Radicalism and Rebellion in Nineteenth-Century Ireland : The Case of Thaddeus O'Malley.' In Devlin, Judith and Fanning, Ronan, eds. *Religion and Rebellion*. Dublin, 1997.
——. 'Federalist, Social Radical and Anti-Sectarian; Thaddeus O'Malley (1798–1877).' In Moran, Gerard, ed. *Radical Irish Priests 1660–1970*. Dublin, 1998.
Darnton, Robert and Roche, Daniel, eds. *Revolution in Print: The Press in France, 1775–1800*. London and Berkeley, 1989.
Delheim, Charles. 'The Creation of a Company Culture: Cadburys, 1861–1931.' In *The American Historical Review*, vol. xcii, no. 1 (February 1987), pp. 13–44.
Doyle, Eugene. *Justin McCarthy*. Dundalk, 1996.
Dungan, Miles. *The Stealing of the Irish Crown Jewels*. Dublin, 2003.
Dutt, Paramananda. *Memoirs of Moti Lal Ghose*. Calcutta, 1935.
Elliott, Marianne. *The Catholics of Ulster*. London, 2000.

———. *Robert Emmet: The Making of a Legend*. London, 2003.
Ellis, Stephen. 'Writing Irish History: Revisionism, Colonialism, and the British Isles.' In *Irish Review*, no. 19 (1996), pp. 1–21.
Eriksen, Thomas Hylland. *Ethnicity and Nationalism: Anthropological Perspectives*. 2nd edn, London, 2002.
Fisher, Michael. *Counterflows to Colonialism: Indian Travellers and Settlers in Britain, 1600–1857*. New Delhi, 2004.
Fitzpatrick, David. 'Ireland and the Empire.' In Porter, Andrew, ed. *The Oxford History of the British Empire, vol. III: The Nineteenth Century*. 5 vols, Oxford, 1999, pp. 495–521.
Foley, Tadhg and O'Connor, Maureen, eds. *Ireland and India: Colonies, Culture and Empire*. Dublin, 2006.
Foster, Roy F. *Charles Stewart Parnell: The Man and His Family*. Hassocks, Sussex, 1976.
———. *Paddy and Mr Punch*. London, 1993.
———. *W. B. Yeats: A Life vol. 1: The Apprentice Mage, 1865–1914*. Oxford, 1997.
Gandhi, Leela. *Affective Communities: Anti-Colonial thought, fin-de-siécle Radicalism and the Politics of Friendship*. Durham and London, 2006.
Geiss, Immanuel. *The Pan-African Movement*. Trans. Ann Keep. London, 1974.
Gellner, Ernest and Breuilly, John. *Nations and Nationalism*. London, 2005.
Gibbons, Luke. *Gaelic Gothic: Race, Colonization and Irish Culture*. Galway, 2004.
Goodbody, Rob. *A Suitable Channel: Quaker Relief in the Great Famine*. Bray, Wicklow, 1995.
Gray, Peter. 'Famine and Land in Ireland and India, 1845–1880: James Caird and the Political Economy of Hunger.' In *The Historical Journal*, vol. xlix, no. 1 (2006), pp. 193–215.
———, ed. *Victoria's Ireland? Irishness and Britishness, 1837–1901*. Dublin, 2004.
Grubb, Isabel. *Quakers in Ireland*. Dublin, 1929.
Haggis, Jane and Allen, Margaret. 'Imperial Emotions: Affective Communities of Mission in British Protestant Women's Missionary Publications c. 1880–1920.' In *Journal of Social History*, vol. xli, no. 3 (Spring 2008), pp. 691–716.
Hall, Catherine. *Civilising Subjects: Metropole and Colony in the English Imagination, 1830–1867*. Oxford, 2002.
Harrison, Richard S. *Richard Davis Webb: Dublin Quaker Printer (1805–72)*. Skibbereen, 1993.
———. *A Biographical Dictionary of Irish Quakers*. Dublin, 1997.
Harvie, Christopher. 'Ideology and Home Rule: James Bryce, A. V. Dicey and Ireland, 1880–1887.' In *The English Historical Review*, vol. xci, no. 359 (1976), pp. 298–314.
Hatton, Helen E. *The Largest amount of Good: Quaker Relief in Ireland 1654–1921*. London, 1993.
Hearn, Mona. *Thomas Edmondson and the Dublin Laundry: A Quaker Businessman 1837–1908*. Dublin, 2004.
Hooper, Glenn and Graham, Colin, eds. *Irish and Postcolonial Writing: History, Theory, Practice*. Houndmills, 2002.
Hopkins, A. G. 'Viewpoint: Back to the Future: From National History to Imperial History.' In *Past & Present*, vol. clxiv (1999), pp. 198–243.

Howe, Stephen. *Ireland and Empire: Colonial Legacies in Irish History and Culture.* Oxford, 2000.

Hunt, Lynn and Jacob, Margaret. 'The Affective Revolution in 1790s Britain.' In *Eighteenth-Century Studies*, vol. xxxiv, no. 4 (2001), pp. 491–521.

Hurst, Michael. 'Ireland and the Ballot Act of 1872.' In *The Historical Journal*, vol. xiii, no. 3 (1965), pp. 343–348.

Isichei, Elizabeth. *Victorian Quakers.* London, 1970.

Jackson, Alvin. 'Irish Unionism and the Russellite Threat, 1894–1906.' In *Irish Historical Studies*, vol. xxv, no. 100 (November 1987), pp. 376–404.

———. *Ireland 1798–1998.* Oxford and Malden, MA, 1999.

———. *Home Rule: An Irish History 1800–2000.* London, 2003.

Jeffery, Keith, ed. *An Irish Empire?: Aspects of Ireland and the British Empire.* Manchester, 1996.

Jones, D. K. 'Lancashire, the American Common School, and the Religious Problem in British Education in the Nineteenth Century.' In *British Journal of Educational Studies*, vol. xv, no. 3 (October 1967), pp. 292–306.

Jordan, Donald. 'The Irish National League and the "Unwritten Law": Rural Protest and Nation-Building in Ireland 1882–1890.' In *Past and Present*, vol. clviii (February 1998), pp. 146–171.

Kendle, J. E. 'The Round Table Movement and "Home Rule All Round."' In *Historical Journal*, vol. xi, no. 2 (1968), pp. 332–353.

Kelly, M. J. *The Fenian Ideal and Irish Nationalism, 1882–1916.* Woodbridge, 2006.

Kennedy, Liam. *Colonialism, Religion and Nationalism in Ireland.* Belfast, 1996.

Kennedy, Liam and Martin W. Dowling. 'Prices and Wages in Ireland, 1700–1850.' In *Irish Economic and Social History*, vol. xxiv (1997), pp. 62–104.

Kennedy, Thomas C. *British Quakerism 1860–1920: The Transformation of a Religious Community.* Oxford, 2001.

Kenny, Kevin, ed. *Ireland and the British Empire.* Oxford, 2004.

Kinane, Vincent. *A History of the Dublin University Press, 1734–1976.* Dublin, 1994.

Kincaid, Andrew. *Postcolonial Dublin: Imperial Legacies and the Built Environment.* Minneapolis, 2006.

King, Carla. 'Michael Davitt, Irish Nationalism and the British Empire in the Late Nineteenth Century.' In Gray, Peter, ed. *Victoria's Ireland? Irishness and Britishness 1837–1901.* Dublin, 2004.

Lee, J. J. *The Modernisation of Irish Society, 1848–1918.* Dublin, 1989.

Legg, Marie-Louise. *Newspaper and Nationalism: The Irish Provincial Press 1850–1892.* Dublin, 1999.

Lennon, Joseph. *Irish Orientalism: A Literary and Intellectual History.* London, 2004.

Logan, Thad. *The Victorian Parlour: A Cultural Study.* Cambridge, 2001.

Loughlin, James. 'The Irish Protestant Home Rule Association and Nationalist Politics, 1886–93.' In *Irish Historical Studies*, vol. xxiv, no. 95 (May 1985), pp. 341–360.

Luddy, Maria. 'Women and the Contagious Diseases Acts 1864–1886.' In *History Ireland*, vol. i, no. 1 (spring 1993), pp. 32–34.

———. *Women and Philanthropy in Nineteenth-Century Ireland.* Cambridge, 1995.

———. 'Isabella M. S. Tod (1836–1896).' In Luddy, Maria and Cullen, Mary, eds. *Women, Power and Consciousness in Nineteenth Century Ireland: Eight Biographical Studies.* Dublin, 1995, pp. 197–230.

Lyons, F. S. L. *John Dillon: A Biography*. London, 1968.
———. *The Irish Parliamentary Party, 1890–1910*. 2nd edn, Westport, CT, 1975.
———. *Charles Stewart Parnell*. London, 1977.
———. *Culture and Anarchy in Ireland 1890–1939*. Oxford, 1979.
MacKenzie, John MacDonald, ed. *Imperialism and Popular Culture*. Manchester, 1986.
Martin, Briton, jr. 'Lord Dufferin and the Indian National Congress, 1885–1888.' In *Journal of British Studies*, vol. vii, no. 1 (November 1967), pp. 68–96.
———. *New India 1885*. Berkeley and Los Angeles, 1969.
Masani, R. P. *Dadabhai Naoroji: The Grand Old Man of India*. London, 1939.
Maume, Patrick. *The Rise and Fall of Irish Ireland: D. P. Moran and Daniel Corkery*. Coleraine, 1996.
———. *The Long Gestation: Irish National Life, 1891–1918*. Dublin, 1999.
McCaffrey, Lawrence J. 'Home Rule and the General Election of 1874 in Ireland.' In *Irish Historical Studies*, vol. ix, no. 34 (September 1954), pp. 190–212.
McClintock, Ann. *Imperial Leather: Race, Gender and Sexuality in the Colonial Context*. New York, 1995.
McConnel, James. ' "Fenians at Westminster": the Edwardian Irish Parliamentary Party and the Legacy of the New Departure.' In *Irish Historical Studies*, vol. xxxiv, no. 133 (May 2004), pp. 41–64.
McCormack, W. J. 'Isaac Butt (1813–79) and the Inner Failure of Protestant Home Rule.' In Brady, Ciaran, ed. *Worsted in the Game: Losers in Irish History*. Dublin, 1989, pp. 121–131.
McCracken, J. L. *New Light at the Cape of Good Hope: William Porter, the Father of Cape Liberalism*. Belfast, 1993.
McDonough, Terence, ed. *Was Ireland a Colony? Economics, Politics and Culture in Nineteenth-Century Ireland*. Dublin, 2005.
McMahon, Cian. 'Struggling against Oppression's Detestable Forms: R. R. Madden and Irish Anti-Slavery, 1833–1846.' In *History Ireland*, vol. xv, no. 3 (May/June 2007), pp. 24–29.
Mehrotra, S. R. *The Emergence of the Indian National Congress*. 2nd edn, New Delhi, 2004.
Metcalf, Thomas R. *Forging the Raj: Essays on British India in the Heyday of Empire*. Oxford, 2005.
Milne-Smith, Amy. 'A Flight to Domesticity? Making a Home in the Gentlemen's Clubs of London, 1880–1914.' In *Journal of British Studies*, vol. xlv (2006), pp. 796–818.
Moody, T. W. *Davitt and Irish Revolution 1846–82*. Oxford, 1981.
Mosse, George L. 'Nationalism and Respectability: Normal and Abnormal Sexuality in the Nineteenth Century.' In *Journal of Contemporary History*, vol. xvii, no. 2 (1982), pp. 221–246.
———. 'Friendship and Nationhood: About the Promise and Failure of German Nationalism.' In *Journal of Contemporary History*, vol. xvii, no. 2 (1982), pp. 351–367.
Nagai, Kaori. *Empire of Analogies: Kipling, India and Ireland*. Cork, 2007.
Newby, Andrew G. 'Landlordism is Soon Going Skye-High: Michael Davitt and Scotland 1882–1887.' In *History Scotland*, vol. iii, no. 4 (2003), pp. 45–52.
O'Brien, Conor Cruise. *Parnell and His Party 1880–90*. 2nd edn, Oxford, 1964.

O'Callaghan, Margaret. *British High Politics and a Nationalist Ireland: Criminality, Land and the Law under Forster and Balfour.* Cork, 1994.
Ó Ciosáin, Niall. *Print and Popular Culture in Ireland, 1750–1850.* London, 1997.
O'Connor, Emmet. *A Labour History of Ireland 1824–1960.* Dublin, 1992.
O'Day, Alan. *Irish Home Rule 1867–1921.* Manchester, 1998.
———. *The English Face of Irish Nationalism: Parnellite Involvement in British Politics 1880–1886.* Dublin, 1977.
Ó Gráda, Cormac. *Ireland: A New Economic History 1780–1939.* Oxford, 1994.
O'Malley, Kate. *Ireland, India and Empire: Indo-Irish Radical Connections 1919–1964.* Manchester, 2008.
O'Neill, Marie. 'The Dublin Women's Suffrage Association and Its Successors.' In *Dublin Historical Record*, vol. xxxviii, no. 4 (September 1985), pp. 126–140.
Paseta, Senia. *Before the Revolution: Nationalism, Social Change and Ireland's Catholic Elite, 1879–1922.* Cork, 1999.
Prakash, Gyan. 'Subaltern Studies as Postcolonial Criticism.' In *American Historical Review*, vol. xcix, no. 5 (December 1994), pp. 1475–90.
Preston, Margaret H. *Charitable Words: Women, Philanthropy, and the Language of Charity in Nineteenth-Century Dublin.* Westport, CT, 2004.
Prochaska, F. K. *Women and Philanthropy in Nineteenth-Century England.* Oxford, 1980.
Putnam, Robert D. *Making Democracy Work: Civic Traditions in Modern Italy.* Princeton, 1993.
Quinlan, Carmel. *Genteel Revolutionaries: Anna and Thomas Haslam and the Irish Women's Movement.* Cork, 2002.
Raftery, Deirdre. 'Frances Power Cobbe.' In Cullen, Mary and Luddy, Maria, eds. *Women, Power and Consciousness in Nineteenth-Century Ireland: Eight Biographical Studies.* Dublin, 1995, pp. 89–124.
Ralph, Omar. *Naoroji: The First Asian MP.* Antigua, 1997.
Regan, Jennifer M. ' "We Could Be of Service to Other Suffering People": Representations of India in the Irish Nationalist Press, c. 1857–1887,' In *Victorian Periodicals Review*, vol. xli, no.1 (Spring 2008), pp. 61–77.
Rich, Paul B. *Race and Empire in British Politics.* 2nd edn, Cambridge, 1990.
Roberts, Daniel Sanjiv. ' "Merely Birds of Passage": Lady Hariot Dufferin's Travel Writings and Medical Work in India, 1884–1888.' In *Women's History Review*, vol. xv, no. 3 (July 2006), pp. 443–457.
Rodgers, Nini. *Ireland, Slavery and Anti-Slavery: 1612–1865.* Basingstoke, 2007.
Rolston, Bill. ' "Ireland of the welcomes"? Racism and Anti-Racism in Nineteenth-Century Ireland.' In *Patterns of Prejudice*, vol. xxxviii, no. 4 (December 2004), pp. 355–370.
Schneer, Jonathan. *London 1900: The Imperial Metropolis.* New Haven and London, 1999.
Seal, Anil. *The Emergence of Indian Nationalism: Competition and Collaboration in the Later Nineteenth Century.* Cambridge, 1968.
Shyllon, Folarin. *Black People in Britain 1555–1833.* London, 1977.
Silvestri, Michael. 'The Sinn Féin of India: Irish Nationalism and the Policy of Revolutionary Terrorism in Bengal.' In *Journal of British Studies*, vol. xxxix, no. 4 (October 2000), 454–486.

———. ' "An Irishman is Specially Suited to be a Policeman": Sir Charles Tegart and Revolutionary Terrorism in Bengal.' In *History-Ireland*, vol. viii, no. 4 (Winter 2000), pp. 40–44.
Smith, Anthony D. *Nationalism and Modernism: A Critical Survey of Recent Theories of Nations and Nationalism*. London, 1998.
Spiers, Edward M. 'Army Organisation and Society in the Nineteenth Century.' In Bartlett, Thomas and Jeffery, Keith, eds. *A Military History of Ireland*. Cambridge, 1996, pp. 335–357.
Swart, Sandra. ' "A Boer and his gun and his wife are three things always together": Republican Masculinity and the 1914 Rebellion.' In *Journal of Southern African Studies*, vol. xxiv, no. 4 (1998), pp. 737–751.
Swift, Roger and Gilley, Sheridan, eds. *The Irish in the Victorian City*. London, 1985.
Taylor, G. P. 'Cecil Rhodes and the Second Home Rule Bill.' In *The Historical Journal*, vol. xiv, no. 4 (December 1971), pp. 771–781.
Thornley, David. 'The Irish Conservatives and Home Rule, 1869–73.' In *Irish Historical Studies*, vol. xi (1958–9), pp. 200–222.
———. *Isaac Butt and Home Rule*. London, 1964.
Tosh, John. 'Masculinities in an Industrializing Society: Britain, 1800–1914.' In *Journal of British Studies*, vol. xliv, no. 2 (2005), pp. 330–342.
———. 'The Making of Masculinities: The Middle Class in Late Nineteenth-Century Britain.' In John, Angela V. and Eustance, Claire, eds. *The Men's Share? Masculinities, Male Support and Women's Suffrage in Britain, 1890–1920*. London, 1997. pp. 38–61.
Townsend, Charles. 'Religion, War, and Identity in Ireland.' In *The Journal of Modern History*, vol. lxxvi (December 2004), pp. 882–902.
Tusan, Michelle. 'Gender, Class and the Printing Trade in Victorian Britain.' In *Journal of Women's History*, vol. xvi, no. 1 (2004), pp. 103–126.
Van Heyningen, Elizabeth B. 'The Social Evil in the Cape Colony 1868–1902: Prostitution and the Contagious Diseases Acts.' In *Journal of Southern African Studies*, vol. x, no. 2 (April 1984), pp. 170–197.
Varouxakis, Georgios. ' "Patriotism", "cosmopolitanism", and "humanity" in Victorian Political Thought.' In *European Journal of Political Theory*, vol. v, no. 1 (2006), pp. 100–118.
Vernon, Anne. *A Quaker Businessman: The Life of Joseph Rowntree, 1836–1925*. London, 1958.
Visram, Rozina. *Asians in Britain: 400 Years of History*. London, 2002.
Walkowitz, Judith R. *Prostitution and Victorian Society: Women, Class and the State*. Cambridge, 1980.
Weekes, Anne Owens. 'A Trackless Road: Irish Nationalisms and Lesbian Writing.' In Kirkpatrick, Kathryn, ed. *Border Crossings: Irish Women Writers and National Identity*. Tuscaloosa and London, 2000.
White, Chris, ed. *Nineteenth-Century Writings on Homosexuality: A Sourcebook*. London, 1999.
White, Terence de Vere. *The Road of Excess*. Dublin, 1946.
Whyte, J. H. *The Independent Irish Party, 1850–9*. Oxford, 1958.
Wigham, Maurice J. *The Irish Quakers: A Short History of the Religious Society of Friends in Ireland*. Dublin, 1992.

Young, Robert. *The Idea of English Ethnicity*. London, 2007.
Zaidi, A. M. and Zaidi, Shaheda, eds. *The Encyclopedia of Indian National Congress, vol. II: 1891–1895, the Age of Reforms*. 17 vols, Delhi, 1977.

II. Reference

Berry, W. Turner and H. Edmund Poole. *Annals of Printing: A Chronological Encyclopedia from Earliest Times to 1950*. London, 1966.
Boylan, Henry. *A Dictionary of Irish Biography*. New York, 1978.
Clair, Colin. *A Chronology of Printing*. London, 1969.
Feather, John. *A Dictionary of Book History*. London, 1986.
Glaister, Geoffrey Ashall. *Glaister's Glossary of the Book*. 2nd edn, London, 1979.
Goodbody, Olive C. and Eustace, P. Beryl, eds. *Quaker Records Dublin: Abstracts of Wills*. Dublin, 1957.
Hayes, Richard J., ed. *Manuscript Sources for the History of Irish Civilization*. Boston, 1965.
Munter, Robert. *A Dictionary of the Print Trade in Ireland, 1550–1775*. New York, 1988.
Pollard, Mary. *A Dictionary of Members of the Dublin Book Trade, 1550–1800*. London, 2000.
List of Recipients of Honorary Freedom of City of Dublin, Dublin City Council (http://www.dublincity.ie/your_council/history/0050_freedom_of_the_city.asp) (28 April 2007).
Various authors. *Oxford Dictionary of National Biography*. Oxford, 2004.

III. Unpublished Work

Bradley, Pamela. Index of Persons named in Alfred Webb's autobiographical manuscript. Dublin Friends Historical Library, 1996.

IV. Unpublished Theses

Brasted, Howard V. 'Irish Home Rule Politics and India 1873–1886: Frank Hugh O'Donnell and Other Irish "Friends of India."' PhD Thesis, University of Edinburgh, 1974.
Regan, Jennifer M. 'Perceptions of India in the Irish Nationalist Press, c. 1857–1887.' M.A. thesis, Queen's University Belfast, 2004.
Riach, Douglas C. 'Ireland and the Campaign against American Slavery, 1830–1860.' PhD thesis, University of Edinburgh, 1975.

Index

abolitionism, *see* anti-slavery
Act of Union (1801), 52, 63, 67, 76, 131
alcohol, *see* Government Licensing Bill; temperance
Allen, clothing business, 16
Allen, Richard, 21
Amnesty Association, 63, 65
Amrita Bazar Patrika, 125
anti-everythingarians, 17–18, 21, 22–4, 26, 43, 120, 172
anti-imperialism, *see* Empire, British; *Fraternity*; Indian Politics; Naoroji, Dadabhai; Webb, Alfred
anti-slavery, 17–18, 21, 22–4, 26
  World Anti-Slavery Convention (1840), 23
apprentices, 14, 16, 18, 25
Argentina, 73
Arnold, Matthew, 125
Ashworth, Lillian, 43
atheism, 138
Athy and Riley, 27
Australia, 18, 25, 39, 48, 117, 129, 133, 156, 162–3
Austria, 18, 133

Ballantyne, Tony, 3
Ballitore, County Kildare, 14, 26
Banerjea, Surendranath, 149
Barker, Joseph, 18
Barrington, family and soap business, 16, 37, 51
Barrington lectures, *see* Statistical and Social Inquiry Society of Ireland
Barry, John, 77, 103
Barry O'Brien, Richard, 103
Bath, 43
Becker, Lydia, 43
Belfast, 37, 43, 44, 45, 52, 95, 108, 131
Besant, Annie, 6, 116, 152
Bewley, family import business, 16, 25–6

Biggar, Joseph, 75, 77, 81, 88, 91, 100, 109, 119, 122, 124, 137
Birmingham, 43, 72
Blake, Edward, 146–8, 156–7
Blennerhassett, Roland Ponsonby, 70–1
Blunden, John, 76–7, 82
Bonnerjee, Womesh Chandra, 137, 140, 143, 148
Boston, 23
bourgeoisie, concerns of, 38, 44, 62, 65, 75
Boylan, Henry, 57
Bradlaugh, Charles, 110, 138, 140, 142–3
Brasted, Howard V., 6, 137
Brennan, T., 88
Briggs, David, 95
Bright, family, 32, 116
Bright, Jacob, 14, 108, 116
Bright, John, 128, 138
British Friend, 31, 130, 158
British Hibernian India Society, 128, 137
Brown, John, revolt, 64
Brown, William, 26
Bryce, James, 107–8
Buckingham, James Silk, 23
Burton, Antoinette, 7, 46
business, 2, 10, 16, 23, 25–8, 32, 53, 166
  see also Dublin exhibitions; printing; Quakers
Butler, Josephine, 44, 116, 172
Butt, Isaac, 60–70, 74–6, 80–4

Cadbury, family, 28
Caine, W. C., 116
Cairnes, John Elliott, 38, 42
Callanan, Frank, 104, 105, 138
Callan, Philip, 76, 77
Campbell Bannerman, Henry, 108
Canada, 6, 73, 76, 129, 133, 146–7

Cape Colony, *see* South Africa
CDAs, *see* public health
Celts, *see* race
Central Relief Committee, *see* famine and famine relief
Ceylon, 49
Chapman, Richard, 25
Charlu, Panambakkam Ananda, 149
chartism, 18, 32
Chennai, *see* Madras
China, 2, 18, 23, 129
Church of Ireland, 16, 55–6, 62–3
civil servants, Indian, 117, 131, 134, 139, 141
Claidheamh Soluis, An, 165–6
Clancy, J. J., 88, 97–8
Clark, G. B., 116
Cló Chumann, 166
Clonmel, County Tipperary, 14–15
Cobbe, Frances Power, 40
Cobh, 44
Coffy, Mr and Mrs, 166
Colley, Linda, 9
Combe, George, 14
Comerford, Richard Vincent, 64, 70, 79, 111
Compendium of Irish Biography, 8, 56–8, 83
Congress, *see* Indian National Congress
Conradh na Gaeilge, *see* Gaelic League
Conservative party, and its members, 78, 81, 86, 141, 143, 144
conservatives, 63, 66, 78, 89, 119, 170
Contemporary Club, 41
Cook, Scott, 6
Corbett, William J., 97, 109
Cork, 15, 24, 44, 64, 74, 136
cosmopolitanism, 11, 17–19, 23–4, 42–3, 58–9, 110–19, 154
Cousins, James, 6
Cousins, Margaret, 6
Croke, Archbishop Dr. Thomas, 99, 102
Cullen, M. J., 37
Cumpston, Mary, 137, 145
Curragh, the, 44

Curtin affair (1885), 90, 100
Curzon, George, 142
cycling, 167

Daly, Mary, 35, 38
Dana, 167–8
D'Arcy Magee, Thomas, 129
Dargan, William, 52
Daunt, William O'Neill, 8, 61–2, 68, 71–2, 74, 76, 77–8, 122
Davitt, Michael, 42, 88, 102–3, 114, 130, 155, 160–1, 163, 171
former Fenian, 120, 147
friendship with Webb, 57, 86, 91, 119–21, 124
involvement in Indian affairs, 139, 142–3, 145, 147, 157
on Irish industry, 53, 87–8
on land issues, 85, 108
see also Fenianism; home rule; Land War; Naoroji, Dadabhai; treasury matters, home rule movement
Dawson, Charles, 88
Deasy, John, 109
Delaney, George, 82, 88, 109
depression, personal, 60, 79, 107, 120–2, 169
Devoy, John, 86–7
Digby, Kenelm, 77
Digby, William, 115–16, 125, 141–2, 143
Dilke, Charles, 108
Dillon, John, 88, 102–4, 107, 113, 144, 147, 148, 154, 159, 163, 166, 168
Dillon, John Blake, 62
Disestablishment, *see* Church of Ireland
Disraeli, Benjamin, 79, 81, 82
Douglass, Frederick, 17, 23–4, 26, 162
Dublin City Council, 51–2
Dublin Convention (1888), 96–7
Dublin Exhibitions, 52–5, 88
Dublin Friends Historical Library, 7
Dublin Port and Docks Board, 51–2
Dublin Statistical Society, *see* Statistical and Social Inquiry Society of Ireland
Dublin University Review, 92

Dufferin, Marquess of (Frederick Hamilton-Temple Blackwood), 131
Duffy, Charles Gavan, 57, 96, 129
Dunn, Miss, 48

Eason, Charles, 42
Eastern question, 133
East India Company, 6, 23, 76
Edmondson, family laundry business, 16, 28
Edmondson, Thomas, 28
Edmondson, William, 15
education, 14, 28, 37, 41, 43, 47, 87, 88, 99, 134, 139
  Catholic University question, 120, 164
Edwards, Celestine, 117, 173
Eglinton, John, 167
Elections
  1872, 70–1
  1874, 77–9
  1886, 139
  1890, Webb's election to Parliament, 97–8
  1892, 111, 117, 143
  1895, 144
  1902, 158
  see also Naoroji, Dadabhai; home rule
Emmet, Robert, 21
Empey, Catherine, 116
Empire, British
  analytical models of, 3–6, 110, 172–3
  Irish atttitudes towards, 39–40, 67, 75–6, 80, 95, 129, 131–6, 151, 160–2
  Irish involvement in, 5–7, 79–80, 131–2
Express, 57

'Faction,' The, 22–3, 30, 38
Famine and famine relief
  Indian, 115, 132, 157, 159
  Irish, 17, 19, 26, 52, 108, 161
Fawcett, Henry, 58, 138, 140
Fawcett, Millicent, 42, 58

Fenianism, 57, 61–5, 85–6, 119, 125, 131, 138, 145, 147, 164
Ferguson, John, 77
Ferguson, Samuel, 38
Field, D. J. and testimonial, 89
Fiji, 46
Flag of Ireland, 132
Foley, Tadhg, 6
Forster, William, Lord Lieutenant, 86, 114
Forster, William, senior, 19, 28
Foster, R. F., 41
Fox, George, 14, 162
France, 18, 53, 107, 133
  French language, 14, 57, 86
  French Revolution, 19, 24, 91, 126
  see also Paris funds
Fraternity, 117–18, 145–6
Freeman's Journal, 36, 43, 53, 54, 55, 57, 83–4, 86, 89, 98, 104, 130, 132, 157, 160–1, 164, 165
'Friend of India', 137–8
Friendship, 5, 48–9, 68, 99, 100, 105, 106, 119, 142, 147, 152, 156, 159
Friends Institute, 31, 36, 41, 159

Gaelic Athletic Association, 97
Gaelic League, 165–8
Galbraith, Rev. Joseph A., 68, 71, 76, 82, 109, 122, 131, 132
Gallery of Modern Art, for Dublin, 55
Galway, 98, 99, 112, 134, 146
Garibaldi, Giuseppe, 18
Garrison, William Lloyd, 10, 14, 17–18, 23–4, 48, 150
Geddes, Samuel, 118
George, Henry, 108
Ghose, Motilal, 125, 143
Gibraltar, 46
Gill, Michael Henry, 51, 56, 166
Gladstone, William E., 62–3, 77, 92, 93, 95, 96, 97, 110, 111, 129, 134, 139, 147
Gogarty, Oliver, 167
Gokhale, G. K., 159
Gonne, Maude, 161, 166
Government Licensing Bill, 1904, 22
Grant, Ulysses S., 97
Gray, Edward Dyer, 51, 88

Gray, Sir John, 42, 51
Griffith, Arthur, 111
Guinness, Arthur (Lord Ardilaun), 89
Gwynn, Stephen, 166

Hancock, William Neilson, 38
Hardie, James Keir, 116, 142
Harrington, Timothy, 88, 89, 91, 97, 102, 107, 113, 158
Harris, Sarah, 48
Harvey, family, 45
Haslam, Anna, 27, 30–1, 32, 43, 44–5, 50
Haslam, Thomas, 27–8, 30–1, 32, 41, 42, 44–5, 49, 50, 57
Haughton, James, 20–3, 38, 45
Healy, Maurice, 109
Healy, Timothy M., 88, 91, 94, 100, 102, 104–5, 109, 113, 119, 121, 124, 127, 155–6, 164, 166
Henry, Mitchell, 70, 77
Hibernian Peace Society, 23
Hishon, Daniel, 88
Hodgson, Dr William Ballantyne, 14
home rule
　Home Government Association, 61, 66–74
　Home Rule Confederation of Great Britain, 72, 81–3, 85
　Home Rule Conference (1873), 74–7, 78, 84, 132
　Home Rule League, 74–9, 81–3, 85–8, 90
　INLGB (Irish National League of Great Britain), 117
　Irish National Federation, 101, 103–5
　Irish National League, 85, 87–97, 101, 119, 171
　Irish National League of America, 122
　Irish Parliamentary Party, 11, 28, 48, 52, 58, 78, 80, 82, 94, 95, 99–105, 107, 110, 111, 113, 114, 118–9, 123–4, 126, 128, 132–6, 138, 143, 144–5, 148, 155–8, 162–8
　IPHRA (Irish Protestant Home Rule Association), 93–6, 100
　Protestant home rulers, 73, 99, 133
　UILGB (United Irish League of Great Britain), 117–18
　United Irish League, 163–4, 166
　see also Elections; friendship; Liberal Party, British; treasury matters, home rule movement; *or under individual members*
homosexuality, 49, 122, 124
Hong Kong, 46
Hume, Allan Octavian, 125, 139–41, 148, 150, 155
Hunt, Lynn, 126
Hyde, Douglas, 166

India, 141, 142, 144, 148, 149, 150, 156–7, 158
Indian-Irish Independence League, 6
Indian Mutiny, 18, 132
Indian politics
　British Committee of the Indian National Congress (BCINC), 141, 143–9, 151, 157
　Constitutional Association of India, 140
　Indian National Congress, 3, 9, 46, 115, 116, 117, 135, 136–7, 139–41, 144–53, 156–7, 161, 171
　Indian Parliamentary Committee, 143–6, 149, 151, 154
　Indian Political Agency, 141
　Indian Telegraph Union, 140
　India Reform Society, 137
Industrial Resources of Ireland, The, 52
industry, Irish, 25, 52–5, 87–8, 112, 168
Ingram, John Kells, 38, 42
Irish Builder, 53–4
Irish Club (London), 118
Irish Federalism, 67
Irish Ireland, 154, 166–8
Irish Labour and Industrial Union, 88
Irish language, 164–8
Irish Literary Society, 57
Irish Literary Theatre, 166
Irish National Press, 101
Irish Party, *see* home rule
Irish Press Agency, 28

Irish Race Convention (1896), 163–4
Irish Republican Brotherhood, see Fenianism
Irish Tenant League, 61
Irish Times, The, 56
Irish Weekly Independent, The, 105
Isichei, Elizabeth, 99
Italy, 18, 48, 50, 83, 133

Jackson, Alvin, 73–4, 82, 119
Jacob, Margaret, 126
Jacob, W. R. and Co, 53
Johnston, William, 42, 62, 119
Jordan, Jeremiah, 119, 124, 171
journalists, 70, 78, 109, 114, 115, 134, 136

Kane, Sir Robert, 42, 52
Kenny, Dr Joseph, 102, 122–3
Kerry, County, 26, 70, 90
Kettle, Andrew, 124
Kickham, Charles Joseph, 64
King-Harman, Captain E. R., 75, 76, 77, 78
King's Inns, Dublin, 56
Krapotkin, Prince Peter, 130
Kruger, Paul, 160

Labouchere, Henry, 108, 110
Ladies' Gallery, Parliament, 48
Land War
  evictions, 108
  Irish Land League, 52–3, 85–8, 140
  Ladies Land League, 27, 86, 87
  Land Act (1870), 62–3
  Land Convention (1880), 86
  tenant farming, 79
Larcom, Thomas, 38
Lawson, James, 38
Lawson, Sir W., 110
League Against Imperialism, 6
Leamy, Edward, 88, 113, 140
Legg, Marie-Louise, 7
liberalism, 19, 32, 38, 43, 58, 60, 66, 78, 109, 114, 119, 129, 140, 170–1

Liberal Party, British, 43, 58, 62, 99, 110, 115, 118, 132, 141, 145–6
  alliance with Irish Party, 92, 95–6, 104–5, 107–12
  see also Elections; Indian politics; Naoroji, Dadabhai; National Liberal Club
Liberator, The, 18
libraries and reading rooms, 8, 25, 38, 41, 43, 45, 51, 56, 98, 141
  see also under individual names
Limerick, 24
Lincoln, Abraham, 64, 79
Little, Judge, 88
Logan, Thad, 20
London, 106–13, 117, 151–2, 172
  Indians in, 114–16, 118, 137–41, 143, 149, 158
  Irish in, 76, 101, 124, 136
  see also Naoroji, Dadabhai; National Liberal Club; Parliament, Westminster
London Indian Society, 137
Loughlin, James, 94–6
love, *see* friendship
Luby, Thomas Clarke, 64
Luddy, Maria, 35, 45
Lurgan, 15
Lyons, F. S. L., 92, 103, 111, 154

McCaffrey, Lawrence, 74
McCarthy, Justin, 101–5, 107, 109, 114, 136–7, 142, 144, 154
McConnel, James, 119
MacDonnell, Sir Antony, 131
McKenna, Sir Joseph, 76
McLaren, Eva, 116, 152
McLaren, Walter Stowe Bright, 116
Mac Neill, Eoin, 165–6
Madden, Dr Richard Robert, 17, 20
Madden, Judge, 166
Madras, 146–51, 158, 162
Mahaffy, John P., 42
Malone, Rev. William, 77
Malthusianism, 38
Manchester, 14, 42, 43, 72, 77
Manchester Examiner and Times, 65
Manchester Guardian, 36, 153
Manchester Martyrs, 65

Mansion House Evicted Tenants Fund, 88
Marks, Alfred, 107
Martin, Briton, jr, 140
Martineau, Harriet, 17, 47
Martin, John, 62, 65, 69, 70, 73, 75, 77, 122
masculinity, 74, 97, 122–7
Mathew, Fr. Theobald, 22
Mayo, County, 85
Mayo, Lord (Richard Southwell Bourke), 131–2
Mazzini, Giuseppe, 18
Mechanics Institutes, 37, 41, 87
Mehta, Sir Pherozeshah, 149
Melbourne Advocate, 56
Methodists, 24
Military, 6, 43–4, 46, 65, 76, 80, 124, 129, 131, 151, 160
Mill, John Stuart, 42, 50
Mitchel, John, 18, 162
Monroe and Co, *see* Paris funds
Mooney, Joseph, 101
Moonlighters, the, 57
Moran, D. P., 111, 168
Morley, John, 96–7, 107, 110, 113
Morrogh, John, 155
Mott, Lucretia, 17
Muller, Henrietta, 151–2
Murphy, William Martin, 101, 103, 104
Museum of Irish Industries, 42

Naoroji, Dadabhai, 4, 137, 142, 145–53, 154, 159, 172–3
  biographical details, 114–15
  daughter Manakbhai, 159
  election campaigns, 118, 143, 158
  member of clubs and societies, 115–18
  in Parliament, 143–4
  potential Irish MP, 116, 138–9, 142–3, 157
National Association, 62, 67
nationalism, 38, 118–19, 122, 124–7, 129–31, 132–3, 139, 145, 165–8, 171–2
  see also cosmopolitanism; home rule; Indian politics

Nationalist Party, *see* home rule
National League, *see* home rule; Irish National League
National Liberal Club, 108–12, 115–16, 118, 154–5, 157
National Library of Ireland, 8, 25, 98
National Roll, 78
Nation, newspaper, 36, 78, 83, 132
Native Americans, 17
networks, *see* anti-slavery; cosmopolitanism; liberalism; nationalism; public health
New Age, 41
New Defence Fund, 163
New Internationalist Review, 158
New Ireland, 66
newspapers, *see* press
New York Catholic World, 82
New York Nation, 21, 36, 91
New Zealand, 6, 48, 73
Nicholson, Asenath, 17
Ninety Club, 57
Norman, Henry, 108
novels, 16, 25, 57, 136

O'Brien, Charlotte Grace, 57
O'Brien, J. F. X. (James Francis Xavier), 100–3, 110, 114, 119–20, 122, 144, 155–6, 163
O'Brien, Sophie Raffalovich, 48, 91, 109, 121, 130
O'Brien, William, 97, 113, 123–4, 164
O'Callaghan, Margaret, 90
O'Connell, Daniel, 17, 19, 24, 54, 71, 140, 142, 150, 165
O'Connor, Arthur, 104
O'Connor, Maureen, 6
O'Connor Power, John, 109
O'Connor, T. P., 109, 114, 116, 136
O'Day, Alan, 74, 108, 111
O'Donnell, Charles J., 118
O'Donnell, Frank Hugh, 81, 82–3, 118, 134–42
Oldham, Alice, 92
Oldham, Charles, 41, 92–6
O'Leary, John, 42, 64
O'Malley, Rev. Thaddeus, 75
Opinions of some Protestants, 9, 93
opium, 23, 99, 116, 129, 151

Orange Young Ireland, 63, 75
orangism, 42, 43, 62, 66, 119
Ordnance Survey, 18, 38
O'Reilly, Rev. Charles, 122–3
O'Shea, Captain W. H., 98
O'Shea, Katherine, 100

pacifism, 15, 21, 23, 64, 80, 86, 131
Paris funds, 88, 102–3
Parliament, Westminster, 4, 71, 82, 92, 135, 144
  Irish independent opposition, 61
  Ladies' Gallery, 48
  obstructionism in, 61, 81, 145
  petitions to, 42, 43, 45, 144
  Webb as MP in, 99, 109–10, 149, 155
  see also Elections; home rule; Indian politics; Naoroji, Dadabhai
Parnell, Anna, 27, 86–7, 107
Parnell, Charles Stewart, 84, 100, 107
  financial attitudes, 88, 91, 101–2
  ideas about Empire, 133–4
  in Parliament, 81
  as a party leader, 85, 87–8, 90, 97–8, 100
  see also France; home rule; Parnell split
Parnell, Fanny, 86
Parnell split, 2, 100–6, 164
Party Processions Act, 62
peace, *see* pacifism
Pease, Sir Joseph, 129
peat industry, 88
Penal Era, 16
People, The, 18
Phoenix Park murders, 31
Pim, family, 37
Pinkerton, John, 99, 112, 119, 124, 133
Presbyterians, 49, 73–4, 93, 112
press, periodical, 55, 91, 96, 111–12, 132, 139–41, 147, 153
  see also under individual titles
printing, 2, 24–30, 86, 98, 166
prisons and imprisonment, 41, 57, 62, 64–5, 86–7, 96–7, 120–1, 123, 130, 162

Protestants, *see* home rule; Methodists; Presbyterians; Quakers; religious questions
public health, 18, 36–7, 39
  birth control, 27, 50, 65, 170
  British, Continental and General Federation for the Abolition of Government Regulation of prostitution, 27, 43–6, 116, 170
  CDAs (Contagious Diseases Acts), 43–50
  hospitals, 36, 65, 159
  NARCDA (National Association for the Repeal of the Contagious Diseases Acts), 34, 44, 45, 50, 116
  Dublin Branch, NARCDA, 27
Public Record Office of Northern Ireland, 61
Pyne, J. D., 97

Quakers, 7, 10, 19, 24, 31, 37–8, 42, 47, 58, 108, 116–17, 128, 130, 160
  community in Ireland, 13–15, 24, 26, 63
  elected politicians, 32, 51, 99, 129, 138
  resignations from, 22, 24, 29, 30
  rules and propriety, 16–17, 25, 28
  theological concerns, 21–2, 32
  see also British Friend; business; Webb, Alfred
Quinlan, Carmel, 42
Quinn, Joe, 123

race, 39, 113, 117, 123–5, 164
railways, 25–6, 52
Ratnam, R. Venkata, 151–2
Redmond, John, 88, 113, 124, 144, 163–4
Redmond, Willie, 161
Reeves, Rev Dr William, 56
religious questions
  anti-Catholicism, 19
  clergymen in public life, 45, 56, 61, 68, 70, 75, 77, 93, 99, 102
  disestablishment of the Church of Ireland, 55, 62–3

Index

repeal, of the Act of Union, 62–3, 67, 75, 80
Rhodes, Cecil, 133–4
Ripon, Marquess of (George Robinson), 96–7, 139–40, 158
Robertson, Annie, 42
Ronayne, Joseph, 77, 137
Rosebery, Lord (Archibald Primrose), 95, 147
Rowntree, Joseph, 19
Royal Dublin Society, 56
Royal Hibernian Academy, 55, 56
Royal Irish Academy, 56
Rules of Discipline of the Yearly Meeting of Friends in Ireland, 15–16, 21
Russell family, London, 107
Russell, George (AE), 42
Russell, T. W., 42, 119
Russia, 130–1
Ryan, Frederick, 167

St. Patrick's day, 117
St. Stephen's Green, 55, 56
Salisbury, Lord (Robert Cecil), 143
Samoa, 50
Saxons, *see* race
Schneer, Jonathan, 6
Schneer, Jonathan, 6–7, 117
Schwann, Sir Charles, 107
Scotland, 14, 49, 72, 88, 114, 169
  Scottish politicians, 110, 139, 141, 142, 149
Seal, Anil, 140, 173
severed head, in Webb home, 20–1
Sexton, Thomas, 88, 104, 147, 148, 166
Shackleton, Abraham, 51, 88
Shackleton, Elizabeth, *see* Webb, Elizabeth (Lizzie) Shackleton
Shackleton family, 14, 26, 37, 47
Shaw-Lefevre, George, 95, 107
Shaw, William, 73, 77, 84–5
Sheares, *see* severed head, in Webb home
Sheehy, David, 109, 144, 166
Shillington, Thomas, 95
slavery, *see* anti-slavery
Smith, Samuel, 116
Smyth, P. J., 70

social activism, *see* anti-slavery; public health; suffragism
socialism, 119, 142, 158
Society of Friends, *see* Quakers
South Africa, 46, 133–4, 152, 160–2
Special Commission (1888), 86, 147
spiritualism, 48
SRUBM (Society for the Recognition of the Universal Brotherhood of Man), 117
Statistical and Social Inquiry Society of Ireland, 37–41, 52, 59, 133
Steel, Donald, 49
strikes, 28
Sturge, Eliza, 43
suffragism, 40, 42–3, 46, 50, 58, 66
  Dublin Women's Suffrage Association (DWSA), 28, 34, 43, 50, 92
  National Society for Women's Suffrage (NSWS), 42–3
  National Union of Women's Suffrage Societies, 116
  Women's Franchise League, 116
Sullivan, Donal, 109, 111
Sullivan, A. M., 66–9, 70–1, 77–8, 82
Sullivan, Maurice, 109
Sullivan, T. D., 88, 96–7, 109
Swift MacNeill, J. G., 95, 109, 133, 136, 141–3, 154

Tagore, Mohun, 140
Tagore, Rabindranath, 6
taxidermy, 20
temperance, 21–3, 38, 42, 97, 99, 112, 116, 119
  Anglo-Indian Temperance Association, 116
  ITU (Irish Temperance Union/Hibernian Temperance Society), 21–3
  United Committee for the Prevention of the Demoralization of Native Races by the Liquor Traffic, 116
Thom, Alexander, 38
Thornley, David, 60, 78
Thoughts in Retirement, 9, 167
Tibet, 162

Times of India, The, 150
Tod, Isabella, 42–3, 45, 119
tory, *see* conservative party, and its members
Tosh, John, 122, 124
treasury matters, home rule movement, 67, 88, 89, 90, 101–4, 171
 debt, of home rule organizations, 28, 62, 69, 78, 81, 91, 103–4
 Evicted Tenants Fund, 28, 88, 103, 163, 171
 Irish Parliamentary Fund, 117, 156, 163
 New Defence Fund, 163
 remittances, 91, 103–4
 see also under home rule; O'Brien, J. F. X. (James Francis Xavier); Paris funds; Parnell, Charles Stewart; Webb, Alfred
Trinity College Dublin, 37, 42, 56, 92
Tweedmouth, Lady (Fanny Spencer-Churchill), 112
Tweedmouth, Lord (Edward Marjoribanks), 111
Tyabji, Badruddin, 148

Ulster, 80, 95, 134, 139
Ulster custom, 63
Uncle Tom's Cabin, 18
unionists, 38, 43, 89, 119
United Ireland, 18
United Irishmen, 17, 19, 20, 21, 47
United States of America, 17–19, 21, 23, 64, 88, 117, 122, 162
University College Dublin, 92

Varouxakis, Georgios, 110, 117
Victoria, Queen, 19

Wacha, Dinshaw, 146, 150–3
Wars
 American Civil, 21, 64, 120
 Boer, 160–1
 Crimean, 18, 43
 Franco-Prussion, 18, 83
 Mexican, 18
 Opium, 2, 18
 Spanish-American, 162

Washington, Booker T., 162
Waterford, 14–16, 24, 97–8, 100, 134
Webb, Alfred
 attitudes towards Catholics, 92–6, 99, 110, 151, 162, 164, 168
 on being a Protestant, 73, 79–80, 93, 121, 151, 168
 biographical details, 13–14
 concerns about political apathy, 68–9, 79, 83, 167–8
 resignations, 24, 29–30, 51–2, 55, 82, 89, 90–1, 100, 155–7, 163
 as a treasurer, 28, 67, 74, 78, 82, 86, 88, 89, 91, 101, 103, 163, 171
Webb, Anna Dunville, 57
Webb, Anne, 14, 49–50
Webb, Deborah, 8, 14, 48–50, 98, 160
Webb, Elizabeth (Lizzie) Shackleton, 14, 47–50, 98, 109, 131, 156, 169
Webb, Emily, 28
Webb, Hannah Waring, 14, 17–18, 30, 47, 49–50
Webb, Helen, 28, 45
Webb, Maria, 45
Webb, R. D. (Richard Davis), 14–19, 21, 23–4, 25, 30, 38, 42, 47, 120, 128, 137
Webb, Richard, 14, 25, 50, 56
Webb, Thomas Henry, 51, 93, 101
Wedderburn, William, 125, 141–4, 146, 148, 149, 154
Welby Commission, 144, 159
Wells, Ida, 107
Westminster, *see* Parliament, Westminster
Wexford, 24, 47
Why I desire Home Rule, 79
Wilde, Sir William, 42
Wilson, Henry, 107
Women's Liberal Federation, 116

Yeats, William Butler, 6, 42, 57, 154, 166–7
Young Ireland, 18, 20, 61, 63, 64, 124
Young, Mr and Mrs Thomas, printing clients, 30
Yule, George, 115